READING MEDIEVAL STUDIES

Volume XLVII

READING MEDIEVAL STUDIES

Volume XLVII

Editors
Aisling Byrne
Anna Campbell
Katie Phillips

Graduate Centre for Medieval Studies

UNIVERSITY OF READING
2021

Published by the Graduate Centre for Medieval Studies
University of Reading

ISSN 0950-3129

ISBN 9780704915848

© University of Reading Graduate Centre for Medieval Studies

Printed and Bound in Great Britain by
Design and Print Studio,
University of Reading

Advisory Board

Table of Contents

Warfare, Poetry and the Community of the Realm in Later Anglo-Saxon England

Andrew Holland

This paper will explore the relationship between conflict and collective identity in later Anglo-Saxon England. I will primarily focus on three Old English poems from the tenth or early eleventh centuries, *The Battle of Brunanburh*, *The Capture of the Five Boroughs*, and *The Battle of Maldon*, to discuss how the representation of conflict in textual sources communicates collective identity and integrates different 'layers' of identity within a heterogeneous realm. These poems have sometimes been seen as straightforward 'patriotic' expressions of a homogeneous Anglo-Saxon identity.[1] However, ethnicity is much less important in the poems than social relationships between the king and his leading subjects. By centring collective identity around the military success of the royal dynasty through a distinctly non-ethnic lens, these poems contributed to the West Saxon dynasty's rhetoric of protection and military leadership.

  Brunanburh and *Five Boroughs* are found in *The Anglo-Saxon Chronicle*, where they appear in entries under annals for 937 and 942 respectively, though there is some confusion regarding chronology for the 940-3 annals, which will be discussed below.[2] The poems are inserted at a point where the *Chronicle's* record becomes notably more attenuated than in previous decades. Entries for the period between 865 and 924 are almost annual, while the forty-nine years between 926 and 975 receive only thirty-five entries across the various versions of the *Chronicle*, occasionally offering significant chronological challenges. Unlike the other poems, *Maldon* is not in the *Chronicle*; the eleventh-century manuscript containing the poem was destroyed in the Cotton fire of 1731.[3] All three poems are usually believed to have been composed within a few decades of the events they purport to describe. It is sometimes suggested that *Brunanburh* and *Five Boroughs* date to the reign of Edmund because of his prominence in the poems.[4]

However, Stenton's suggestion that the poems should be dated to the late 950s deserves attention, and a case will be made below that the reign of Edgar provides a plausible context for the composition of *Brunanburh* and *Five Boroughs*.[5] Meanwhile, the dating of *Maldon* is controversial, but it was composed no later than the first quarter of the eleventh century, and it may be nearly contemporary to the battle itself.[6]

The Battle of the Brunanburh and *The Capture of the Five Boroughs* were incorporated into MSS A-D of the *Chronicle*, suggesting that they derived from a common source.[7] They seem to be directly related to the political project of the Cerdicing kings and specific to the political contexts of the mid-tenth century. *Maldon*, on the other hand, may not have emanated from a royal court *per se* – the king receives only a single mention, for instance – but it will be seen that the poem uses similar techniques and strategies to *Brunanburh* and *Five Boroughs*. This might suggest that the effect of the chronicle poems in the decades after their production and dissemination was to help foster a common cultural mode between the royal court and the aristocracy that emphasised the interpersonal relationships between the king and his subjects in martial terms, representing a link between the royal court and the provinces communicated through agents such as Ealdorman Byrhtnoth, the protagonist of *Maldon*.

Ethnicity is a cultural identity that encompasses a range of shared attributes, including language, law, religion, dress and accessories, and the belief in a common descent, homeland, or kinship. These attributes need not all align with each other, and one should be wary of being too rigid. Furthermore, an ethnicity does not require a corresponding polity. An ethnic identity can encompass other 'nested' expressions of identity, and regional variation regarding legal practice, dress and accessories, and dialect, among other things, must also be acknowledged. The point at which regional variation flows into a new ethnicity is not fixed, and there could be considerable ambiguity in this regard. Much important work in the past decades on early medieval ethnicity has emphasised that it was 'functional', and it could be deployed strategically to draw distinctions between in-groups and out-groups.[8] The question of identity in Anglo-Saxon England has been a matter of no small importance to historians. In particular, seminal work by Patrick Wormald and Sarah Foot has been influential in shaping the contours of the debate, establishing a framework for understanding the development of a later Anglo-Saxon – or *Englisc*, to use the vernacular – identity ultimately derived from Pope Gregory I and Bede's *Historia Ecclesiastica*, in which a sense of cohesion was mobilised by the court of Alfred, and which expanded under Alfred's heirs as hitherto independent groups in Britain submitted to the Cerdicing dynasty in the tenth century.[9]

As early as 731, Bede could write of the *gens Anglorum*. In doing so, he particularly emphasised shared language. In one of the most famous passages of the *Historia Ecclesiastica*, Bede describes the five languages of the *gentes* of Britain: English, British, Irish, and Pictish, with the unifying language of Latin being common to them all.[10] Bede also dwells on the shared homeland and common descent of the *Anglorum siue Saxonum gens*, who he claims arrived in Britain in three ships from among 'three powerful peoples of *Germania* (*Germaniae populis*), the Angles, Saxons, and Jutes'.[11] The use of the vernacular was important in both literature and history writing. Various versions of *The Anglo-Saxon Chronicle* were kept in English through the end of the Anglo-Saxon period. English also served as the language of law codes and other legal documents, and the vernacular was used prominently in sermons, biblical translations, translations of patristic writing, hagiography, and poetry, among much else.[12] Newcomers were encouraged to adopt English names at times. For instance, when Guthrum was baptized in 878, he adopted the baptismal name of Æthelstan, and when Emma of Normandy married Æthelred II in 1002, she took (or was given) the English name Ælfgifu.[13] The alleged common descent of the Anglo-Saxon dynasties was emphasised in genealogical material that stressed common descent from Woden.[14] Law codes suggest a common legal culture. For instance, the introduction to the laws of Alfred notes that the king collected laws that seemed good from his own West Saxon predecessors as well as from Mercia and Kent.[15] Shared religious custom could also signal ethnicity. This need not *always* be the case, but after the conversion, the adoption of paschal conformity, and the universal acceptance among the Anglo-Saxons of the primacy of Canterbury, it could be useful to frame an Anglo-Saxon Christian identity in contrast to, say, pagans. This oppositional relationship is articulated in textual sources when, for example, external invasion by heathens was described as the result of widespread sin among the *gens*.[16] As shall be discussed below, however, such oppositional techniques of communication were situationally useful and could bely a more complex political reality.

As the West Saxon dynasty expanded in the tenth century, previously independent polities were incorporated – sometimes tenuously – into a single kingdom, and by the middle of the century, most Angles and Saxons were subjects of the descendants of Alfred of Wessex. Historians of the so-called 'Late Anglo-Saxon State' have often focused on the relative strength of the Cerdicing kings during this period, the homogeneity of administrative structures such as shires and hundreds, and an apparent sense of 'national' unity.[17] At the same time, however, the tenth- and eleventh-century kingdom could tend toward regionalism and it was ethnically diverse, encompassing populations of Anglo-Saxons, Britons, and Scandinavians.[18]

With this diversity in mind, Susan Reynolds argued in 1985 that the tenth-century Cerdicing kings were '*reges Anglorum*,' and their subjects, correspondingly, were *Angli*,' whatever their ethnic background, as opposed to newcomers recently arrived from Scandinavia and who were enemies of the king.[19] Indeed, much recent work on ethnic identities has emphasised this ambiguity. For example, both Dawn Hadley and Matthew Innes have written about the longstanding regional distinctiveness of Northumbria and the East Midlands within the English kingdom, in which a specifically 'Danish' identity was situational and could be articulated at need.[20]

Reynolds's point is further supported by the work of Edward James and Patrick Geary on the Franks. They have focused particularly on how military activity could centre collective identity around kingship. Geary has written that 'Essentially, the terms *Franci, Alamanni, Burgundiones, Gothi* and the like appeared in connection with kings and with war. The kings were kings of peoples, as were dukes, and by far the most common use of the ethnic labels was to modify the names of kings. When Gregory, Fredegar, or the author of the *Liber Historiae Francorum* speak of peoples, they normally meant the warriors, the army. The *gens Francorum* was the *exercitus Francorum*, led by its king or its *duces*.'[21] As Edward James wrote, Gregory of Tours is 'best known for doing something he did not do: [writing] an ethnic history, the

History of the Franks.[22] James notes that Gregory only uses 'Frank' or 'Franks' in forty-eight passages of his lengthy history, normally in formulae such as *regnum* or *reges Francorum*. The word seems to be used to describe people who were politically active, those at the king's court or assembled in the army. This suggests a layering of identity, in which local identities, perhaps organised around one's *civitas*, ran alongside one's 'public' or political identity, in which those within the Frankish kingdom and subject to the king of the Franks *were* Franks.[23] One might mostly think in terms of being an Arvernian at home, but a Frank when associated with the king or on campaign against, say, the Burgundians.

Was it the same in Anglo-Saxon society? There is evidence to suggest that this could be the case during the Anglo-Saxon period. The *gens Anglorum* was something that could be conceptualised before there was any semblance of political unity. However, the creation of a unitary English kingdom did not obliterate other layers of collective identity. The continued relevance of a Mercian political identity, for instance, manifested itself at several points.[24] This can be seen in other guises, as smaller groups of peoples that together comprised the *gens Anglorum* flit in and out of the textual record. For example, in the *Chronicle's* account of the Battle of *Assandun* in 1016, the chronicler describes how Edmund Ironside gathered together his army from *ealle Engla þeode* ('all the people of the English'). After Edmund's defeat at the hands of Cnut, the chronicler ascribes blame to the *Magonsæte*, the people of modern Herefordshire and Shropshire who were allegedly the first to flee the field.[25] This suggests that these sublayers of collective identity within the broad umbrella of the *gens Anglorum* continued to be relevant in the eleventh century. In this case, the lesser-order identity was used as a scapegoat for military defeat. If the account is accurate, it suggests that such strata of collective identity could have also remained relevant for the purposes of military organisation.

As the Cerdicing dominion expanded, varied groups needed to be accommodated within a wider community of the realm. Kingship provided a means to centre political identity. Warfare, in both its conduct and memorialisation, provided a medium through which to communicate such identity around the royal dynasty. Multi-ethnic aristocratic solidarities expressed in martial terms can be seen throughout the Anglo-Saxon period. In his 734 *Letter to Ecgberht*, Bede complains that, without available land to be granted as a reward for service, the sons of nobles and discharged soldiers will 'go across the sea' to take service with foreign lords 'and abandon their country, which they ought to fight for.'[26] In the eighth-century *Vita Sancti Guthlaci*, the hagiographer Felix wrote of how during his warlike youth, Guthlac 'gathered together companions from diverse *gentes* and from all directions' and amassed 'immense plunder'.[27] In the 890s (probably 893), Asser wrote of Alfred's household that 'many Franks, Frisians, *Galli*, pagans, Britons, Irish and Bretons willingly subjected themselves to his lordship.'[28] This latter example does not explicitly say that being subject to Alfred's lordship required military service, but it should not be ruled out. We see in these examples how elite cohesion was centred upon the construction of a household or retinue that was diverse and heterogeneous; the examples suggest class-based rather than 'ethnic' solidarities that relied upon the interpersonal connections between lords and their men.

A final example that is particularly instructive is the 1014 will of the *ætheling* Æthelstan, the eldest son of King Æthelred II. When Æthelstan died, he made the following bequest:

> [To Old Minster, Winchester:] the sword and silver hilt wrought by Wulfric, and the golden belt and arm-ring which Wulfric wrought, and the drinking-horn which I had bought from the community at Old Minster... the silver-hilted sword that belonged to Ulfketel, and the byrnie which Morcar has, and the horse which Thurbrand gave me, and the white horse which Leofwine gave me, and to my brother Edmund I grant the sword which belonged to King Offa, and the sword with the pitted hilt, and a blade, and a silver-inlaid trumpet... and I grant to my brother Eadwig a silver-inlaid sword... and I grant to Bishop Ælfsige... a black stallion... and to my mass priest Ælfwine... the ornamented sword which belonged to Wihtar, and a horse with tack, and to my 'dish-thegn' Ælfmær a roan stallion and a damaged sword... and I grant to Sigeferth a sword, and a horse, and my curved shield... and I grant to Eadric, the son of Wynflæd, the sword on which the hand is marked. And I grant to my retainer Æthelwine

the sword which he has given me. And I grant to Ælfnoth my
sword-sharpener, the damaged ornamented sword... [29]

Many of the men named in Æthelstan's will were notable in their own
right: Ulfketel – a Scandinavian name – who had given the *ætheling* a
silver-hilted sword was the ealdorman of East Anglia who fought against
Sweyn Forkbeard at Thetford in 1004 and at Ringmere in 1010.[30]
Morcar, to whom Æthelstan had given a mail byrnie, was a landholder
in Derbyshire and Leicestershire.[31][32] Thurbrand the Hold, another man
with a Scandinavian name, was a prominent magnate in Northumbria,[33]
and Leofwine was the Ealdormen of the Hwicce.[34] Æthelstan's brothers,
Edmund and Eadwig are self-explanatory, and Ælfsige was the Bishop
of Winchester. Thus, the will demonstrates the way Æthelstan
maintained horizontal connections with his brothers and some of the
chief lay and ecclesiastical magnates from across the realm. However,
the will also demonstrates Æthelstan's vertical connections: he
remembers his mass-priest, his 'dish-thegn' (steward), his sword-
sharpener, and some of his retainers. The bequeathing of swords,
shields and horses appears instrumental as a medium through which to
create an affinity between a cross-section of society in a way that was
personally meaningful. It also played on their sense of history and
regional loyalty. Æthelstan gave his brother Edmund a sword belonging
to King Offa of Mercia, which must have been over 200 years old if it
was genuine. The will demonstrates the way interpersonal relationships
were mediated through the imagery and equipment of warfare, which
acted as an agent of social cohesion and helped to forge a solidarity;
presumably the intent was that this would form an important backbone
of support for Æthelstan had he become king. Most importantly for the
purposes of this paper, the affinity described in the will cuts across
apparent ethnic divisions and features beneficiaries who – at least
through their names – signalled a Scandinavian identity.

Old English literature provided a means to communicate the
connection between the king, warfare, and collective identity. The
examples that will be discussed below navigated both the ambiguities
between different Anglo-Saxon groups and between different ethnicities
in the tenth- and eleventh-century kingdom. It is important not to
confuse literary motif with historical reality, but it would also be unwise

to dismiss such sources out of hand.[35] Such literature could still reflect the pretentions or aspirations of the audience and shape perceptions of what was admirable or shameful. Even if such poems seem anachronistic or unrealistic, the depiction of the king and his men in a heroic mode could still be an important way to form an affinity. Such literary motifs had a long lifespan and persisted through the end of the Anglo-Saxon period. Edward the Confessor was provided with an encomiastic obituary in the *Chronicle*, which described the king in martial terms as the ruler of a heterogeneous realm of Angles, Saxons, Britons, and Scots: 'That ruler of heroes lavish of riches... He governed well the Welshmen, Æthelred's son, ruled Britons and Scots, Angles and Saxons, his mighty champions. All that the cold sea waves encompass / brave young warriors faithfully obeyed King Edward the noble... At length he came forth in splendid array, a virtuous king, pure and mild, Edward the noble guarding his homeland, land and people.'[36]

The Battle of Brunanburh describes Æthelstan's great battle of 937.[37] In the poem, Æthelstan is described as a 'lord of nobles, [and the] ring-giver to men.' For he and his brother Edmund, 'it was natural to men of their kindred to be often in the field against every foe, to defend their land, their treasure, and their homes.'[38] The poet immediately establishes the legitimacy of Æthelstan and Edmund through their lineage and their martial prowess in the defence of their homes. The poet mentions the 'mounted companies' (*eoredcystum*) of the West Saxons and stoutness of the Mercians (*Myrce ne wyrndon heardes handplegen...*), but the poet also writes that after the battle the brothers 'sought their kinsmen in the land of the West Saxons (*cyþþe sohton Wessexena land*).[39] The final paragraph is worth quoting in full:

> Never yet in this island before this, by what books tell us and our ancient sages, was a greater slaughter of a host made by the edge of the sword, since the Angles and Saxons came hither from the east, invading Britain over broad seas, the proud assailants, warriors eager for glory, overcame the Britons and won a country (*eard*).

The *Brunanburh* poet was attempting to strike a delicate balance. On the one hand, the prowess of West Saxons and the Mercians is equally recognised, and they are mentioned distinctly, suggesting deference to the regional particularism of both kingdoms. For most of the poem, Æthelstan and Edmund are described in neutral terms, but in the aftermath of the battle they are both explicitly linked to Wessex. It may be that the poet was deliberately seeking to associate Æthelstan with Wessex, given the alleged coolness the West Saxons had toward him.[10] It may also be that the poet's word choice was sufficiently ambiguous to acknowledge Æthelstan's West Saxon lineage without depicting him as a specifically 'West Saxon' king at the expense of the Mercians.

This seems more likely given the final paragraph, in which the battle is put in a broader historical context. For the poet, Brunanburh represents the climax of a series of battles fought for hegemony over Britain. It may be that by 'books... and ancient sages', the poet refers to the early entries of the common stock of the Anglo-Saxon Chronicle (or its sources), in which various origin myths were stitched together.41 The Chronicle's origin legends are largely silent regarding the Angles. Of the thirty-six entries of the Chronicle between s.a. 449, the year given for the arrival of 'Hengest and Horsa', and 601, the year Augustine received the pallium, six entries are devoted to the line of Hengest and Horsa;42 four are given for the Jutes of the Isle of Wight and Hampshire;43 three concern the line of Ælle and the South Saxons;44 and eighteen are devoted to the line of Cerdic, who would become the progenitor of the West Saxons.45 Only five entries concern the Northumbrian Angles: a genealogy for Ida of Bernicia s.a. 547; a genealogy for Ælle of the Deirans s.a. 560 (with an obit for Ida in MS E for the same year); an obit for Ælle and a note of Æthelric's accession s.a. 588; a note of Æthelfrith of Bernicia's accession s.a. 593; and in 601, when Paulinus is introduced, it is noted as an aside that he would convert King Edwin.46 No entries mention the Mercians or any other Angles, and of those five meagre entries, none provide origin stories. Perhaps, then, the intent of the *Brunanburh* poet was to join the Angles and Saxons together by giving them a shared history, as suggested by the final lines of the poem. By depicting the alliance between the Anglian Mercians and the West Saxons in such heroic fashion, the Mercians are woven into the story and put on the path of a common future within the *imperium* of the Cerdicing kings.

If the poem treads carefully around the relationship between the West Saxons and the Mercians, the *Brunanburh* poet was also notably delicate in his treatment of Æthelstan's enemies. Indeed, much is left unsaid. Æthelstan's chief enemies at Brunanburh were Olaf Guthfrithson, (Amlaíb mac Gofraid), the Norse king of Dublin and Constantine (Causantín mac Áeda) of Alba; Owain ap Dyfnwal, king of the Britons of Strathclyde, may also have been among the allies but he is not mentioned in the *Chronicle*.[17] In an omission that seems conspicuous, the poet does not mention Danes at all. This is rather striking. It is plausible – even likely – that there were Danes, long since settled in eastern England, among the Mercian troops fighting with Æthelstan. On the other hand, it is impossible to rule out the possibility that there were Danes among the king's enemies. The *Annals of Clonmacnoise*, which survive in the form of a seventeenth-century English translation specifically claim that Olaf invaded 'with the help of the Danes of that [i.e. Æthelstan's] kingdom.'[18]

In contrast, the Scots are referred to explicitly, and on two occasions Olaf's followers are referred to as 'Northmen'.[19] Otherwise, Æthelstan's enemies are 'pirates', 'sailors', or generically 'northerners': the latter could equally refer to the followers of Olaf, the Scots, or the Britons of Strathclyde. There is also some evidence to suggest that there were Northumbrians among Æthelstan's enemies. These may also be among the 'northerners' referred to. Æthelstan subdued Northumbria in 927, after the death of his brother-in-law Sihtric.[50] While progressing north in 934 to conduct a campaign in Scotland, Æthelstan issued a charter at Nottingham granting land at Amounderness that 'he had bought with no small amount of money' to the church of York, and shortly thereafter he made a grant to the community of St Cuthbert at Chester-le-Street.[51] Nevertheless, it may be that all was not well in the north. In the *Annals of Clonmacnoise*, a certain 'Adulf McEtulfe, king of the North Saxons' has an *obit* for 934.[52] This is probably Æthelwulf son of Eadwulf.[53] It has been suggested that Æthelwulf held some sort of royal authority north of the Tyne, possibly with the support of Constantine, and his death may have provided the impetus for Æthelstan's invasion in 934.[54] Finally, a panegyric devoted to Æthelstan quoted at length by William of Malmesbury suggests that 'with the consent of the king of the Scots, the northern land (*borealis terra*) lends its support [to Olaf] with no misgivings; and now they are swollen with pride, they frighten with their words the very air; the natives, the whole region yields to their presumption.'[55] While hardly conclusive, this does lend support to the notion that at least some Northumbrians, perhaps those north of the Tyne who had been associated with Æthelwulf son of Eadwulf, found themselves with Olaf and Constantine on the eve of Brunanburh.

If this interpretation is correct, the *Brunanburh* poet was attempting to weave together the fate of Wessex and Mercia under the aegis of the Cerdicing dynasty. In doing so, however, the poet obscures the position of both the Northumbrians – whether ethnic Anglo-Saxons or Scandinavians – who had submitted to Æthelstan's rule in 927 and who may have been in rebellion in 934, as well as the position of the Danes dwelling within the kingdom, constructing instead a triumphant narrative centred upon the royal dynasty. This elision may have served to integrate both a territorial layer of collective identity (i.e. Mercia, Northumbria) and an ethnic layer of identity (i.e. Danes subject to Æthelstan's lordship) within the Cerdicing realm.

This receives more attention in the poem known as the *Capture of the Five Boroughs*. *Five Boroughs* is entered under the *Anglo-Saxon Chronicle's* annal for 942, only the second entry after *Brunanburh*. The poem refers to Edmund's capture of five fortified places in eastern Mercia in 942/3. The entire poem runs as follows:

Her Eadmund cyning, Engla þeoden,
Mæcga mundbora, Myrce geeode,
Dyre dædfruma, swa Dor scadeþ;
Hwitanwyllesgeat and Humbra ea,
Brada brimstream. Burga fife,
Ligoraceaster and Lincylene,
And Snotingham, swylce Stanford eac,
and Deoraby. Dæne wæran æror
under Norðmannum nyde gebegde
on hæþenra hæfteclommum
lange þrage, oþ hie alysde eft
for his weorþscipe wiggendra hleo,
afera Eadweardes, Eadmund cyning.[56]

Though Stenton found the poem to be 'overloaded with clichés', it nevertheless is instructive regarding concepts of royal protection.[57] In the poem, Edmund is portrayed as 'lord of the English and protector of kinsmen' (*Engla þeoden mæcga mundbora*) and the 'protector of warriors' (*wiggendra hleo*), emphasising the role of the king as a protector and military leader. Edmund's capture of the Five Boroughs is not depicted as conquest, but as redemption or liberation (*alysde*) from heathen captivity (*hæþenra hæfteclommum*).[58] As 'lord of the English', Edmund is cast as the protector of both the Mercians and West Saxons, *and* Christian Danes living in the Five Boroughs, demonstrating a heterogeneous construction of collective identity that stems from the king, their protector and lord.[59] This supports a multi-ethnic reading of the sources, in which Christian Danes had a place within the Mercian political community under the protection of the king.[60]

Five Boroughs presents a simplification of the chaotic politics of the 940s. Instead of a straightforward triumph leading to the 'liberation' of Christian Danes from the subjugation of heathen 'Northmen', it seems more likely that in 940 the *imperium* won by Æthelstan was deeply divided in Northumbria and eastern Mercia. Clare Downham has recently argued that the perception of a rivalry between 'Hiberno-Norse' (*Norðmenn*) and Danes (*Dene*) is anachronistic and that the two terms were often used interchangeably, particularly in Latin writing from the ninth and tenth centuries. Thus, rather than 'The Danes had before been subjected by force under the Northmen, and for a long time were bound in captivity to the heathens,' it would be viable to read that the Five Boroughs 'were previously *Dene* [i.e. under Danish rule] – oppressed in need under the Northmen, in the fetter-chains of heathens.'[61] However, it is worth noting that the *Chronicle* did occasionally distinguish between Danes and 'Northmen' in the kingdoms of Britain. In an entry for 920, the chronicler wrote of 'all those who live in Northumbria, both English and Danish, Northmen and others.'[62] It may indeed be anachronistic to think in terms of 'Northmen' and 'Danes' as distinct *ethnicities*, but this does not necessarily mean the words were always used interchangeably. It is worth recalling the argument made by Susan Reynolds cited above, which draws a distinction between 'recently arrived' pagan Scandinavians hostile to the king and those Scandinavians with whom the king had dealings and who may have been Christian. In other words, the distinction need not necessarily be ethnic to remain valid; what is more important is whether these peoples were within the king's peace and if they were Christian. *Brunanburh*, it should be noted, explicitly refers to Olaf's followers as 'Northmen', and it does not seem unreasonable to suppose that in the 940s, there may have been wariness among some Scandinavians in eastern Mercia toward Olaf and his kinsmen (perhaps particularly after Brunanburh). A picture should be emphasised in which communities of Angles and Danes in eastern Mercia were forced to respond to the death of Æthelstan and the competing claims made by Olaf and Edmund.

Rather than drawing a straightforward ethnic binary, *Five Boroughs* emphasises unity under Edmund as a protector and war-leader and paints a celebratory picture of Edmund's campaigns in 942/3. However, when the chronology is untangled, it becomes clear that the situation on the ground was rather complicated. After the death of Æthelstan in October of 939, Olaf Guthfrithson – having escaped to Dublin after his defeat at Brunanburh in 937 – quit Dublin, according to the *Annals of the Four Masters*.[63] According to the D manuscript of the *Chronicle*, in 941 the Northumbrians withdrew their pledges and accepted 'Olaf of Ireland' (*Anlaf of Yrlande*) as their king. Olaf Guthfrithson died in 941, so if the D manuscript is correct, this was probably Olaf Guthfrithson's cousin and successor, Olaf Sihtricson (Amlaíb Cuarán).[64] It was probably after Olaf Guthfrithson's death that war in Mercia was renewed. In 942, Edmund was in a position to make grants in Derbyshire to Wulfsige the Black, and in (probably) 943 Edmund stood as sponsor to Olaf Sihtricson and Ragnald Guthfrithson (Ragnall mac Gofraid), who was then ruling in Northumbria.[65] This truce evidently did not hold as Edmund drove Olaf and Ragnald from Northumbria in 944.

The D manuscript includes an entry for 943 claiming that Olaf invaded Mercia and captured the old Mercian royal centre of Tamworth, which had been fortified by Edmund's aunt Æthelflæd in 913.[66] The entry also claims that in the same year, Olaf and his ally Archbishop Wulfstan I of York were besieged in Leicester by Edmund, but they escaped under the cover of night.[67] According to the *Historia Regum*, Archbishops Odda of Canterbury and Wulfstan brokered a truce between the two kings.[68] At this point, the entry of the D manuscript specifically calls Edmund's enemies 'Danes', but the composition of Edmund's foes must have been heterogeneous. If Wulfstan of York was with Olaf in Leicester, there is reason to suppose that some of his men would be Northumbrian Angles, not to mention possible Anglian supporters from the Five Boroughs, in addition to Olaf's 'Northmen' and any Danes from eastern Mercia and/or Northumbria who threw in their lot with him.

The 943 entry of the D manuscript is particularly vexing. The use of the word '*Her*' ('In this year') twice, first to describe the attack on Tamworth and then to describe the siege of Leicester suggests that the chronicler had stitched together the events of two years. Downham has argued that the attack on Tamworth occurred in 942, the same year that Edmund captured the Five Boroughs, and that the siege of Leicester took place in 943, after which Olaf and Ragnald were baptized, apparently implying that there was a revolt against Edmund's rule in Leicester after the Five Boroughs campaign.[69] However, perhaps the chronology that makes the most sense is to suppose that the attack on Tamworth did indeed take place in 942; this was followed by the Five Boroughs campaign across 942 and 943, and that the D manuscript's account of the siege of Leicester in 943 marks the final action of that campaign.

This reconstructed narrative is not at all clear in the *Five Boroughs* poem, which elides Edmund's compromises and setbacks. The defection of the Northumbrians in 941, Olaf's successful attack on Tamworth, the siege of Leicester, and the alliance between Olaf and Wulfstan are only recorded in MS D. Taking the manuscripts together, it is clear that north-eastern Mercia was in the balance in the early 940s, and its political community was deeply divided. It is not surprising, therefore, that the poet should wish to strike a tone that emphasises collective identity tied to Edmund and his position as a leader in war and as a defender of his people, rather than a simple oppositional relationship between English and Danish ethnicities.

It seems likely that *Brunanburh* and *Five Boroughs* were intended to be read together to provide a narrative of Cerdicing triumph while navigating the complex politics and questions of collective identity in the 930s and 940s. Both poems are careful in their treatment of the dynasty's enemies and expansive in their understanding of the kings' dominion and the protection bestowed upon heterogeneous subjects.

When were the poems composed? A good case can be made for the reign of Edgar. If the poems date to Edgar's reign, then reading them as a comment on royal legitimacy in relation to the partition of Wessex and Mercia between Eadwig and Edgar could be viable. When reading *Brunanburh* and *Five Boroughs* together, one would be reminded of the alliance of the West Saxons and the Mercians that achieved such a remarkable victory in 937, and of the legitimacy of the Cerdicing kings and their ability to protect their people. This receives further support from Bately, who argues that the common material for MSS A-D for the annals between 933-946 was in existence by the 950s, and that the poems themselves contain non-West Saxon dialect features.[70] Thus, the poems may be a product of Edgar's court in Mercia between 957-9. If so, then they are royal, but not necessarily West Saxon. This may explain the poems' responsiveness to regional sensitivities, and they could be seen as instruments of integration, rather than the simple imposition of West Saxon authority. In this case, rather than blunt tools of royal propaganda emanating from the royal court in Wessex, the poems, and their incorporation in the manuscripts of the *Chronicle*, represent a dialogue between the royal dynasty and the provinces.

The broader political ideologies of Edgar's reign also seem to suit the composition and dissemination of the poems. There is a hint that Edgar attempted to redefine the position of the Danes in the kingdom through his legislation. Edgar's fourth code (962 or 963) declares that while the Danes had hitherto been allowed to keep their own laws because of the loyalty they had always shown the king, nevertheless the king wished that his pronouncements regarding cattle theft were to be obeyed even among the Danes.[71] Perhaps *Brunanburh* and *Five Boroughs* are ambiguous regarding potential disloyalty among Danes in Northumbria and Mercia in the 930s and 940s as part of a wider agenda of integration in the late 950s and early 960s. At the same time, more explicit foils are made of the Scots and the Uí Ímair, who were by this time a more distant threat. According to the *Annals of Ulster*, Olaf

Sihtricson faced a challenge from Cammán mac Amlaíb/Sihtric Cam, the son of Olaf Guthfrithson in 960.[72] The increasing security of the Cerdicing realm in the 960s, after bursts of instability in Mercia and the north between 937 and 954, provided the context for Edgar's famously robust display of self-assurance on the Dee in 973, when a meeting was held at Chester with the kings of the Irish Sea in a ceremony that may have entailed some form of submission to Edgar's authority.[73] It is sometimes overlooked, but the Battle of Brunanburh took place a mere thirty-six years before Edgar's procession on the Dee, and it is likely that the battle was fought quite near to Chester.[74] It is plausible that some men who were at the end of their political careers in 973 had just grown into political maturity in 937. Perhaps some of Edgar's senior councillors had been young men in Æthelstan's army?

Our final poem is the famous *Battle of Maldon*, which celebrates Ealdorman Byrhtnoth of Essex's heroic but doomed stand against a viking army in 991. As in *Brunanburh* and *Five Boroughs*, *Maldon* rarely uses ethnic terminology to describe the antagonists. Typically, they are *wicinga* (vikings), *sæmen, sæ-mannum, sæ-lida, brim-manna, flotan* (seamen, sailors, etc.), or even more vaguely as 'enemies' or 'warriors' (*beorn, guma, cempa, wiga, feða* etc.).[75] Twice, the enemies are 'heathens'.[76] There is only one occasion in the 325 surviving lines of the poem in which the word 'Dane' is used, in which Byrhtnoth encouraged his men 'to gain fame from the Danes.'[77] As Robinson noted, Byrhtnoth's enemies are presented 'not as heinous villains, but as a vague inimical force.'[78]

Historians often understand *Maldon* to represent a strong sense of national identity in the face of a common foe.[79] However, while the Danes are only mentioned once in the poem, the English are not mentioned *at all*. *Maldon* is not about ethnic animosity, nor is it about 'English' unity; it is about Byrhtnoth and his retainers. If the poem has any higher aspirations in regard to collective identity, they are twofold: the first objective is to draw upon a Christian identity in opposition to pagan enemies, as when Byrhtnoth looks to heaven and says a final prayer before being slain by *hæðene scealcas* ('heathen fighters').[80] The second is to emphasise the *regional* identities that comprise Æthelred's kingdom. Thus, Byrhtnoth and his men make up the *Eastseaxena ord*.[81] Later, one of Byrhtnoth's men declaims: 'I want my nobility known to all men, that I was among the Mercians of a mighty kindred,' thereby representing the Mercians in the battle.[82] Then, a Northumbrian hostage takes up arms to avenge Byrhtnoth, and he is mentioned fighting bravely 'as long as he was able to wield weapons.'[83] The heroes of the poem also represent the vertical relationships of Anglo-Saxon society.[84] Most of the poem concerns the ealdorman and his noble retainers, but at one point, 'a simple ceorl' (*unorne ceorl*), exhorts the warriors to avenge their lord. What unifies these men is not ethnicity, but their social relationships with each other, with Byrhtnoth, and the king. In this way the poem recalls the will of Æthelstan *ætheling*, discussed above. Instead of referring to 'England', the poet refers to the kingdom as *Æþelredes eard* (Æthelred's land). Through his references to the East Saxons, Northumbrians, and Mercians, the poet suggests a realm that is an accretion of regionally distinctive territories and peoples; they were united not necessarily by their 'Englishness', but by their allegiance to Æthelred, and the vertical and horizontal social relationships of the nobility.

All three poems use conflict to communicate collective identity, but none of them are about ethnic solidarity in the face of a common foe; instead, they are about the interpersonal relationships predicated upon the king as a military leader and the protector of his subjects. These are social relationships, but they are also relationships of mutual military obligation: Byrhtnoth is fulfilling his military obligations to the king, Byrhtnoth's retainers fulfil their obligation to their lord, and the king has an obligation of protection to his subjects.

The *Maldon* poet included a warning about treachery and the consequences of these obligations being left unfulfilled. The battle was lost when some of Byrhtnoth's retainers fled from the fighting.[85] This suggests something broader about the regional and ethnically diverse tenth-century kingdom: it required the active participation of the aristocracy, who were unified through their interpersonal relationships with each other and their loyalty to the dynasty. But when the dynasty was perceived as being militarily unsuccessful, or when members of the aristocracy no longer 'bought in' to the project, the results could be disastrous. As the military situation worsened around the turn of the century, we see just this in the *Anglo-Saxon Chronicle*. What the *Maldon* poet understood to be the strength of the kingdom – the diverse regions that were united in their loyalty to the king – is suggested to be a weakness in the *Chronicle*.

For example, in 1006 the chronicler complained about the king spending Christmas north of the Thames in Shropshire while a viking army ravaged through Berkshire and Hampshire.[86] In 1009, it is reported that the men of East Kent made a separate peace with Thorkell the Tall, paying a tribute of £3000 and allowing the army to overwinter in the province as they harried the surrounding shires.[87] In 1010, the chronicler described the battle of Ringmere, and noted that the men of East Anglia fled, abandoning the men of Cambridgeshire to their fate as they held their ground. The chronicler ended the annal for 1010 bitterly: 'there was no leader who would raise an army, but each fled as best he could, and in the end no shire would even help the next.'[88]

The aristocratic solidarities of the tenth century came under great strain in the eleventh century. If we return to the will of Æthelstan *ætheling* discussed above, we see the effects of this. Of all the associates and companions remembered by the prince in 1014, most of them would be dead soon after, and many died violently: Morcar was murdered in 1015,[89] Ulfketel was killed in battle in 1016.[90] Leofwine survived, but his son, Northman, was killed by Cnut in 1017.[91] Eadwig was banished in 1016 or 1017, and was murdered by Cnut the following year.[92] Æthelstan's other brother Edmund died suddenly in 1016 after fighting a series of battles against Cnut.[93] Thurbrand the Hold was killed by his rivals in the north in 1024.[94] However, we should not take this *too* far: Cnut's conquest did not have the same sort of structural impact on the aristocracy that the Norman Conquest had fifty years later, but there was probably enough disruption among the military elite and enough disillusionment with the regime for Cnut to consolidate his position in England.[95]

Historians have often been impressed by the homogeneous administrative institutions of the English kingdom and the extent of royal authority in the tenth and eleventh centuries. Though the maximal view of the Anglo-Saxon 'state' may have receded slightly, the strength and durability of these institutions across two conquests in fifty years remains impressive. Institutions such as shires and hundreds provided a means by which the English kingdom was consolidated. The literary evidence discussed here provides another angle. These poems suggest a regional, ethnically diverse, and potentially fractious kingdom that was held together in no small part due to the interpersonal relationships of the military aristocracy under the leadership of the royal dynasty. Conflict, and the memorialisation of conflict, provided a way to frame and communicate collective identity under the king in a way that could respond to political nuance and was appropriate to the heterogeneous nature of the English kingdom. None of the poems discussed here celebrate the 'English' at the expense of 'the Danes', and in most cases references to the dynasty's enemies are left rather ambiguous. The use of these poems as instruments of a dynastic political project should be recognised. This may be particularly true of the *Brunanburh* and *Five Boroughs*, the so-called 'chronicle poems', which may be more profitably understood as subtle texts that were put to work in order to smooth over some of the rougher edges of recent history and help define 'in-groups' and 'out-groups' in the coalescing kingdom.

The evidence discussed here emphasises the notion of the kingdom as a network of interpersonal relationships between the king and his leading subjects that are expressed through military idioms. Poetry may have flattered the pretensions of the warriors and aristocrats who sustained and participated in the dynasty's success. To put it another way, the poems provide a heroic veneer to the more prosaic reforms brought about by the implementation of shires and hundreds.[96] Were these poems archaizing celebrations of a heroic mode that never existed? Perhaps, but that may be just what the audience liked to hear. Crucially, ethnicity is less important in these texts than social relations. This is not to say that ethnicity was not important in early medieval Britain, but the poems all recognise other salient aspects of collective identity: regionalism, dynastic loyalty, class, and social obligation.

A certain amount of fragility needs to be recognised: the rhetoric of the poetry discussed in this paper was oriented around noble solidarities and the relationships held by the king. This worked while the nobility was engaged, and the king was – generally speaking – strong and successful in war. As those who were loyal to the dynasty died, were killed in battle, or became disillusioned, the communication of collective identity through military success ultimately rang hollow during the wars of the 990s and early 1000s. Poetry in the heroic mode that celebrated the military aristocracy and the royal dynasty may have been helpful in binding together the dynasty's potentially disparate and fractious subjects, but perhaps these men would have been better served studying their gospels, where they would have recalled that those who take up the sword shall perish by it.

Notes

1   P. Wormald, 'Anglo-Saxon Society and its Literature', in *The Cambridge Companion to Old English Literature*, ed. by M. Godden and M. Lapidge (Cambridge, Cambridge University Press, 1991), pp. 1-22 (15).
2   The *Anglo-Saxon Chronicle* (*ASC*) is cited from S. Keynes, D. N. Dumville et al, (eds.), *The Anglo-Saxon Chronicle: A Collaborative Edition* vols. 3-8 (Cambridge, D.S. Brewer, 1983-2004), referenced by year after *The Anglo-Saxon Chronicle: A Revised Translation*, ed. and trans. by D. Whitelock, D.C. Douglas and S.I. Tucker (London, Eyre and Spottiswoode, 1961) unless otherwise noted.
3   *The Battle of Maldon*, ed. and trans. by D.G. Scragg (Manchester, 1981). The poem was incorporated into the manuscript known as London, British Library, Cotton MS Otho A.XII. The poem survives due to a transcription made shortly before the fire. See also Scragg, '*The Battle of Maldon*: Fact or Fiction?', in *The Battle of Maldon: Fiction and Fact*, ed. by J. Cooper (London, Hambledon, 1993), pp. 19-31.
4   A. Woolf, *From Pictland to Alba, 789-1070* (Edinburgh, Edinburgh University Press, 2007), pp. 168-73, p. 169; C. Downham, 'The Chronology of the Last Scandinavian Kings of York, AD 937-954', *Northern History* 40 (2003): 27-51 (31).
5   F.M. Stenton, *Anglo-Saxon England* (3rd ed., Oxford, Clarendon, 1971), p. 689.
6   For the date of poem, J.D. Niles, '*Maldon* and Mythopoesis', in *Old English Literature: Critical Essays*, ed. by R.M. Liuzza (New Haven, Yale University Press, 2002), pp. 289-305, favouring an early date. L. Neidorf, 'II Æthelred and the Politics of the *Battle of Maldon*', *JEGP* 111 (2012): 451-73 argues that the promulgation of *II Æthelred* in 994 may have presented a useful context for the composition of the poem; cf. G. Clark, '*The Battle of Maldon*: A Heroic Poem', *Speculum* 43 (1968): 52-71.
7   Keynes, 'Manuscripts of the *Anglo-Saxon Chronicle*', in *The Cambridge History of the Book in Britain*, ed. by R. Gameson (Cambridge, Cambridge University Press, 2011), pp. 537-52, provides an overview.
8   The debate surrounding early medieval ethnicity is often fraught. A sample of the main positions are: P. Heather, *The Goths* (Oxford, Blackwell,

1996), who argues that barbarian ethnicity was stable and coherent across a broad section of society characterised by 'warrior freemen'. The *traditionskern* model, on the other hand, argues that heterogenous groups were led by cores of aristocratic dynasties that retained traditions of genuine 'ethnic memory' from a Scandinavian homeland: R. Wenskus, *Stammesbildung und Verfassung: Das Werden der frümittelalterlichen gentes*, (Cologne, Böhlau Verlag, 1961); H. Wolfram, *History of the Goths* (Berkeley, University of California Press, 1988). For the 'Vienna School', which adds significant nuance to the *traditionskern* model, see e.g. W. Pohl, 'Conceptions of Ethnicity in Early Medieval Studies', in *Debating the Middle Ages*, ed. by L. K. Little and B. H. Rosenwein (Oxford, Blackwell, 1998), pp. 13-24; Pohl, 'Telling the Difference: Signs of Ethnic Identity', in *Strategies of Distinction: The Construction of Ethnic Communities, 300-800*, ed. by W. Pohl and H. Reimitz (Leiden, Brill, 1998), pp. 17-70, and many of the assembled papers in H-W Goetz, J. Jarnut and W. Pohl (eds.), *Regna and Gentes: The Relationship between Late Antique and Early Medieval Peoples and Kingdoms in the Transformation of the Roman World* (Leiden, Brill, 2003). Opposition to the 'Vienna School', which denies the existence even of that so-called 'kernel', is demonstrated by W. Goffart, 'Two Notes on Germanic Antiquity Today', *Traditio* 50 (1995): 9-30; C. Bowlus, 'Ethnogenesis Models and the Age of Migrations: A Critique', *Austrian History Yearbook* 26 (1995): 147-64; and the papers in A. Gillett (ed.), *On Barbarian Identity* (Turnhout, Brepols, 2003). P. Amory, *People and Identity in Ostrogothic Italy* (Cambridge, Cambridge University Press, 1997), takes a very situational view of ethnicity.

9   Wormald, 'The Venerable Bede and the Church of the English', in *The English Religious Tradition and the Genius of Anglicanism*, ed. by G. Rowell (Wantage, Ikon, 1992), pp. 13-32; Wormald, 'Bede, the Bretwaldas and the Origins of the *Gens Anglorum*', in *Ideal and Reality in Frankish and Anglo-Saxon Society: Essays Presented to J.M. Wallace-Hadrill*, ed. by P. Wormald, D. Bullough and R. Collins (Oxford, Clarendon, 1983), pp. 99-129; Wormald, '*Engla Lond*: The Making of an Allegiance', *Journal of Historical Sociology* 7 (1994): 1-24; S. Foot, 'The Making of *Angelcynn*: English Identity Before the Norman Conquest', *TRHS* 6 (1996): 25-49. In addition, see: J. Campbell, 'The United Kingdom of England: The Anglo-Saxon Achievement', repr. in his *The Anglo-Saxon State* (London, Bloomsbury, 2000), pp. 31-54.

10   Bede, *Historia Ecclesiastica Gentes Anglorum*, ed. by B. Colgrave and R.A.B. Mynors (Oxford, Clarendon, 1969), i.1: 'quinque gentium linguis... Anglorum uidelicet Brettonum, Scottorum, Pictorum et Latinorum'.

11 Bede, *HE* i.15. For more on this, see N. Howe, *Migration and Mythmaking in Anglo-Saxon England* (New Haven, Yale University Press, 1989).

12 A. Hastings, *The Construction of Nationalism: Ethnicity, Religion and Nationalism* (Cambridge, Cambridge University Press, 1997), sees this as particularly important to the creation of the English kingdom.

13 The evidence for Guthrum comes from the numismatic record. See: P. Grierson and M.A.S. Blackburn, *Early Medieval Coinage, with a Catalogue of the Coins of the Fitzwilliam Museum, Cambridge*, vol. 1 (Cambridge, Cambridge University Press, 1986), p. 318. For Ælfgifu-Emma: *Encomium Emmae Reginae*, ed. and trans. by A. Campbell with a supplementary introduction by S. Keynes (Cambridge, Cambridge University Press for the Royal Historical Society, 1998), pp. xli, 55-8; P. Sawyer, *Anglo-Saxon Charters: An Annotated List and Bibliography* (London, Royal Historical Society, 1968), no. 902 [charters cited hereafter as 'S.'+ Sawyer number, e.g. 'S. 902'], revised and annotated at <https://esawyer.lib.cam.ac.uk/about/index.html>.

14 *De Rebus Gestis Ælfredi*, in *Asser's Life of King Alfred together with the Annals of St Neots erroneously ascribed to Asser*, ed. by W.H. Stevenson (Oxford, Clarendon, 1904), 1; D. Dumville, 'The Anglian Collection of Royal Genealogies and Regnal Lists', *ASE* 5 (1976): pp. 23-50; 'The West Saxon Genealogical Regnal List: Manuscripts and Texts', *Anglia* 104 (1986): 1-32.

15 Af. Int.49.9, in *Die Gesetze der Angelsachsen*, vol. 1, ed. by F. Liebermann (Halle, M. Niemeyer, 1903), p. 46.

16 This was assimilated into Anglo-Saxon culture through the Old Testament and the writing of Gildas, who argues in his *De Excidio Brittanniae*, ed. and trans. by H. Williams (Lampeter, Llanerch Press, 1901) that the *adventus* of the Saxons was sown by the sins of the Britons. This story is repeated in Bede, *HE* i.22 and then in 1010 x 1016 in Wulfstan II of York's *Sermo Lupi ad Anglos*, ed. D. Whitelock (3rd ed., London, Methuen, 1963).

17 Campbell, 'United Kingdom', pp. 37-40; Hastings, *The Construction of Nationalism*, pp. 35-65, draws on Campbell considerably. But see now G. Molyneaux, *The Formation of the English Kingdom in the Tenth Century* (Oxford, Oxford University Press, 2015).

18 For Britons, see e.g. C.P. Lewis, 'Welsh Territories and Welsh Identities in Late Anglo-Saxon England', in *Britons in Anglo-Saxon England*, ed. by N.J. Higham (Woodbridge, Boydell & Brewer, 2007), pp. 130-43; and D.E. Thornton, 'Some Welshmen in Domesday Book and Beyond: Aspects of Anglo-Welsh Relations in the Eleventh Century', in *Britons in Anglo-Saxon England*, pp. 144-64. More recently, see L. Brady, *Writing the Welsh Borderlands in Anglo-Saxon England* (Oxford, Oxford

University Press, 2017). Britons are accorded a *wergild* in the eleventh-century legal tract *Norðleoda laga: Norðleod 7*. For Scandinavians in later Anglo-Saxon England the literature is too numerous to cite here but see for instance the papers in R. Lavelle and S. Roffey (eds.), *Danes in Wessex: The Scandinavian Presence in Southern England, c. 800-c. 1100* (Oxford, Oxbow, 2015); D.M. Hadley, *The Northern Danelaw: its Social Structure, c. 800-1100* (Leicester, Leicester University Press, 2000).

19 S. Reynolds, 'What do we mean by "Anglo-Saxon" and "Anglo-Saxons"?', *Journal of British Studies* 24 (1985): 395-414.

20 Hadley, 'Viking and Native: Re-Thinking Identity in the Danelaw', *EME* 11 (2002): 45-70; M. Innes, 'Danelaw Identities: Ethnicity, Regionalism, and Political Allegiance', in *Cultures in Contact: Scandinavia Settlement in England in the Ninth and Tenth Centuries*, ed. by D.M. Hadley and J.D. Richards (Turnhout, Brepols, 2000), pp. 65-88.

21 P. Geary, 'Ethnic Identity as a Situational Construct in the Early Middle Ages', *Mitteilungen der anthropologischen Gesellschaft in Wien,* 113 (1983): 15-26 (22).

22 E. James, 'Gregory of Tours and the Franks', in *After Rome's Fall: Narrators and Sources of Early Medieval History*, ed. by A. C. Murray (Toronto, University of Toronto Press, 1998), pp. 51-66 (52).

23 James, 'Gregory of Tours', pp. 60, 65-6.

24 e.g. *Vita Sancti Oswaldi,* in *Byrhtferth of Ramsey: The Lives of St Oswald and St Ecgwine*, ed. and trans. by M. Lapidge (Oxford, Clarendon, 2009). iv.12.

25 *ASC* CDE 1016.

26 Letter of Bede to Ecgbehrt, Archbishop of York, in *Venerabilis Bedae Opera Historica*, ed. by C. Plummer (Oxford, Clarendon, 1896), vol. 1, pp. 405-23: 'filii nobilium aut emeritorum militum... patriam suam pro qua militare debuerant trans mare abeuntes relinquant.'

27 Felix, *Vita Sancti Guthlaci*, ed. by B. Colgrave (Cambridge, Cambridge University Press, 1956), 17: 'conrasis undique diversarum gentium sociis inmensas praedas gregasset.'

28 Asser, 76: 'Franci autem multi, Frisones, Galli, pagani, Britones, et Scotti, Armorici sponte se suo dominio subdiderant.'

29 *Anglo-Saxon Wills*, ed. Whitelock (Cambridge, Cambridge University Press, 1930), no. 20, pp. 56-63; S. 1503.

30 *ASC* C 1004, 1010.

31 Prosopography of Anglo-Saxon England (PASE) Morcar 2. Accessed at: <https://pase.ac.uk/>.

32 C. Insley, 'Politics, Conflict and Kinship in Early Eleventh-Century Mercia', *Midland History* 25 (2000): pp. 28-42.

33 J.G. Hudson, 'Feud, Vengeance and Violence in England from the Tenth to the Twelfth Centuries', in *Feud, Violence and Practice: Essays in Medieval Studies in Honor of Stephen D. White*, ed. by B.S. Tuten and T.L. Billado (Farnham, Ashgate, 2010), pp. 29-53. Thurbrand is described in the *Historia Regum* as a 'Turebrando nobili et Danico viro': *Historia Regum*, in *Symeonis Monachi Opera Omnia*, ed. by T. Arnold, Rolls Series 75 (London, Longman, 1882-5), p. 148.

34 PASE Leofwine 49.

35 R. Woolf, 'The Ideal of Men Dying with Their Lord in the *Germania* and in *The Battle of Maldon*', *Anglo-Saxon England*, 5 (1976): 63-81.

36 *ASC* CD 1065: 'weol[an] brytnode... / hæleða wealdend, / weold wel geþungen Walum 7 Scottum / 7 Bryttum eac, byre Æðelredes / Englum 7 Sexum oretmæcgcum [mighty champions], / swa ymbclyppað ceald brymmas, / þæt eall Eadwarde, æðelum kinge, / hyrdon holdlice hagestealde menn... /Syððan forð becom freolice in geatwum / kyninge kystum god. Clæne 7 milde, / Eadward se æðela eðel bewerode, / land 7 leode...'

37 S. Foot, *Æthelstan: The First King of England* (New Haven, Yale University Press, 2011), pp. 169-83; Downham, *Viking Kings of Britain and Ireland: The Dynasty of Ívarr to A.D. 1014* (Edinburgh, Dunedin, 2007), pp. 104-5; Woolf, *Pictland to Alba*, pp. 168-73. There has been an enormous amount of literature devoted to the battle, see for instance *The Battle of Brunanburh*, ed. by A. Campbell (London, W. Heinemann, 1938) for text and commentary; *The Battle of Brunanburh: A Casebook*, ed. by M. Livingston (Exeter, Exeter University Press, 2011), for a collection of sources related to the battle. Recent reassessments include: K. Halloran, 'The Brunanburh Campaign: A Reappraisal', *Scottish Historical Review* 84 (2005): 133-48.

38 'Her Æþelstan cing, eorla drihten, / beorna beahgyfa... swa him geæþele wæs / fram cneomægum, þæt hi æt campe oft / wiþ laþra gehwæne land ealgodon, / hord 7 hamas.'

39 Whitelock, *ASC*, p. 70 prefers 'their own country' for *cyþþe*; while it is true that *cyþþe* can mean 'native country, homeland,' etc., as per *University of Toronto Dictionary of Old English s.v. Cyþþ* 3, in this case I prefer sense 2.b, 'kindred', because it allows the poet to strike a more ambiguous line by *not* suggesting that Mercia was in any sense 'foreign' to the brothers. For the poet, such nuance may have been preferable in this instance. Admittedly, the close relationship between the two senses of the word is undeniable. See: *University of Toronto Dictionary of Old English: A to I Online*, ed. A. Cameron et al. (Toronto, 2018), consulted at <https://doe.utoronto.ca>.

40 *Liber Vitae of the New Minster and Hyde Abbey Winchester, British Library Stowe 944*, ed. S. Keynes (Copenhagen, Rosenkilde og Bagger, 1996), pp. 19-20.

41 As discussed by B. Yorke, 'The Jutes of Hampshire and Wight and the Origins of Wessex', in *The Origins of Anglo-Saxon Kingdoms*. ed. by S. Bassett (Leicester, Leicester University Press, 1989), pp. 84-96 and elsewhere.

42 *ASC s.a.* 449, 455, 456, 473, 488.

43 *ASC s.a.* 501, 514, 534, 544.

44 *ASC s.a.* 477, 485, 491.

45 *ASC s.a.* 495, 508, 514, 519, 527, 530, 534, 552, 556, 560, 568, 571, 577, 584, 591, 592, 593, 597.

46 However, *ASC* E *s.a.* 449 does include a notice that the Angles came from Angeln, 'which ever after remained a waste'.

47 *Historia Regum*, p. 93.

48 *Annals of Clonmacnoise Being the Annals of Ireland from the Earliest Period to A.D. 1408*, ed. by D. Murphy. (Dublin, Royal Society of Antiquaries of Ireland, 1896), 931 (=937), p. 151.

49 *Brunanburh* line 33: *Norðmanna bregu* ('prince of the Northmen'), and lines 53-6: 'Gewitan him þa Norþmen nægledcnearrum, / dreorig daraða laf, on Dinges mere / ofer deop wæter Difelin secan 7 eft Hiraland' ('Then the 'Northmen', sorrowful survivors of the spears, departed in their nailed ships on to *Dingesmere* / seeking Dublin over deep water, back to Ireland.'), and see below.

50 *ASC* D 927.

51 *ASC* 934; S. 407; *Historia de Sancto Cuthberto: A History of a Saint and a Record of His Patrimony*, ed. T. Johnson South, Anglo-Saxon Texts 3 (Woodbridge, Boydell & Brewer, 2002), pp. 26-7.

52 *Annals of Clonmacnoise*, 928 (=934), p. 149.

53 N. McGuigan, 'Ælla and the Descendants of Ivar: Politics and Legend in the Viking Age', *Northern History* 52 (2015): 20-34.

54 Woolf, *Pictland to Alba*, pp. 164-5.

55 William of Malmesbury, *Gesta Regum Anglorum*, ed. by R.A.B. Mynors, R.M. Thompson and M. Winterbottom (Oxford, Clarendon, 1998), vol. 1, ii.135, p. 220; and see Foot, *Æthelstan*, p. 172.

56 *ASC* ABCD 942: 'In this year King Edmund, lord of the English, defender of kinsmen, the beloved doer of great deeds, went to Mercia, as bounded by Dore, the Whitwell Gate, and the River Humber, the broad flowing stream. Five boroughs, Leicester and Lincoln, Nottingham and also Stamford and Derby each. The Danes had before been subjected by force under the northmen, and for a long time were bound in captivity to the

heathens, until they were redeemed by the defender of warriors, the son of Edward, Edmund the king, to his glory.'

57 Stenton, *Anglo-Saxon England*, p. 358

58 Those derived from A. Mawer, 'The Redemption of the Five Boroughs', *EHR* 38 (1923): 551-7; see e.g. Stenton, 'The Danes in England', in *Preparatory to Anglo-Saxon England*, ed. by D. Stenton (Oxford, Clarendon, 1970), p. 162.

59 As noted by Foot, 'Where English Becomes British: Rethinking Contexts for *Brunanburh*', in *Myth, Rulership, Church and Charters: Essays in Honour of Nicholas Brooks*, ed. by J. Barrow and A. Wareham (Aldershot, Ashgate, 2008), pp. 127-44 (131-2).

60 S.J. Harris, *Race and Ethnicity in Anglo-Saxon Literature* (London, Routledge, 2003), pp. 107-29 sees a similar message discussed through an Old Testament 'logic' in Archbishop Wulfstan's *Sermo Lupi ad Anglos*.

61 Downham, '"Hiberno-Norwegians" and "Anglo-Danes": Anachronistic Ethnicities in Viking-Age England', *Medieval Scandinavia* 19 (2009): 139-69, with a translation at p. 148; see also Halloran, 'The War for Mercia, 942-943', *Midland History* 41 (2016): 96-106.

62 *ASC* A 920: 'ealle þa þe on Norþhymrum bugeaþ, ægþer ge Englisce, ge Denisce, ge Norþmen, ge oþre...'

63 *The Annals of the Kingdom of Ireland by the Four Masters from the Earliest Times to the Year 1616*, ed. by John O'Donovan (Dublin, Hodges, Smith & Co., 1856), ii, *s.a.* 937 (=939), pp. 638-9.

64 According the *Annals of the Four Masters*, Olaf Sihtricson left for York *s.a.* 938 (=939).

65 S. 479, 484, 1606.

66 *ASC* MR 913.

67 *ASC* D *s.a.* 943.

68 *Historia Regum*, pp. 93-4.

69 Downham, 'The Chronology': 32-41.

70 J. Bately, *The Anglo-Saxon Chronicle: Texts and Textual Relationships*, Reading Medieval Studies Monograph no. 3 (Reading, University of Reading, 1991), p. 10.

71 IV Eg.12-15.

72 *ASC* MS D 954; *The Annals of Ulster to AD 1131*, ed. and trans. by S. Mac Airt and G. Mac Niocaill (Dublin, Dublin Institute for Advanced Studies, 1983) 960.

73 J. Barrow, 'Chester's Earliest Regatta? Edgar's Dee-Rowing Revisited', *EME* 10 (2001): 81-93; D. Thorton, 'Edgar and the Eight Kings, A.D. 973: *Textus* and *Dramatis Personae*', *EME* 10 (2001): 49-79.

74 The location of the Battle of Brunanburh is fraught, but see P. Cavill, S.
   Harding and J. Jesch, 'Revisiting *Dingesmere*', *Journal of the English Place-
   Name Society* 36 (2004): 25-38.
75 'Vikings': lines 26, 73, 97, 116, 139, 322; 'sailors, seamen, etc.': 27, 29, 38,
   45, 49, 72, 134, 164, 227, 286, 295; 'heathens': 55, 181; 'enemy, foe': 82;
   'loathsome guests, people': 86, 90; 'champions, warriors, etc.': 119, 131,
   270, 277.
76 *Maldon* 55, 181
77 *Maldon* 127-9.
78 F.C. Robinson, 'Some Aspects of the *Maldon* Poet's Artistry', *JEGP*, 75
   (1976): 25-40 (27).
79 Campbell, 'England, *c.* 991', repr. in his *The Anglo-Saxon State*, pp. 157-
   78 (pp. 176-7); Clark, 'The Battle in *The Battle of Maldon*',
   Neuphilologische Mitteilungen 69 (1968): 374-9.
80 *Maldon* 171-80.
81 *Maldon* 69: 'vanguard of the East Saxons'.
82 *Maldon* 216-17.
83 *Maldon* 265-72.
84 A. Williams, 'The Battle of Maldon and "The Battle of Maldon": History,
   Poetry and Propaganda', *Medieval History*, 2 (1992): 35-44.
85 *Maldon* 185-201.
86 *ASC* CDE 1006.
87 *ASC* CDE 1009.
88 *ASC* CDE 1010.
89 *ASC* CDE 1015.
90 *ASC* CDE 1016.
91 *ASC* CDE 1017
92 *ASC* CDE 1017.
93 *ASC* CDE 1016; Neither the *Chronicle* nor *Encomium Emmae Reginae*
   ii.14 suggest that Edmund died violently, but Henry of Huntingdon claimed
   he was murdered in his privy, while Gaimar stated that he was murdered
   with a crossbow: Henry of Huntingdon, *Historia Anglorum*, ed. Greenway,
   iv.14; Gaimar, *L'Estorie des Engles*, ed. Hardy and Martin, lines 4408-20.
94 *De Obsessione Dunelmi*, ed. by T. Arnold, pp. 215-20; Hudson, 'Feud,
   Vengeance and Violence', pp. 29-53.
95 For the debate surrounding the structural impact of Cnut's conquest on the
   aristocracy, see: R. Fleming, *Kings and Lords in Conquest England*
   (Cambridge, Cambridge University Press, 1991), esp. pp. 21-52; K. Mack,
   'Changing Thegns: Cnut's Conquest and the English Aristocracy', *Albion*
   16 (1984): 375-87; Williams, '"Cockles amongst the Wheat': Danes and
   English in the Western Midlands in the First Half of the Eleventh Century',

Midland History 11 (1986): 1-22; Keynes, 'Cnut's Earls', in *The Reign of Cnut: King of England, Denmark and Norway*, ed. by A. Rumble (Leicester, Leicester University Press, 1994), pp. 43-88 for a judicious take.

96 For Anglo-Saxon military obligation, see: R. Abels, *Lordship and Military Obligation in Anglo-Saxon England* (Berkeley, University of California Press, 1988).

Is there a medieval legal theology? Legal learning, legal careers, and historical methodology in twelfth-century England

Philippa Byrne

University of Oxford

Law by other means

What was legal knowledge in the twelfth century, and how was it measured? The question is far less straightforward than it appears, for our medieval sources tend to elide what we might consider to be distinct categories of legal education, legal experience, and legal reputation. This paper offers a series of methodological suggestions on that point, on the need for circumspection and specificity when we speak of 'legal learning' (or its cognate terms) in the later twelfth-century. The first is that the most distinguished judges were not always distinguished jurists, or even jurists at all. Our categories do not always align neatly. In recent decades, historians have suggested that the legal expertise of some of the celebrated 'lawyer popes' of the Middle Ages has been overstated.[1] Even popes learned law on the job, through the support of specialised administrators. This article aims to explore legal knowledge more broadly, by examining the lives of some less prominent lawyers and judges. Many individuals are lauded in the surviving sources as sound judges, but such accolades are often better read as praise of personal virtue rather than evidence of technical legal knowledge. Legal reputation was a complex and slippery thing. There is a counterpoint to this observation: there were a significant group of men who were trained in law but who ultimately abandoned legal careers, and then used their legal knowledge to lay claim to authority in non-legal matters. Substantial time spent in the schools, even years of legal study, could be used to give authority to moral and social critiques. In short, this article invites us to recognise the complexity and diversity of twelfth-century 'legal' careers. While the unit of study is twelfth-century England (a place which provides both a rich and focused body of material), its conclusions are intended to speak more widely to our understanding of legal learning in this period.[2]

It is worth first defining the term, 'legal education', 'legal experience', and 'legal reputation'. By legal education, I mean those who had studied law in the schools as part of a formal course of study; those who had engaged academically with jurisprudence. Legal 'experience', by contrast, equates to practice. It describes those who had acted in a formal role in cases involving the canons – either as advocates or as judges, delegated either by a bishop or by the papal curia. Finally, legal reputation was a matter of contemporary judgment: those men singled out by our medieval sources as distinguished by their facility with the law; the kind of commendation which ones finds in chronicles, memorials or letters.

These distinctions may appear to be small ones, but historians have often inadvertently blurred the lines between training, professional expertise, and reputation, either assuming that one quality sprang from another, or that the three were typically in alignment.[3] This, in turn, means we fail to appreciate which qualities medieval sources are praising. This leads me to my second point. It is only when we recognise how medieval authors choose to elide or separate these different categories of legal experience that we can properly understand how law and legal study related to the other scholastic subjects and other categories of knowledge and learning in the medieval schools.[4] Praise of legal learning did not exist in isolation; it was closely connected to claims about moral probity and personal virtue. This is particularly important for the twelfth century, the moment at which the relationships between the different subjects in the medieval schools were beginning to be more sharply defined.[5] Finally, this paper re-examines two under-studied legal careers – those of Gerald of Wales and Baldwin of Forde – in an attempt to place law within a twelfth-century life.

It is often the evidence of jurisprudential education which has spoken the loudest in the ears of historians. This is perhaps unsurprising: a faculty or school of law provides a useful institutional focus, as well as the increased likelihood of copying and preservation of manuscripts.[6] The evidence for this learning has survived in a significant body of sources, both for the study of canon law and Roman law: the collections, *summae*, glosses, *distinctiones* and *ordines*, all part of a process in which learned masters in the schools attempted to epitomise and expand upon existing legal knowledge. For canon law, such works were the substantial focus of the seminal study of Kuttner and Rathbone, which provided them with the evidence for the prolific writing of Anglo-Norman canonists.[7] Kuttner and Rathbone's research remains the starting point for any work on canon law and lawyers in twelfth-century England; it is hard to overstate its enduring influence. It was an analysis constructed from those Anglo-Norman canonists who left evidence of their academic work. Thus, by the very nature of the work, those men who had no formal legal education, left no legal commentaries, or who came to legal activity through the schools of theology, rather than law, have never quite come into focus.

One of the chief problems is the ambiguity of titles and the difficulty of reconstructing 'legal' careers. We might take the career of *magister* John Grim. In the first years of the thirteenth century, John, who had been teaching theology in the schools of Oxford, was called upon to act as judge on behalf of the Archbishop of Canterbury on at least two occasions. He heard an appeal by the abbot of Eynsham against a knight accused of spoiling the abbey's lands and assaulting the abbey's clerks.[8] John also heard a dispute concerning a marriage, in which a potential new wife was alleged to be too closely connected by blood to the first.[9] He acted, at least once, as a papal judge-delegate for Innocent III.[10] These three records of judgments represent almost sum total of his surviving biography.[11] Evidently, John Grim's expertise lay in theology. His fellow judge in the case of Eynsham abbey was one Simon of Gloucester, similarly described as a student in the schools of theology at Oxford.

At Canterbury, Archbishop Hubert Walter called on several *magistri* from outside his household to settle judicial disputes for the see. In the late twelfth century, Jordan de Ros and Alexander of Hadham acted on his behalf, settling an argument over a disputed composition.[12] This was an unremarkable example of delegation to *magistri*; further examples can be found in the records of many other late twelfth-century English see.[13] Indeed, Baldwin, Hubert Walter's predecessor at Canterbury, rated two of his servants so highly that he recommended them – Roger of Rolleston and Robert of Bedford – to Hugh of Lincoln, as capable servants to assist the newly-appointed bishop.[14] We do not know if they had served Baldwin as judges-delegate, but Roger of Rolleston certainly did so for the bishop of Lincoln.[15] Baldwin, commending Robert of Bedford to Hugh, explained that he possessed a distinguished theological education and a particular 'passion for righteousness' (*zelo iustitie*).[16] This perhaps is to be read as a comment on Roger's moral probity: the kind of standing which made him capable of issuing good, just verdicts.

Magistri were often employed to perform specific judicial tasks for bishops – they did not need to be permanent members of the episcopal household to do so. It will come as no surprise to any historian who has consulted these records to observe that the title 'magister' was a flexible one; it could denote several different kinds of learning, or administrative capacity, or it could simply represent a title bestowed by a writer to indicate respect. But this prompts a further question: what was it about these particular *magistri* that made them fit to judge? It may be the case that John Grim, Simon of Gloucester, Jordan de Ros, Alexander of Hadham, Roger of Rolleston, and Robert of Bedford were all recipients of significant formal legal education in the schools, and that the evidence for it has not survived.[17] Rather more likely, however, is that when bishops looked to appoint judges-delegate in the late twelfth century, it was not, primarily, a legal education that they sought – at least in cases which seemed to present straightforward problems for resolution. What qualified them for these temporary appointments seems to have been a combination of qualities: procedural knowledge of judicial processes gained from having been present in the courts and following cases, along with a reputation for learning and administrative efficiency. In the case of John Grim, knowledge of the higher subject of theology must have recommended him further: in part because of the closeness of the canons and theological principles; some significant overlap between theology and the canons. Moreover, a reputation as a theologian might offer a guarantee that the act of judgment would adhere to moral standards. These were judgments which, for the most part, did not require legal expertise in the sense of a deep knowledge of the law; most cases required the ability to handle plaintiffs, consider and weigh testimony, and decide on a course of action that would satisfy the demands of morality and probity. It required the ability to explain and justify a decision: thus, as C. R. Cheney noted in passing in his work on bishops' chanceries, capacity in law was closely connected to facility in rhetoric – legal training did not instil eloquence, but without eloquence, no lawyer could hope to gain renown.[18]

Another figure who deserves more serious attention when tracing out the boundaries of the twelfth-century legal world is Benedict, prior of Canterbury and abbot of Peterborough (1177-93). Benedict is best known to posterity as the careful gardener who tended Becket's incipient cult, not least through bringing relics with him when he made his journey from Canterbury to Peterborough.[19] Benedict had no formal legal education, but in 1190 he served as the head of panel of itinerant royal justices; on several other occasions, he acted as a papal judge-delegate.[20] His legal knowledge must have accrued over time; as prior of a significant Benedictine house there would have been legal matters he could not avoid attending to.

At Canterbury, Benedict had enjoyed access to one of the best-stocked libraries in twelfth-century England, with significant canon law collections.[21] It is significant, therefore, that Benedict took with him to Peterborough a considerable collection of law books. This numbered a full volume of the *Corpus iuris civilis*, the *Institutes*, the *Authenticum*, the *Summa* of Placentinus, alongside the *Decretum*.[22] That choice looks purposeful: Benedict selected the key texts he might need on his elevation to the abbacy; both for disputes that might pertain to Peterborough's holdings, but also texts which he might need to utilise if called upon to judge. His book collection – whether the texts were read by Benedict himself or by his assistants – represents an acknowledgment that law had to be 'got up', sometimes only after one had been appointed to judicial office. While we cannot do more than speculate about how Peterborough's legal collections may have compared to those of other abbots, bishops, or monasteries, we might infer from this collection that there was a world of legal learning and study which did not depend upon contact with the schools.[23]

As Jane Sayers' work on thirteenth-century papal judges-delegate has emphasised, the factors at play in appointing a judge-delegate were largely extra-legal. The 'localness' and local reputation of a judge may often have been the decisive factor in their appointment. The process in the twelfth century is unlikely to have been vastly different: depending on a judge's local knowledge, his personal reputation, and/or past service. Legal expertise, after all, could be brought in where it was needed. Judges could be advised.[24]

The principle that judicial reputation did not depend, exclusively, or even for the most part, on legal learning seems to hold true at both the highest and the lowest levels in twelfth-century England. In his *Vita Sancti Remigii*, written at Lincoln in the first decades of the thirteenth century, Gerald of Wales commended and commemorated the two most accomplished judges of the later twelfth-century English episcopate: Bartholomew, bishop of Exeter (1161-84), and Roger, bishop of Worcester (1163-79). Their reputation, Gerald explains, rested on the fact that Alexander III considered them to be preeminent in judicial matters – entrusting the two of them with the greatest number of cases as judges delegate.[25] Indeed, Gerald's claim is borne out by the surviving decretal collections: along with Gilbert Foliot, bishop of London, Bartholomew and Roger seem to have been the two most frequently employed papal judges-delegate in England in the 1160s and 1170s.[26]

The judicial activities of Bartholomew and Roger cannot be in doubt; what deserves scrutiny, however, are the rationale for these appointments. This should prompt us to consider what was really being praised. By Gerald's own admission, Bartholomew was more learned in the *leges* than the *canones*.[27] Bartholomew knew the canons; that much is demonstrated by his *Penitential*. But, as his biographer Morey observed, by the 1160s and 1170s, this was far from cutting-edge jurisprudence – his knowledge was formed by the older collections of Ivo of Chartres and Burchard of Worms, not the more recent work of Gratian or Peter Lombard.[28] Gerald had studied law at Paris in the 1170s – perhaps this accounts for his comment on Bartholomew's learning in the canons. Nonetheless, however, a lack of knowledge of the most recent developments in the canon law was not enough to diminish Bartholomew's reputation as a judge. Indeed, Gerald's praise for the two men is couched in terms of their moral excellence. This includes their *probitas* (probity) – a word which might be associated with impartial and scrupulous judgment; but he praises too a wider range of moral virtues possessed by the two bishops: *eloquentia, religio, honestas, bonitas.*[29]

There is a similar challenge in interpreting Gerald's praise of his other great judge, Roger of Worcester. Roger had certainly studied arts and theology in the schools (the latter subject under the distinguished theologian Robert of Melun); whether he had undertaken any law is more difficult to assess; historiographical opinion is split.[30] We might take this as a comment on just how difficult it is to reconstruct the early careers of twelfth-century bishops, but we should at least entertain the possibility that formal jurisprudential expertise was not the reason for his appointment by Alexander. Alexander's trust in Roger could well have been vested in ties of personal friendship, founded in their time in the schools of Paris.[31] Roger's judicial reputation may have been a matter of his expertise in the canons; but it may also be (at least in part) explained by proven efficiency or trustworthiness, especially when acting at a remove from Rome. Like a rolling stone gathering moss, the more one judged – and judged without throwing up problems or complaint – the more one was trusted to judge again.

The criteria for having judged well, or having resolved a matter properly, lay somewhere between the administrative, moral, and the legal. This could produce some strange hierarchies and rankings in texts which praised moral probity under the guise of legal judgments and vice-versa. There were men in the English episcopate who could boast jurisprudential training which far outstripped that of either Bartholomew or Roger, and who acted in a similar fashion as judges, but who did not receive such laudatory notices (of one such individual, more will be said below).[32]

Whether on a national stage or a local one, a judge's accomplishments might be measured on a variety of criteria: formal legal learning in the schools was only one element of this (and not always determinative). This may have been the case in later centuries, when learning (of all scholastic kinds) became more formalised; it does not hold true for the twelfth century. Some of this is a problem of evidence: where we cannot 'flesh out' a master's early career – where, what or when they studied – we should not assume that law was a more likely object of study than theology. However, this is also a matter of recognising what kinds of knowledge our medieval sources prize.

Chronicles, hagiographies, and narrative sources of all types rarely treat jurisprudential facility as a discrete category. Rather, they tend to approach legal education and legal expertise as only one aspect through which good moral standing or personal virtue might be indicated or assessed. Those categories had – for the most part – porous borders. The corollary of this, moreover, was that knowledge of law was frequently set to other purposes. There were many men for whom law was not an end in itself, but could serve rhetorical, historical, and theological purposes.

Gerald of Wales: a little law goes a long way

How, then, did those men who had made an academic study of the law understand its purpose and place in their careers? One of the rare personal accounts we can turn to is that of Gerald of Wales. Gerald had studied the arts curriculum in Paris between 1165 and 1172; after the disappointment of seeing Peter de Leia elected to the see of St David's in 1176 – the office he had hoped to occupy – Gerald decided to find his comfort in the study of the law. He returned to Paris in 1176 with a new intellectual purpose. In his *Autobiography*, Gerald presents the study of the law as a necessary (indeed, integral) part of his vision for his own education and improvement.

> Thus, above the foundation of the arts and literature, I would build high walls of the law and canons [*legum et canonum*], and finishing above them with a holy roof of the study of theology. And then this threefold structure would stand strong, held together by the firmest bonds.[33]

Gerald's description of his own education accords with Richard Southern's characterisation of scholastic education as a project which sought to bring together the different kinds of knowledge of the created world in order to serve a higher purpose; each part of the school curriculum contributing something towards the work of 'restoration'.[34] The liberal arts, law, and theology support and inform one another. Indeed, Gerald's desire for completeness was such that he studied both 'imperial' and 'pontifical' constitutions – that is to say, both civil and canon law.[35]

Gerald's *Autobiography* recounts his rapid success in the laws. In the schools of Paris, Sundays were set aside for discussion of the Decretals: there Gerald's abilities won him both praise and acclaim. Crowds would come to hear him; there was scarcely a hall large enough to hold his audience, and his fellow students would write down each precious word which fell from Gerald's lips. One lecture was so commended that Gerald takes the trouble to describe his argument in his text. The lecture addressed the question of whether it was ever acceptable for a judge to judge out of his private knowledge (i.e. to determine his decision based on information which had not been presented to him by witnesses).[36]

Lest his readers fail to appreciate the innovation of his argument, Gerald explains that the prevailing legal orthodoxy was that a judge should not judge from 'private' knowledge, but only according to the information set before him in the court – although it should be noted that Gerald rather exaggerates how infrequently this question was subject to debate. Gerald defended the right of the judge to adjudicate on the basis of private knowledge. He reports that the scholars of Paris were so impressed with the lecture and the proofs of his argument that they sought to appoint Gerald as a lecturer, in place of the recently-departed Master Matthew of Anjou. But Gerald could not accept this offer, as he had plans to travel to Bologna. Instead, he hoped the scholars of Paris would be content by providing them two daily lectures on Gratian while he remained in the city: one on the distinctions, one on special cases.

The cynical reader of Gerald's *Autobiography* may doubt whether such a job offer was ever made. As in so much of Gerald's career, it is difficult to separate event from characteristic embellishment. The reality of the lectureship in Paris, however, is less pertinent to the matter under discussion. Gerald, in giving his own account of his life, set his second Parisian period in the context of his longer career. The study of the laws was no mere footnote; it was the culmination (and coming-together) of long-developing intellectual interests. Yet in the volume of scholarship recently produced on Gerald in recent decades (which in itself constitutes a minor Geraldine Renaissance), the legal dimensions of his life and work have rarely come into direct focus. Recent research has documented Gerald's interest in ethnography, identity, in ghosts and in dreams, but his engagement with the law has not received the same attention.[37] The neglect is made more acute by the fact that Gerald, throughout his writing, repeatedly draws his readers' attention to his own legal learning and legal accomplishments. Gerald's evident pride in his legal knowledge, and his enthusiasm for inserting legal arguments, proofs, or talking points into texts which are not, *sensu stricto*, about law, exemplifies one of the most significant trends in the later twelfth century. Legal learning was increasingly a feather in the cap of young, ambitious men. Even for men who had no intention of becoming 'professional' lawyers, a claim to some level of legal expertise was one way of demonstrating one's suitability for office.

Gerald's career allows us to probe the idea of a spectrum of legal learning. There was no strict division between lawyer and non-lawyer; in fact, there was a sizeable group of young men who had picked up some level of legal training (either at the schools, or in episcopal households), but for whom law was not their full-time occupation. Gerald spent three years in Paris studying both civil and canon law; the usual course was to spend three years on civil law before three more on the decretals. That did not put him among the first rank of lawyers when he returned to England: Gerald was no Simon of Sywell or John of Tynemouth. But as an archdeacon and as one who aspired to a bishopric, he would have known enough of the law (canon and civil) to understand its principles, to receive and offer legal advice, and to navigate his way through key legal texts. More than that, Gerald was capable of using legal quotations to give strength and support to claims he made in other arenas, when writing. Most importantly, his ability to navigate the authoritative texts and principles of late twelfth-century law provided him with a further tool in his moral writing. It allowed him to claim a further kind of legal authority when he wrote or spoke about how law might be used in the creation of a virtuous society. Gerald never wrote a 'legal' work, but his writings are peppered with moral arguments which depend on legal principles, or which draw their strength or illustrations from legal ideas.

This much is evident from reading the first book of *De principis instructione*, Gerald's *speculum principis*, written and added to at intervals between 1191 and 1217.[38] While the second two books work through historical examples from Angevin and French monarchies, the first examines virtue and the moral qualities needed to rule. Those qualities are demonstrated with reference to biblical and classical examples (as one might expect), but, also through reference to the principles of Roman law. To explain the importance of gentleness (*mansuetudine*) in the ruler, Gerald relies on *Codex* 1.14.4 and 6.23.3.[39] In the same chapter he records that the great Julius Caesar showed elaborate respect for advocates when entering the courts, putting aside his imperial dignity, and was himself willing to appear as a lawyer for a poor veteran.[40] Gerald elsewhere commends Roman laws which treated those who slander the imperial name with mildness and patience,[41] arguing that in this Roman law is in accordance with Solomon's proverbial praise of patience (Prov. 16.32). On show is a wide-ranging knowledge of the *Codex* and *Digest*, and an assumption that where virtue was to be found in the Roman polity, it was to be found in its laws. It was law which compelled Rome's rulers to fulfil their duties, and to conduct themselves with piety in office.[42]

Gerald's use of the law to engage his readers on the subject of virtue, however, goes beyond quotation. He includes in his work on the instruction of princes a comparative passage, discussing the difference between Roman law and English law on shipwreck. The comparison is intended to illustrate the matter of royal piety: a pious and compassionate ruler ensures that the law of shipwreck takes care of those who have lost goods or loved ones. Rulers should thus understand that they can shape the laws for public good. The very best of these laws concerning shipwreck, Gerald argues, were the 'ancient' laws of England, which decreed that any goods salvaged from a shipwreck were to be used to benefit the very poor and the heirs of those who had died in the wreck.[43]

In short, legal fluency allowed Gerald to elaborate on and enhance his moral arguments; to explain, moreover, how good moral principles could be properly codified in law. Of course, some of the display of legal learning was self-serving, and it would be naïve to think otherwise – Gerald was keen to demonstrate his own legal brilliance. At the same time, however, Gerald used the law he knew in the service of moral reformation. That was as true of his knowledge of the Decretals as it was for the *Corpus Juris Civilis*. Gerald deploys the same type of techniques in his *Gemma ecclesiastica* (c. 1198), his case for the moral reform of the church.

Ostensibly, the *Gemma ecclesiastica* is quite the opposite of a legal work. It begins with an attack on lawyers who are merely interested in the study of law as a means of advancement and who embark on legal studies without establishing the basics of logic and the *trivium*.[44] This was by no means an uncommon complaint in the mid-twelfth century.[45] But the *Gemma ecclesiastica* itself provides a series of references to canon law and summaries of canonical arguments. There are principles of canon law which a priest must understand in order to perform his role in the church; principles which Gerald helpfully sets out. Those legal principles include the difference between clerical acceptance of gifts (a prohibited activity) and receiving a freely-given stipend (acceptable),[46] and the canonical support for the principle that the Eucharist is never to be denied to anyone seeking it at the moment of death.[47] In both the *Gemma ecclesiastica* and the *De principis instructione*, Gerald saw himself as distilling legal principles for the benefit of those who were unlearned in law, but who required some basic understanding of its rules in order to fulfil their office (royal, administrative, priestly). The legal knowledge which Gerald claimed made his arguments more potent; it supported his cry for moral reform.

When read in this fashion, Gerald's overlapping legal, moral, and literary activities bear a striking similarity to those of his more accomplished and acclaimed contemporary, Master Vacarius. Vacarius, who had studied at Bologna or Pavia in the 1130s, was the leading master of Roman law in twelfth-century England. As Jason Taliadoros has recently demonstrated, Vacarius' endeavours were not strictly 'legal': as a master he aimed at building bridges between theology and law, putting law in the service of pastoral theology, and using jurisprudential techniques to aid in the comprehension of matters of Christology. Gerald, of course, did not have the same depth of legal learning as Vacarius. But that did not prevent him from using the law he did know in the service of moral theology. Indeed, seen in this way, Vacarius' theological interests, as catalogued by Taliadoros, represent only the tip of the iceberg in twelfth-century England. Vacarius' work was, perhaps, the most refined and conceptually sophisticated – but exchanges between theology and law happened at every level of legal literacy.[48]

Gerald is an important example, whose engagement with the law has been – unaccountably, given the volume of writing on other aspects of his life – overlooked. But there were still other men in twelfth-century England who, though they were not legal masters, utilised the law they knew. John Cotts has noted the case of Peter of Blois, who had studied for a period at Bologna.[49] Peter's attitude to his own legal learning was ambivalent. In his later years, he made much of the distinction between the world of law and the world of moral theology; however, as a young man, he repeatedly emphasised the utility of law – as a kind of rhetoric which could be made to speak to certain audiences. For much of his life, Peter thought that some level of legal training could be useful to the theologian or preacher. Indeed, he employed the 'language' of law as part of his persuasive rhetoric as a Christian orator: invoking a court setting, borrowing legal ideas and principles – all of these could give weight to his arguments.[50]

Two more authors – historians – should be added to this list. The first is Ralph of Diss, dean of St Pauls and author of two historical works, the *Abbreviationes chronicorum* and the *Ymagines historiarum*. Bruce Brasington has examined the legal dimensions of Ralph's learning. Ralph was no jurist, but was able to follow the norms of canon law and to utilise legal texts pertinent to his argument; bringing his legal learning to bear when discussing contemporary politics.[51] The second is Richard de Morins (d. 1242) who, before he was abbot of Dunstable, was a graduate of the university of Bologna; who, even after his entry into the religious life as an Augustinian canon, remained keenly engaged in legal matters – both as litigant and as a judge.[52] Richard, like Ralph and Gerald, wrote legally-minded history. While one might expect a monastic chronicle to keep a record of legal cases which affected the well-being and properties of the priory, or legal events which had considerable national political fallout, the *Annals of Dunstable Priory* are distinguished by their consistent attention to the technical detail of legal matters and legal process. They report, for example, how evidence was used in legal cases;[53] the wording and form of oaths which were sworn before itinerant justices;[54] how royal justices were dispatched in response to a crimewave;[55] how judicial combat was used to decide a verdict; and a dispute over how appropriate punishment for specified offences was to be determined.[56]

Law and history were mutually reinforcing, in a way which should not surprise us. Legal details represented a useful embellishment of history – showing how legal decisions, legislation or judgment could be used as a spur (or obstacle) to moral improvement. Legal action was also the proper subject matter of history: like theological or classical texts, it showed the good engaged in a battle with the wicked. Men who had first studied the liberal arts curriculum and had then come to law (or who had picked up law in a non-academic setting) viewed it as merely another kind of knowledge to be borrowed and drawn upon: it was not a kind of knowledge set apart from all the others. If we take together the works of Gerald of Wales, Peter of Blois, Ralph of Diss, and Richard of Morins, we end up with a category we might call 'legal theology'; where law is layered into theological and moral thinking; where law is another type of rhetoric through which moral arguments can be advanced.

Baldwin of Forde and the occasional silence of the lawyers

Legal learning was – for the most part – rarely a distinct category; 'legal' virtues bled into others. The advocate or judge admired for his facility with law was praised too for his moral probity; men who had picked up parts of a legal education put that knowledge to work in the service of moral reform. Many who were not considered *iurisperiti* still claimed a level of legal expertise that gave them moral authority. In short, below the level of academic jurisprudence, further down the food-chain, legal, historical, rhetorical and moral arguments were often deliberately run together. This blurring of legal, historical, rhetorical, and moral was the norm. However, for twelfth-century England, there is at least one important and high-profile exception to this blurring. This was Baldwin of Forde, Archbishop of Canterbury (1185-90). Baldwin represents an important case for two reasons. First, because he has been surprisingly understudied. Despite his well-documented career, very little has been written about him.[57] Secondly, and perhaps more importantly, Baldwin has been positioned as someone whose moral and ascetic writings were indelibly marked by his legal training, and who presented a distinctive 'legal' kind of theology.[58] This is not an accurate reading of Baldwin. Indeed, unlike most of his similarly-learned contemporaries like Gilbert Foliot or Vacarius, Baldwin's moral writings exhibit almost no trace of his legal education.

In order to appreciate the novelty of Baldwin's intellectual orientation, one must first grasp the outlines of his career. Born in Exeter, likely the son of the archdeacon of Totnes, Baldwin was sent to the schools, most likely under the patronage of the Bishop of Exeter. At Bologna he studied canon law and theology, probably alongside the future Pope Alexander III and the canonist Stephen of Tournai. Baldwin's reputation as a canonist was such that he was appointed as tutor to the nephew of Eugenius III. He eventually returned to Exeter where he became archdeacon of Totnes, possibly teaching at the cathedral school there.[59] A promising career in the English church must have seemed on the cards, but, in around 1170, Baldwin's career took a less predictable turn – he entered the Cistercian order, becoming a monk at the abbey of Forde. Baldwin had played a role on the fringes of the Becket conflict; it may have been this which propelled him into the cloister. Entry into the Cistercian order did not, ultimately, arrest his progress. Baldwin quickly became of abbot at Forde, and from there to the see of Worcester in 1180, and from there to Canterbury. On this evidence, Baldwin must have been one of the more accomplished canon lawyers in the English church. Nor did Baldwin retire from the legal world after his entry into Forde: he served the papacy as judge-delegate as abbot, as bishop of Worcester and as archbishop.[60]

In the 1180s, at Worcester, Baldwin played a significant role in the creation of the decretal collection now known as the *Collectio wigorniensis*.[61] The *Collectio* is one of the most significant decretal collections in late twelfth-century England, primarily built upon papal letters to Worcester and Exeter. Baldwin himself is unlikely to have assembled the collections single-handedly; he must have drawn upon earlier endeavours at Worcester, possibly associated with his predecessor Bishop Roger. The *Collectio* is in itself, of course, evidence for the vitality and importance of legal writing and compilation outside the schools. As a canonist of some considerable reputation, Baldwin evidently fostered a circle in which members of his household devoted time to the collection and organisation of recent decretals.[62] There is no doubt, therefore, that Baldwin continued to make significant use of his high-profile legal education. The argument I make here is not that Baldwin *lacked* legal expertise. It is rather that his legal knowledge was rarely, if ever, imported into his theological writing. This, in turn, reveals something about the limits of legal learning and its utility in the twelfth century.

David Bell has discussed Baldwin's surviving spiritual works at length. These include a series of nineteen surviving sermons, and two treatises, *De sacramento altaris* and *De commendatio fidei*. Most, if not all of these writings seem to have been produced while Baldwin was at Forde; the two treatises provided spiritual guidance and a distillation of the most important themes of faith and redemption for the monastic community. One further work – an anti-heretical treatise – seems to have been the product of his time in Canterbury; a small number of letters also survive relating to Baldwin's dispute with the monks of Canterbury over the foundation of a secular college of canons.[63] Bell has characterised Baldwin as a theologian who drew on all his legal expertise to make theological arguments, and who sometimes breaks into the language of the courts to express himself.[64] On Bell's account, Baldwin drew on his legal knowledge to frame a number of theological concepts for his audience, and utilised several technical legal terms to define his theology. For Bell, the culmination of this is found in the *De commendatio fidei*, in which Baldwin presents the Father, Son, and Holy Spirit each giving 'testimony' (*testimonium*), as if in a court, as a demonstration of the truth of the Christian Faith.[65] It is worth noting that Bell's characterisation of Baldwin as a writer of 'legal theology' stands in marked contrast to Landgraf's description of Baldwin as a writer in the 'ascetic-mystical' style.[66]

On closer inspection, however, there is very little which is evidently 'legal' in Baldwin's sermons or spiritual treatises. We might also wonder exactly what advantage Baldwin would have derived from presenting legal arguments to such an audience. There are, to be sure, a number of references to justice and judgment. But these are no more than one would expect given the themes on which Baldwin is sermonising; and they do not invoke any technical language. Indeed, across the corpus of sermons, the references to any kind of law, advocacy, or judicial scenes are scanty. What mentions there are of matters of judgment come from biblical models, not those of contemporary law.[67] One would not need to be a canonist to access or utilise these sets of ideas. There are occasional, stray references to the contemporary law – but even then, these are used a point of general illustration. Discussing the principle that God does not punish twice, Baldwin glosses: 'just as in civil judgments, when those expert in law have determined that the damages be doubled in cases where debts are reneged...'.[68] This is a concept which most monks in the community of Forde would have been familiar with, but it hardly stands as a demonstration of any kind of technical legal expertise.

A secondary point of Bell's argument is to draw attention to the vocabulary deployed Baldwin. But, again, this is rather less 'jurisprudential' and technical than Bell suggests. In the *De commendatio fidei*, for example, Baldwin uses the term 'sententia' to describe the firmness of judgment arrived at by faith.[69] While this could be a deliberately 'legal' term, we should recognise the flexibility of this word in medieval Latin. The idea of divine *sententia* was a commonplace in moral theology; on its own it is not much substantial evidence of the deliberate employment of a 'legal' vocabulary. Elsewhere in the same text, Baldwin uses 'reatus' for sin, using the term to describe those guilty of the sin of unbelief.[70] Again, 'reatus' could bear a technical legal meaning, but that is in no way suggested by the context of the discussion, which is an examination of the Old Testament (Nb. 20.11-13); and it is not deployed in relation to any other legal terms. Moreover – as Bell himself notes – this was a term which Augustine and the Church Fathers had also used to describe sin. There is nothing here which can be claimed as distinctly legal, demonstrating that Baldwin was tapping into an expert jurisprudential vocabulary. These supposedly 'legal' terms would more likely have been familiar to the monks of Forde from the Vulgate, and in their 'theological' usage.

The most important part of Bell's case for Baldwin's integration of law into theology are the parts of the *De commendatio fidei* in which Father, Son, and Holy Spirit are asked to provide 'testimony' of the Christian faith, serving as witnesses (*testes*): 'quod tres testimonium dant in celo, et tres in terra'.[71] Once again, however, this is a term which is being used by Baldwin in a non-technical, non-legal sense. The chapters which describe these 'testimonies' have no other legal framing or terminology: there is no suggestion, for example, that the reader or listener should imagine himself in a court-like setting. While the term *testimonia* might have legal implications, it was being used in twelfth-century theological and scholastic circles simply to mean proof, evidence, or demonstration. This is how the term is used by Alan of Lille, also writing in the later twelfth century. Alan's *Distinctiones* define *testimonium* in a purely spiritual way, through the use of biblical citations: 'testimonies' are merely proof of the greatness and goodness of the Lord; often worked through the Holy Spirit.[72] The term is used similarly in other of Alan's writings; testimony is a proof from scripture, a demonstration of God's power.[73] Indeed, when Baldwin expands on his definition of 'testimony' in a later chapter, his definition is solidly 'theological', not legal: 'the testimonies of our faith, therefore, are the works of the righteous, those works of righteousness and devotion which...please God and glorify God in himself'.[74] By testimony, Baldwin means signs and miracles, those worked and magnified by God. The idea of witness is tied up in making confession (90.4), most associated with the prophets and apostles.[75] To place this in a legal setting obliges us to imagine a connection which Baldwin never invokes.

I can find only one passage of the *De commendatio fidei* (a substantial treatise) which discusses law or legal frameworks in any detail. That is a passage which discusses a historical example: Pilate's condemnation of Christ.[76] But none of that discussion contains any material relevant to the practices and procedures of the twelfth-century courts that Baldwin knew: it is an account based on Mark 14 and Matthew 26, a re-telling and paraphrase of the events described in the New Testament. If the reader did not know that Baldwin – a trained jurist – was the author of these sermons and treatise, they would not be struck by any significant 'legal' character to the argument. A much stronger theme throughout the sermons is not law, but the traditionally monastic concept of obedience within the community.[77]

There is also a more fundamental historical problem for anyone looking to find Baldwin the lawyer in his writings from Forde. It is difficult to see what benefit Baldwin would find in speaking to a Cistercian audience in technical legal terms. While the order did not forbid its members from learning law, it did not consider legal learning appropriate for most of its brothers. The General Chapter of 1188 restricted those in the monastery who might have access to the 'corpus canonum et decretum graciani'.[78] Of course, the Cistercians were – in reality – not able to distance themselves from the world as much as their claims suggested. Cistercian monasteries certainly engaged in legal disputes, and dividing lines between 'law' and the cloister were not hard and fast.[79]

One complication which must be considered here is the possibility that certain English Cistercian monasteries did have a distinctive canon law tradition. Peter Landau has argued for considerable interest in canon law at Fountains Abbey in the late 1170s and early 1180s, culminating in the creation of the *Collectio Fontanensis*.[80] This was a repository of the kinds of law that particularly touched Cistercian houses, such as on property and tithes, as well as decretals which might be particularly useful for an abbot to study if he were called upon to serve as a judge-delegate – for example, on matters of marriage and judicial appeals. The creation of the *Collectio* seems to be connected to a more comprehensive project of canonical collection Durham. However, legal engagement at Fountains is not a particularly good guide to intellectual life at Forde. Fountains was particularly distinguished amongst English Cistercian houses; Forde was not of the same rank. Moreover, the intellectual tradition at Forde, as we can recreate it, seems to have been literary, spiritual, and even mystical, rather than legal.[81] The leading figure at the abbey in the late twelfth century was John (abbot 1191-1214). John, who had been a close friend of Baldwin, and possibly even his student, was known for writing a *Life* of the hermit Wulfric of Haselbury and a commentary on the Song of Songs. The latter followed a traditional, Bernadine model. Also associated with twelfth-century literary production at the abbey were Roger of Forde, the 'author' (more accurately, redactor) of the *Revelations* of Elizabeth of Schönau, and William, abbot of Bindon, who compiled a collection of miracle stories about the Virgin.[82] Holdsworth, making a survey of twelfth-century Cistercian writing, has characterised Forde as representing a traditional 'conservative' monastic tradition, associated with the Church Fathers, earlier Cistercian writers, and Victorine texts.[83]

In such a context, invoking legal language would have been unlikely to help Baldwin make his case before a monastic audience. Even recognising that there could be some measure of legal expertise attached to individuals within Cistercian houses, the prestige of law must have been limited when talking to a broad audience of Cistercian brothers. By contrast, when Gerald of Wales wrote for an audience of courtiers and princes, the invocation of Roman Law and the concomitant Roman imperial authority packed a persuasive punch. Baldwin, who had studied the *trivium*, would surely had recognised the principle of classical rhetoric – that once adjusts one's material to suit one's audience. One adapted one's preaching according to those whom you addressed; a different language was suited to monks than to kings; to knights than to nuns.[84] Law was but one register; it was not rhetorically effective for every audience. Alain Boureau has suggested that one pattern that can be discerned in twelfth-century monastic recruitment is the deliberate attempt, by certain monasteries, to bring in highly-trained lawyers from the schools, offering them rapid advancement within the community.[85] That offer might in turn be appealing to those students of law who found limited academic success and no security. Baldwin, however, does not seem to fit this pattern, and Boureau's examples are from Benedictine monasteries – Battle and Evesham.[86]

The reason it has been worth examining Baldwin's theological lexicon in such fine detail is his place within a wider twelfth-century argument and set of trends. One of the hallmarks of that century was that men who had only a limited legal education sought to integrate that legal learning into their other works – whether in history-writing, in moral theology, or in letter collections for wider circulation. Gerald of Wales demonstrates how *magistri* and *eruditi* might seek to make use of every bit of their legal education, and its accompanying prestige and the persuasive power of legal argument, even many years after their time in the schools. This was a 'legal theology' in which law might be bent to many other uses – although not, it seems, by Baldwin of Forde.

Conclusion

One must, of course, be wary of arguments from silence. There may be questions of survival here: a lost corpus of sermons which might show Baldwin speaking in technical legal language to the monks of Forde (although it seems that most, if not all, of Baldwin's writings have survived to the present day).[87] That possibility notwithstanding, we should recognise a deliberate choice here. Around 1170, the distinguished canonist Baldwin of Totnes joined the monastic order least likely to celebrate his chief intellectual achievement – the legal reputation won in the schools of northern Italy. The Augustinian canons of Dunstable in the early thirteenth century seem to have been rather more impressed by the fame of Richard de Morins – and more receptive to his interests – than the Cistercians at Forde were with Baldwin's previous career. One might speculate as to whether this was a deliberate choice on Baldwin's part, in the aftermath of the Becket controversy? Quite clearly, entry into the Cistercian order did not mean giving up the law, as his continued judicial work and engagement with the papacy makes clear. But it meant entering a community where legal knowledge had much less currency, and where legal knowledge was to be handled with caution.

What do Gerald of Wales and Baldwin of Ford show us if trying to sketch out a model for the 'legal theology' in the twelfth century? First, that the ways in which theology and law might interact were far from predictable. Law was just one kind of *scientia*; it continued to be valued for the contribution legal learning might make towards a man's moral formation. In judges, the lack of a legal education or training could be compensated for by demonstrating the right moral orientation or administrative capacity.[88] While the twelfth century saw the development of a sophisticated technical framework for the teaching of law and jurisprudence, learning in the law was still thought of as a moral attribute, one in a constellation of moral virtues, capable of many varieties of combination – as it had been in earlier centuries. One is tempted to suggest that, in this sense, the twelfth century was a moment of transition. In the thirteenth century, as the distinction between law and the other studies that one might pursue in the schools became more sharply drawn, there would be less room for this kind of 'legal theology', and fewer men who could boast sufficient training in both the *artes* and in *jurisprudentia* to work that combination. But in the twelfth century, that kind of symbiosis was still possible – legal theology was possible because the hard category of 'law' was still in formation.

Notes

1   See, for example, K. Pennington, 'The Legal Education of Pope Innocent III', *Bulletin of Medieval Canon Law*, 4 (1974), 70-7; R. Weigand, 'Magister Rolandus und Papst Alexander III', *Archiv für katholisches Kirchenrecht*, 149 (1980), 3-44.

2   Though working from English material, the present study does not consider the common law tradition, in which processes of legal learning and training and judicial formation were markedly different to that of the canon and Roman lawyers discussed here.

3   This is a point I discuss further in 'Legal Learning and Saintly Authority in Thirteenth-Century Hagiography: the Magna vita sancti Hugonis', *Journal of Medieval History*, 44 (2018), 39-55.

4   For some reflections on how historians try to reconcile the relationship between legal theory and legal practice, see the general remarks of G. R. Evans, *Law and Theology in the Middle Ages* (London, 2002), esp. pp. 83-4.

5   For example, J. H. Baker's *Monuments of Endlesse Labours: English Canonists and their Work, 1300-1900* (London, 1998), looks no further back than the 1190s. It cites the work of Kuttner and Rathbone, but begins from a time at which the disciplinary and professional relationships were more clearly defined; law had a more certain and fixed identity. For further discussion of where 'law' as a separate sphere of study might be seen to emerge, see M. Ascheri, *Diritto medievale e moderno* (Rimini, 1991).

6   See, for example, D. M. Owen, *The Medieval Canon Law: Teaching, Literature and Transmission* (Cambridge, 1990); G. Seabourne, *Royal Regulation of Loans and Sales in Medieval England: Monkish Superstition and Civil Tyranny* (Woodbridge, 2003); or, for an example from legal writing, Heikki Pihlajamäki, and Mia Korpiola, 'Medieval Canon Law: The Origins of Modern Criminal Law', in *The Oxford Handbook of Criminal Law*, ed. by M. D. Dubber and T. Hörnle (Oxford, 2014), pp. 201-24.

7   S. Kuttner and E. Rathbone, 'Anglo-Norman Canonists of the Twelfth Century: An Introductory Study', *Traditio*, 7 (1949), 279-358; the same focus is embodied in Leonard Boyle's important article, 'The Beginnings of Legal Studies at Oxford', *Viator*, 14 (1983), 107-31.

8   C. R. Cheney and E. John, (eds.), *English Episcopal Acta 3: Canterbury, 1193-1205*, ed. (Oxford, 1991), nos. 463 and 464 [hereafter *EEA 3*].

9   Ibid., no. 468.

10   C. R. Cheney and M. G. Cheney, (eds.), *The Letters of Pope Innocent III (1198-1216) concerning England and Wales* (Oxford, 1967), no. 279.

11 See further A. B. Emden, *Biographical Register of the University of Oxford*, 3 vols. (Oxford, 1957-9), ii. 826. John Grim is no longer considered the likely author of a *Summa super canonem missae*, now ascribed to John of Cornwall.

12 *EEA 3*, nos. 548, 549. The case dates to the period between 1198 and 1205. About Alexander of Hadham nothing else is known; Jordan de Ros is probably to be identified with the figure of the same name who became entangled in a legal dispute over land with Abbot Samson of Bury St Edmunds. See *The Chronicle of Jocelin of Brakelond*, ed. by H. E. Butler (London, 1949), pp. 61-2.

13 C. R. Cheney, *English Bishops' Chanceries 1100-1250* (Manchester, 1950), for an overview; pp. 11-17 for the household of Hubert Walter; see also C. E. Lewis, 'Canonists and Law Clerks in the Household of Archbishop Hubert Walter', *Colloquia Germanica*, 4 (1970), 192-201.

14 Adam of Eynsham, *Magna vita Sancti Hugonis*, ed. by D. L. Douie and D. H. Farmer, 2 vols. (Oxford, 1985), book 3, chapter 8, i. 112.

15 *English Episcopal Acta IV: Lincoln, 1186-1206*, ed. by D. M. Smith (London, 1986), nos. 116, 182, 191. Robert of Bedford did not live long after his move to Lincoln.

16 Adam of Eynsham, *Magna vita Sancti Hugonis*, 3.8, i. 112.

17 See the discussion in H. G. Richardson, 'The Oxford Law School under John', *Law Quarterly Review*, 57 (1941), 319-38, and idem, 'The Schools of Northampton in the Twelfth Century', *English Historical Review*, 56 (1941), 595-605.

18 Cheney, *English Bishops' Chanceries*, p. 11.

19 See E. King, 'Benedict of Peterborough and the Cult of Thomas Becket', *Northamptonshire Past and Present*, 9 (1996-97), 213-20.

20 Benedict led a panel of royal justices in 1190: D. M. Stenton, *Pleas before the King or his Justices, 1198-1202*, 4 vols. (London, 1952-67), iii, lxxxi.

21 For a sense of that library, see R. Gameson, *The Earliest Books of Canterbury Cathedral: Manuscripts and Fragments to c.1200* (London, 2008).

22 M. R. James, *Lists of Manuscripts formerly in Peterborough Abbey Library* (Oxford, 1926), p. 21.

23 Compare, for example, Philip de Harcourt, Bishop of Bayeux, who left a collection of legal texts to Bec on his death in 1163, from what must have been an extensive legal library. See A. J. Duggan, 'Roman, Canon and Common Law in Twelfth-Century England: The Council of Northampton (1164) Re-examined', *Historical Research*, 83 (2010), 390-1.

24 J. E. Sayers, *Papal Judges-Delegate in the Province of Canterbury, 1198-1254: A Study in Ecclesiastical Jurisdiction and Administration* (London,

1971), pp. 109-14. See K. Major, 'The "Familia" of Archbishop Stephen Langton', *English Historical Review*, 48 (1933), 529-33 – Major identifies William of Bardney and Adam of Tilney, both distinguished canonists, as Langton's primary legal advisors. For the lawyers associated with the household of Becket in exile, see Herbert of Bosham, *Vita S. Thomae* in *Materials for a History of Thomas Becket*, ed. by James Craigie Robertson, 7 vols. (London, 1875-85), iii. 523-9. See also F. Barlow, *Thomas Becket* (London, 1986), esp. p. 129.

25 Gerald of Wales, *Vita Sancti Remigii*, ed. by J. F. Dimock (London, 1877), c.28, pp. 57-67 (57 for Alexander's commendation of the two men).

26 Sayers, p. 10.

27 Gerald, *Vita Sancti Remigii*, p. 57; for an important discussion of the circumstances surrounding the writing of this text and its construct and purpose, see Matthew Mesley, 'The Construction of Episcopal Identity: The Meaning and Function of Episcopal Depictions within Latin Saints', PhD dissertation, University of Exeter, 2009.

28 A. Morey, *Bartholomew of Exeter* (Cambridge: Cambridge University Press, 1937), esp. pp. 44-78 and 172-4. See also the discussion in Kuttner and Rathbone, 'Anglo-Norman Canonists', p. 295.

29 Gerald, *Vita Sancti Remigii*, p. 57. One should also recognise that by the time Gerald was writing, Bartholomew's legal knowledge would no longer have been cutting edge; something which again points to Gerald as using Bartholomew as a means of praising good judicial conduct, rather than knowledge of specific legal procedure or argument.

30 See M. G. Cheney, *Roger, Bishop of Worcester 1164-79* (Oxford, 1980). For a more recent verdict – and one which is less convinced by the evidence for Roger's legal training – see also R. Helmholz, 'Roger, Bishop of Worcester (c 1134-1179)', *Ecclesiastical Law Journal*, 15 (2013), 75-80. Evans, *Law and Theology*, p. 46, notes the fact of Roger's theological training but does not discuss the implications for Roger's role as a papal judge-delegate.

31 Cheney, *Roger, Bishop of Worcester*, pp. 38-42.

32 Cf. Kuttner and Rathbone, 'Anglo-Norman Canonists', see below, 'Baldwin of Forde'.

33 Gerald of Wales, *De rebus a se gestis*, ed. by J. S. Brewer (London: Longmans, 1861), II.1, p. 45.

34 Southern, *Scholastic Humanism and the Unification of Europe: Volume 1, Foundations* (Oxford, 1995), esp. pp. 3-5.

35 Gerald, *De rebus a se gestis*, II.1, p. 45.

36 For the legal context, see K. W. Nörr, *Zur Stellung Des Richters Im Gelehrten Prozess Der Frühzeit: Iudex Secundum Allegata Non Secundum Conscientiam Iudicat* (Munich, 1967).

37 For example: though Robert Bartlett's *Gerald of Wales: A Voice of the Middle Ages* (Stroud, 2006) contains an entry for 'beavers', there are no references in the index for canon law, common law or Roman law. There is a brief discussion of Irish and Welsh customary law in the context of conquest and the attempts of the English church to reform local customs.

38 For the process of composition see further the discussion in Gerald of Wales, *De Principis Instructione*, ed. by R. Bartlett (Oxford, 2018), xv-xix [hereafter *DPI*].

39 Gerald of Wales, *DPI*, i.2, p. 45.

40 *DPI*, i.2, pp. 46-7.

41 *DPI*, i.5, pp. 66-7; *Codex* 9.7.1.

42 *DPI*, i.20, p. 347; *Codex* 3.1.8. Gerald makes use of quotations from the *Decretum* as a guide for rulers, e.g. *DPI*, i.10, p. 121, citing C. 23, q. 8, c.16.

43 *DPI*, i.20, p. 351, discussing *Digest* 47. For a more comprehensive discussion of these laws, see R. Meikan, 'Shippers, Salvors and Sovereigns: Competing Interests in the Medieval Law of Shipwreck', *Journal of Legal History*, 11 (1990), 163-82.

44 *Gemma ecclesiastica*, ed. by J. S. Brewer (London: Longmans, 1862), II.37, p. 349.

45 For an overview of such complaints, see S. Ferruolo, '"Quid dant artes nisi luctum?": Learning, Ambition, and Careers in the Medieval University', *History of Education Quarterly*, 28 (1988), 1-22.

46 *Gemma ecclesiastica*, II.33, pp. 324-9.

47 *Gemma ecclesiastica*, I.40, pp. 115-16. For other references, see I.2 (Dist. II c.29), pp. 13-14; I.5 (Dist. II. c. 14), p. 16; I.6 (Dist. II. c.8), pp. 20-1; I.9 (Dist. II. c. 16), p. 30.

48 J. Taliadoros, 'Synthesizing the Legal and Theological Thought of Master Vacarius', *Zeitschrift der Savigny-Stiftung für Rechtsgeschichte. Kanonistische Abteilung*, 95 (2009), 48-77.

49 Cotts, *The Clerical Dilemma*, pp. 104-9. Gervase of Canterbury described Peter as 'legis peritus', but this seems an overstatement of Peter's legal abilities: see Gervase, *Chronica* in *Opera Historica*, ed. by W. Stubbs (London: Longmans, 1879-80), p. 356.

50 See PL. 207, Epp. 26, 71, 115, for Peter's references to his study of the law in Bologna.

51 B. C. Brasington, 'A Lawyer of Sorts: Ralph Diss' Knowledge of Canon and Civil Law', in *Law and Learning in the Middle Ages*, ed. by M. Münster-Swendsen and H. Vogt (Copenhagen, 2006), pp. 147-66.

52 C. R. Cheney has questioned whether Richard was the sole author of the chronicle to 1242, suggesting that it is more likely that parts of it were prepared by canons under his direction: see 'Notes on the Making of the Dunstable Annals', in *Essays in Medieval History presented to Bertie Wilkinson*, ed. by T. A. Sandquist and M. R. Powicke (Toronto, 1969), pp. 79-89. For Ricardus more generally, see R. C. Figueira, 'Ricardus de Mores at Common Law – The Second Career of an Anglo-Norman Canonist', *Proceedings of the Eighth International Congress of Medieval Canon Law, 1998*, ed. by S. Chodorow (Vatican City, 1992), pp. 281-99. See too the introduction to the new edition of the *Annals*, translated by David Preest and edited by Harriett R. Webster, *The Annals of Dunstaple Priory* (Woodbridge, 2018).

53 *Annales Prioratus de Dunstaplia*, in H. R. Luard (ed.), *Annales Monastici*, vol. 3 (London, 1866) [1219] p. 55.

54 *Annales Prioratus de Dunstaplia*, [1219] p. 55.

55 *Annales Prioratus de Dunstaplia*, [1225] p. 95.

56 *Annales Prioratus de Dunstaplia*, [1227] pp. 105-6.

57 Baldwin's varied career has largely only been considered in relation to the creation of the legal text known as the *Collectio Wigorniensis* (see below). The best summary of his life is to be found in David Bell's introduction to Baldwin of Ford, *Spiritual Tractates* (Kalamazoo, 1986). For an important addition to recent work on Baldwin, see Suzanne Grace Coley, 'Archbishop Baldwin of Canterbury and the Fear of Heresy in Late Twelfth-Century England', PhD dissertation, University of Southampton, 2018.

58 This argument has been made most strongly by Bell, the most assiduous modern scholar of Baldwin; e.g. *Spiritual Tractates*, p. 23: 'law and precedent were of first importance to him'. See also Bell's comments in his introduction to Baldwin of Ford, *The Commendation of the Faith* (Kalamazoo, 2000), p. 18.

59 For the teaching of law in England in this period, see Boyle, 'The Beginnings'.

60 For Worcester, see *English Episcopal Acta 33: Worcester 1062-1185*, ed. by M. G. Cheney (Oxford: Oxford University Press, 2007), nos. 243, 246, 247, 249, 257. For Canterbury, see *English Episcopal Acta 2: Canterbury, 1162-90*, ed. by C. R. Cheney (Oxford, 1986), nos. 297 and 309 (the latter, however, may have been addressed either to Baldwin or to his predecessor, Richard of Dover.)

61 C. Duggan, 'The Trinity Collection of Decretals and the Early Worcester Family', *Traditio*, 17 (1961), 506-26; and H. Lohmann, 'Die collectio Wigorniensis', *ZRG KA*, 22 (1933), 36-187.

62 Mayr-Harting suggests the work of assembly may itself have been done by Master Silvester – a clerk first to Roger of Worcester and then to Baldwin. H. Mayr-Harting, 'Master Silvester and the Compilation of Early English Decretal Collections', *Studies in Church History*, 2 (1965), 186-96.

63 The surviving writings are catalogued in D. N. Bell, 'The Corpus of the Works of Baldwin of Ford', *Cîteaux* 35 (1984). For the letters: Stubbs, *Chronicles and Memorials of the Reign of Richard I*, vol. II (London, 1865), nos. 8, 22, 32, 84, 111, 140, 191, 338, 345.

64 *The Commendation of the Faith*, p. 24: 'we now encounter Baldwin the papal judge-delegate, Baldwin the lawyer'.

65 For the Latin text: Balduini de Forda, *Opera*, ed. David N Bell (Turnhout, 1991): c. 67, 'Testimonium Patris'; c. 68, 'Testimonium Filii', c. 69, 'Testimonium Spiritus Sancti', pp. 413-16.

66 A. Landgraf, 'The Commentary on St Paul of the Codex Paris Arsenal, Lat. 534 and Baldwin of Canterbury', *The Catholic Biblical Quarterly*, 10:1 (1948): 55-62.

67 E.g. Sermo 2.5, *Opera*, p. 26 (the future judgment of the good and the wicked).

68 Sermo 4.47, p. 79: 'Et sicut in civilibus iudiciis, ut cognitores litium diffiniunt, lis quandoque per inficiationem crescit in duplum'.

69 *De commendatio fidei*, 9.1, p. 352.

70 *De commendatio fidei*, 12.9, p. 359.

71 *De commendatio fidei*, 66, p. 412.

72 Alan of Lille, *Distinctiones*, PL.211.970D-71A.

73 Alan of Lille, *De fide catholica* 3.21, PL.211.420D. For a similar use of *testimonia* in the early thirteenth century, see Robert Grosseteste, *De cessatione legalium*, ed. by R. C. Dales and E. B. King (London, 1986), 2.III.3.

74 *De commendation fidei*, 77.2, p. 422: 'Testimonia ergo fidei nostre sunt opera iustorum, opera iusticie et pietatis...ut Deo placerent et Deum in se glorificarent'. Translation in Bell, *The Commendation of the Faith*, p. 212.

75 *De commendatio fidei*, 90.4, p. 438, 'prophete et apostoli veri testes sunt'.

76 *De commendatio fidei*, 94.3, p. 444.

77 For example, see Sermo 2 and Sermo 7, both 'de obedientia'.

78 C. Waddell, (ed.), *Twelfth-Century Statutes from the Cistercian General Chapter* (Cîteaux, 2002), 1188/7, p. 149. See also 1201/51, p. 500: the abbot of Bellevaux was rebuked and given a penance for acting as a lawyer for a woman in court.

79 See C. H. Lawrence, 'Stephen of Lexington and Cistercian University Studies in the Thirteenth Century', *Journal of Ecclesiastical History*, 11 (1960), 164-78.

80 P. Landau, 'Collectio Fontanensis: A Decretal Collection of the Twelfth Century for an English Cistercian Abbey', in K. Pennington and M. H. Eichbauer (eds.), *Law as Profession and Practice in Medieval Europe* (London, 2016), pp. 201-18. I am grateful to the journal's anonymous reviewer for their helpful suggestions on this point.

81 For the fullest discussion of Forde, see C. J. Holdsworth, 'John of Ford and English Cistercian Writing 1167-1214', *Transactions of the Royal Historical Society*, 11 (1961), 117-36.

82 Holdsworth, 'John of Ford', 125-6. For Roger's redactions, see R. J. Dean, 'Elizabeth, Abbess of Schönau, and Roger of Ford', *Modern Philology*, 41 (1944), 209-20.

83 Holdsworth, 'John of Ford', 127.

84 For a demonstration of this principle, see Alan of Lille's *Summa de arte praedicatoria*, PL. 211.189-91; c.XLIII on how to preach to monks.

85 Alain Boureau, 'How Law Came to the Monks: The Use of Law in English Society at the Beginning of the Thirteenth Century', *Past & Present*, 167 (2000), 29-74.

86 Although it should be noted that extant writing on Baldwin has been coloured by the assumption that his entry into the Cistercian order was the result of a spiritual and psychological crisis precipitated by the Becket affair; but this much is only speculation, a reading-between-the-lines of the facts of his biography. A more sceptical interpretation of the move from archdeacon to monk is sustainable.

87 See the discussion in Bell, 'The Corpus'.

88 When describing Baldwin, Gerald of Wales passes very quickly over his learning (describing him only as 'literarum studiis') and instead chooses to discuss his *moral* character: *Vita Sancti Remigii*, c. 29, p. 71.

The Hybridity of Demons: Perceptions of Demons in Medieval Theology and Iconography

Victoria Burns-Price

University of Reading

The purpose of this article is to consider the hybridity of demons in the medieval period, both in terms of their physical attributes as understood by theologians at the time and their contemporary representation in visual media. There is a stark difference between the nature and physicality of demons as described by theologians and the way in which demons are represented in the visual arts, a conflict which will form the basis of this paper. The idea of demons and their presence in the human world was an increasingly interesting issue for the medieval church and for theologians. This interest can be found as far back as Augustine's writings, who discussed such topics in *De doctrina Christiana, De civitate Dei* and *De trinitate.* Augustine was writing at a time when pagan concepts were being understood through a Christian worldview and ideas such as *daimones,* neutral spirits in the Greco-Roman world, were translated into Christian demons, which warranted significant discussion. An interest in these topics was revived in the medieval period for various reasons. There was a widespread belief that the year 1000 would herald the Last Judgement, based on the reference in Revelation 20 to Satan being bound for 1000 years, after which he would be freed to wreak havoc on the world.[1] As a result of this, ideas around hell, eternal punishment and sin became more prominent at this time. In the following centuries, the Church was increasingly concerned by non-orthodox beliefs, heretical groups, and the influence of other religions such as Judaism and Islam. A drive toward Church reform ensued and as such the influence of the devil and his demons on human life, and the threat to Christian society that this posed, became a priority for the Church. This led to a wide range of literature on the subject of demons, both in the form of Church sermons designed to warn the laity, and through the writings of theologians who were particularly interested in the fundamental nature of demons, their powers, and how they could interact with humans. This coincided with a drive towards more formal theology, beginning in the twelfth century, as a result of the emergence of the universities, and that of Paris in particular. This drive resulted in many theological systems and other works produced at this time which sought to address all aspects of theology, including angels and demons. These theological writings often explored the physical attributes of demons, including how they appeared to and interacted with human beings, and often included physical descriptions of them. The heightened interested in demonic forces at this time also led to an increase in visual representations of demons in the twelfth century.[2]

The concept of demonic physicality has been considered in detail by Dyan Elliott in *Fallen Bodies: Pollution, Sexuality, and Demonology in the Middle Ages*.[3] While this text is primarily concerned with notions of bodily purity and pollution, the chapter "On Angelic Disembodiment and the Incredible Purity of Demons" discusses the perceived physical nature of angels and demons in the medieval period at length. Similarly, Anke Bernau's *Bodies and the Supernatural: Humans, Demons and Angels* discusses the bodies of demons as opposed to those of angels and humans.[4] Bernau also discusses the visual representations of demons and describes them as appearing as both "deceptively beautiful" and "terrifying and awe-inspiring".[5] The focus in this work, however, is on the forms that demons take to deceive humans as discussed in literature, rather than the visual imagery used to depict them. A key text in terms of the concept of hybridity in the Middle Ages is Caroline Walker Bynum's *Metamorphosis and Identity,* published in 2001.[6] This volume considers the two concepts of metamorphosis and hybridity in the medieval period primarily through a consideration of the werewolf trope. However, it considers the idea of hybridity more generally, discussing how it was received in the medieval period by theological scholars, and how it related to their wider understanding of the world. While it does not consider the demonic and can therefore not inform this study's understanding of demons as hybrid forms, its exploration of the medieval understanding of hybridity is important. It is impossible to consider the significance of the representations of demons as hybrid without understanding what hybridity meant to medieval thinkers, what it could be used to represent more widely, and how it impacted the Christian worldview. Bynum concludes that hybridity, and metamorphosis, are 'destabilizings of expectation' which 'shake our confidence in the structure of reality'.[7] This understanding is important to bear in mind when considering the way in which the demonic has been represented in the medieval period and why this has been done.

In this essay hybridity will be studied in through multiple lenses. Firstly, it will consider the conceptual hybridity of demons and the multiplicity of representation between theological understanding and visual imagery, whereby they are simultaneously thought of as both aerial beings, akin to their angelic counterparts, who maintained many of their physical features after their fall, and monstrous forms who are unlike anything seen in heaven or on earth. Secondly, the literal hybridity of the demonic form as represented in visual media in the medieval period will be explored, looking into the origins and consequences of this tradition. The theological understanding of demonic physicality will be explored through a study of some key theological texts which had a wide-ranging impact in the medieval period. The first of these is the twelfth-century *Sententiarum libri quatuor* (hereafter *Sententiarum*) of Peter Lombard. This was one of the most important theological texts of the medieval period and formed an integral part of the theology curriculum at the University of Paris. It was the most successful form of theological system developed in the twelfth century, and the main aim of the text was to provide synthesis between various contradictory authoritative texts, such as the Church Fathers, with regards different areas of theology. Due to its logical structure and its methodology of bringing together different authorities and finding a common conclusion, it became a very important text in the medieval period and was taught at the University of Paris for centuries. Its discussions of topics such as the physical form of demons were highly influential and formed the basis of arguments around this subject by other theologians. Due to the nature of the *Sententiarum,* essentially a compilation of earlier theological thought, the writings of the Church Fathers, and Augustine in particular, make up the foundation of the arguments found within it regarding demons and their nature. Augustine's ideas on the demonic will therefore also be considered here. Similarly, due to the importance of the *Sententiarum* as a teaching text, theology students at Paris throughout the medieval period were required to produce commentaries on it in order to gain their degree. The thirteenth-century theologians St Thomas Aquinas and St Bonaventure were two of the more influential commentators, as, unlike many, their commentaries both greatly expanded on the material of the original text and also provide new ideas and opinions. They also both went on to produce their own important theological texts, the *Summa theologiae* of Aquinas and the *Breviloquium* of Bonaventure. The ideas expressed in their commentaries on the physical form of demons were therefore also influential and can be seen as representative of theological thought at the time. Finally, the twelfth-century *Historia scholastica* of Peter Comestor will be explored. This is another important theological text which was fundamental to the teaching of theology in the medieval period. Jean-Pierre Torrell, in his 2005 work on Thomas Aquinas, states that by the 1230s the three basic texts that Dominican friars were expected to study were the Bible, the *Historia scholastica* of Peter Comestor, and Lombard's *Sententiarum*.[8] This work also considers the nature of the demonic and provides a different viewpoint to the other theologians listed so far, as will be explored below.

With regards the visual imagery surrounding demons, this study will look at both manuscript illuminations accompanying religious or theological writings, and the architectural art of medieval churches. The manuscripts considered range from the twelfth to the fourteenth centuries, covering the same period as the theological writings above, and include texts with a link to theological or biblical literature, thereby providing a contextual link to the theological discussions of demons also being explored. The manuscripts include devotional texts, used by both clergy and the lay community, such as psalters, collections of Psalms used for prayer. The highly illustrated Add MS 21926, known as the Grandisson Psalter and held by the British Library, is a thirteenth-century psalter named for its fourteenth-century owner John Grandisson, Bishop of Exeter.[9] Similarly, the Getty Museum's twelfth-century MS 66, named the Ingeborg Psalter as it was produced for

Queen Ingeborg of France, is another richly illuminated example that will be considered.[10] Also used here are two fourteenth-century illustrated Bibles, also both held by the British Library. The first is MS Kings 5, a Dutch example of a *Biblia pauperum*, a typological Bible focussed on illustrations for the illiterate elite comparing similarities between the New and Old Testaments.[11] The second is Add MS 47682, known as the Holkham Picture Book, a fourteenth-century richly illustrated Bible from England, designed by the clergy for an illiterate audience.[12] The final devotional text to be examined is the Taymouth Hours, Yates Thomson MS 13 in the British Library.[13] It is a fourteenth-century book of hours, a devotional text incorporating prayers and psalms for use by the laity. While many of these works included lots of imagery, this is a particularly richly illustrated version, and was possibly made for a royal patron, explaining this emphasis on illumination. Other imagery to be considered comes from a thirteenth century production of Anselm of Canterbury's *De humanis noribus per similitudines* (hereafter *Similitudines),* a work which was possibly revised and finalised following his death.[14] This text considered human morality and compared vice and virtue in a variety of contexts. Also considered is the fourteenth-century *Breviari d'amor,* a lengthy Occitan poem which incorporates a section discussing theology, by Matfre Ermengau, a French friar and troubadour.[15] These examples have been chosen as they are utilised by both the clergy and laity, they all come from manuscripts with a link to theological or biblical thought, and they are contemporary to the theological discussions being considered. The church art to be incorporated into this study focuses on three examples. These are two twelfth-century tympana, those of the Abbey Church of Sainte-Foy in Conques and of St Lazare in Autun. The last is a thirteenth-century wall painting in the church of St Mary and St Michael in Melbourne, England. These have been selected due to their prominent positions within the church settings themselves, their subject matter, and the contemporary time frame of their completion.[16]

This essay will therefore consider the differences between theological descriptions of demons and how they are visually represented within theological and church settings. It will consider the reasons behind the visual representations of demons and how this differs from their understood physicality. It will also make a case for further research into the implications of this dual understanding of the demonic physical form and how they have both existed within the Christian worldview in the medieval period and beyond.

In the medieval period theological works primarily understood demons as having the same physical attributes as angels. Peter Lombard's *Sententiarum*, explains that '[m]any Catholic writers have agreed on this and have taught unanimously that angels are incorporeal and do not have bodies united to them.'[17] On demons specifically, Lombard cites Augustine:

> All angels before their confirmation or fall had aerial bodies,
> formed from the purer and higher part of the air and suitable for
> acting, but not for suffering. And such bodies were preserved for
> the good angels who remained steadfast, so that they can act in
> such bodies, but not suffer...But the bodies of the evil angels in
> their fall were changed into an inferior quality of thicker air. For
> just as they were cast down from a worthier place to a lower one,
> that is, into this cloudy atmosphere, so their refined bodies were
> transformed into inferior and thicker ones, in which they can
> suffer from a superior element, that is, from fire. And this seems
> to have been Augustine's thought, as he says, in *On Genesis*:
> Demons are called aerial animate beings because they are
> endowed with bodies of an aerial nature;
> Peter Lombard, *Sententiarum*, II.8.1 [18]

This passage, drawn from Augustine's writings, clarifies that demons were angels before their fall. Angels are aerial creatures and those that fell, becoming demons, retained their aerial nature, although they began taking their substance from a lower quality of air given their new habitat. It is therefore possible to draw the conclusion that demons still do not have an intrinsic corporeal form. Bonaventure's commentary on the Sententiarum explicitly confirms this, stating:

> On this point, however, many doubt whether demons have an
> inseparable body tied to them in which they are tortured. But it is

plain enough that just as the good angels do not have a body
unless they voluntarily assume one, neither do the wicked angels.
Bonaventure, *Commentaria,* II.7.1.1.1.[19]

Demons are therefore understood to be aerial and incorporeal, similar
to angels, but of a lower quality of matter.

The passage from Bonaventure above also reflects another facet to
the theological understanding of angelic and demonic form, that both
angels and demons can take on certain forms when required to. The
appearance of God and of supernatural creatures, both angels and
demons, was a common occurrence in the Old Testament of the Bible,
and they took many different forms. God appeared as a burning bush,
as pillars of cloud and fire, and as storms.[20] Angels also took the form
of other humans, as when they appeared before Abraham. Similarly,
demons are seen in the Bible using a variety of forms when they appear
to human beings, or possessing the bodies of both humans and animals,
such as pigs. Aquinas' *Summa theologiae* provides an example of
demons taking different forms when necessary:

> But if from the joining of demons some are occasionally begotten,
> this is not through the seed cut from them, or from assumed
> bodies, but through the seed of some man received for this,
> namely that the same demon which is a succubus to a man, was
> an incubus to a woman;
> Aquinas, *Summa Theologiae,* q. 51, a.3, ad.6. [21]

Here Aquinas is explaining the mechanics of an incubus, a demon
which is able to impregnate a woman using sperm which it has
previously taken from a human man. The demons must therefore be
able to take the form of both genders in order for this to work. This
topic is of interest to theologians as it relates to demons' capabilities and
whether they are able to impregnate women. This was another subject
which Augustine considered at length in his writings, and much of the
discussion in the medieval period was founded on his writings.
Augustine was undecided on whether such occurrences did indeed
happen, but by the thirteenth century the concept of incubi assaulting
women was discussed as fact.[22] As part of his explanation here Aquinas

has clearly stated that demons first take the form of a woman and then take the form of a man, meaning that they are capable of taking the form of both genders.

The most common example given and discussed in theological works is the serpent in the garden of Eden. There is much discussion over whether it was the Devil in the form of a serpent or whether the Devil used a real serpent for his purposes.[23] However, regardless of this difference of opinion, even when it is assumed that it was the Devil in the form of a serpent, there is still much to learn from theological discussions on the topic. In the twelfth century the description of the serpent in the garden as having a woman's head began to become more widespread. This was popularised by Peter Comestor in his late twelfth-century *Historia scholastica* where he described the serpent in Eden as 'having the face of a virgin'.[24] Despite claiming that this description was drawn from an uncited work of Bede, the concept of a female-headed serpent in Eden has no bases in Biblical source material and was refuted both directly and indirectly by other theological writers at the time. Nicholas of Lyra, in the fourteenth century, wrote that 'some say that serpent had a pleasing and virginal face; but this has no scriptural authority...', which directly contradicts Peter Comestor's understanding of the hybrid serpent.[25] Similarly, Lombard's *Sententiarum* indirectly refutes Comestor's account when it explains that:

> But because he could not harm her by violence, he turned to deceit, so that he might overthrow her whom he could not overcome by power. But lest his deception should become too apparent, he did not come in his own form, lest he should be clearly recognised and so rejected. On the other hand, lest his deceit be so excessively hidden it would be impossible to guard against and humankind would also seem to suffer a wrong if God allowed it to be tricked in such a way that it would not be able to take any precautions, the devil was allowed to come in another's form, but in one in which his wickedness would be easily detected. And so, that he came not in his own form was done by his own will; but that he came in a form suitable to his wickedness was done by God. And so he came to the humans as a serpent Peter Lombard, *Sententiarum*, II.21.2.[26]

Lombard is here quite explicit that the Devil was not allowed by God to take on a form that would be too appealing to Eve, such as a human form. This, perhaps, is behind the hybrid nature of the serpent-woman that Comestor describes which does not go so far as allowing the Devil to use the full body of a human woman. However, if the purpose of the virgin's face is for Eve to find the Devil appealing and more easily trusted, then Lombard's logic above would not allow for this.

Nevertheless, in Comestor's serpent-woman, the demonic has begun to take on a hybrid form. This hybrid description was commonly reproduced in the illustrations accompanying discussions of Genesis and the fall.[27] A thirteenth-century example can be found in the Grandisson Psalter, produced in England in the 1270s-80s, and most famously owned by John Grandisson, the Bishop of Exeter in the following century.[28] Accompanying Psalm 109, which is concerned with the deceit of the wicked, an image of the Fall of Man appears, including the woman-headed serpent. This is significant as it is a devotional text, owned by a prominent member of the clergy who would have been familiar with theological commentary around the appearance of the serpent and demons in general. Similar examples include the fourteenth-century Biblia Pauperum from the Netherlands, held by the British Library, in which a female-headed serpent appears to Eve alone, and the fourteenth-century Taymouth Hours, produced in England for a royal woman, which depicts the hybrid serpent between Adam and Eve.[29] Biblia Pauperum were Bibles which focussed on imagery as the primary form of communication with little or no text alongside them. They were designed for the lay population who were often unable to read and relied on visual imagery, although the expense of manuscript versions such as this put them out of reach of most of the population. Books of Hours were devotional works used for prayer by the upper classes. Other interesting examples include the fourteenth-century Holkham Bible Picture Book, produced in London and likely to have been designed for a wealthy lay audience. The illustrations representing Genesis include an image of Adam and Eve eating the forbidden fruit, watched by a serpent with a female head.[30] Like the above examples, this is not necessarily intended for a clerical audience, however, it was produced by clergy, probably Dominicans, and sits well within a Biblical context. Another example can be found in a fourteenth-century manuscript copy of Matfre Ermengau's *Breviari d'amor*, a thirteenth century French poetic work which includes a lengthy section on theology. In this example Eve alone reaches for the forbidden fruit while a female-headed serpent watches her pluck it.[31] Ermengau was himself a cleric and was well versed in the theological arguments of the time. Therefore, despite the secular nature of the work itself, there was a strong link to formal theological discussion accompanying the image of the female-headed serpent in this instance. In all these examples the hybrid nature of the serpent is contrary to the prevailing theological theory at the time, that the Devil appeared as a normal serpent. However, its hybridity is likely to serve to highlight to the viewer of the works its unnatural character and the supernatural element of the situation.

Demons appear as hybrid and monstrous forms in other theological contexts, beyond that of the female-headed serpent in Genesis. Apart from the trope of the female-headed serpent, there were other common elements to the way in which demons were represented. This includes demons as hybrid compilations of other creatures and with overtly monstrous features, including unusual colourings, bat-like wings, enlarged limbs and teeth, or horns. Again, the purpose of this study is not to provide an exhaustive list of examples, however, some instances have been included for demonstration and to consider the possible reasons behind the differences in the visual representation of demons and the theological understanding of their form.

One of the explanations for the female-headed serpent posited above is linked to identification and that the hybridity of the serpent serves to mark it as apart from an ordinary creature. It is possible that the depictions of demons as strange hybrid creatures in visual art more widely was in fact done to ensure that they are easily identified in illustrations as they are often shown alongside humans or angels. This can be seen in a thirteenth-century illustration from St Anselm's *Similitudines*, where the Devil is present alongside saints and sinners.[32] The *Similitudines* were designed to compare the vices and virtues of human morality, using pairs of opposite concepts throughout. One pairing used is between saints and sinners and the illustration depicts God, and angel, and a humble human on the one hand, with an adulterous pair and the Devil on the other. The visual imagery here is important so that the wickedness of the Devil can be distinguished from the goodness of the angel. Another example can be found in the Ingeborg Psalter, a twelfth century prayer book commissioned for Ingeborg, the wife of Philip II of France.[33] As a devotional text used by a member of lay royalty, it is helpful for the viewer to be able to immediately recognise demonic figures from the human or the divine. The illustration for Psalm 53, which begins 'the fool hath said in his heart, there is no God', depicts a man holding a piece of parchment which reads 'non est Deus'. He is flanked by two devils, identifiable as grey imp-like creatures with wings and horns. In stark visual contrast, an angel, who is warning the man, is shown above in robes with golden hair and a divine halo. In both of these examples, were these creatures to be represented according to their true nature, this would not only be impossible due to their incorporeality, but they would also look the same given the Devil's and his demons existence as fallen angels. This highlights two issues facing those tasked with visually representing angels and demons. The first is the impossibility of accurately representing an incorporeal being. The second is how to distinguish between two beings which are identical in their physicality but completely opposite in their fundamental nature, a point which is important to make to clear to the viewer. Standard tropes therefore developed with angels depicted in a similar way to saints with halos to demonstrate their closeness to God, and wings to mark them as supernatural. Demons, on the other hand, were depicted as monstrous and hybrid beings, demonstrating both their wicked nature and distinguishing them from other animals or creatures. As mentioned above Caroline Walker Bynum, in her *Metamorphosis and Identity,* explained that hybridity was seen in the medieval period as conflicting with standard notions of reality and what individuals what expect to encounter.[34] It could be that the hybridity of the demonic, especially incorporating the animalistic, is in contrast with the concepts of man being made in God's image and the incarnation of the divine in Christ. However, elsewhere, Bynum also refers to Bernard of Clairvaux's attitudes to hybridity, which he terms *unitas* in reference to the unity of multiple parts. Bynum explains that Bernard sees Christ as hybrid, combining both the divine and human, and that humans themselves are hybrid as they are made up of the body, the soul, and the spirit.[35] However, these notions are referring to a hybridity of nature, rather than of form, and the visual representation of the demonic as hybrid and animal is still in stark contrast to the concept of the divine as akin to man's form. The hybrid nature of the representation of demons in these instances is therefore a way to demonstrate their otherness and that their very existence is in conflict with the reality that Christianity strives for. This leads to another possible reason for the specific way in which demons were depicted, which was to provoke fear.

One of the concerns of the Church in the medieval period was ensuring that the general populace remained God-fearing and did not stray from the tenets of Christianity. The Church relied on continued piety to retain their position of power within society, to ensure their income from tithes, and to stamp out unorthodox beliefs and heresy. One of the methods utilised to ensure good behaviour and piety was a fear of life outside of the Christian faith and of exclusion from heaven in the afterlife. Church art, including painting, stained glass, and sculpture, was used to reinforce this. Many images within a Church setting were therefore designed to praise divinity, for example, images of saints, Christ, and Biblical scenes. However, some imagery was used to highlight the "other" and to increase fear amongst the laity of transgressing. The imagery within Churches was also able to extend to a much wider audience than illustrations within manuscripts. Some of the examples above would have been accessible only to a scholarly audience, such as the *Similitudines*. Others would have been more widely seen, such as those in devotional texts, but still limited to the wealthy elite. Church art, displayed publicly, would have been seen by a much broader segment of the population. A good example is a wall painting from St Michael and St Mary in Melbourne, Derbyshire.[36] The image is damaged and there is debate over exactly what it depicts, with two figures in the foreground being suggested as either gossiping women or witches involved in sabbat rituals. However, an unmistakable element of the image is the large demon positioned between the two figures, depicted with an enlarged nose and ears, talons on its feet, hair covering its body, and two pairs of wings. It is a striking image and its position in the church meant that it was facing the congregation directly and would have been in full view at all times. The general populace, when faced with this imagery, would not be concerned around the theological details of demonic physicality. They would, however, be frightened by the force of this memorable visual imagery, which would not otherwise be commonplace in the life of a medieval churchgoer. Even for those individuals who did not formally attend church regularly might still be exposed to this kind of visual representation with sculpture featured on the building of the Church itself. Architectural examples can be found in the tympana of two churches in France, those of St. Lazare Cathedral in Autun and the Abbay Church of Sainte-Foy in Conques.[37] The tympanum was a large, semi-circular carving above the main entrance into a Church, and was therefore in a very prominent position. These carvings often portrayed Last Judgement scenes, and demons were a common aspect. The demons in both of these tympana are depicted as grotesque creatures with exaggerated features and long, skeletal limbs. While they are clearly not representing humans, animals, or anything divine, the representation is so extreme that viewers would feel a sense of unease looking at it. Given the context of the Last Judgement, identification of the figures as demons is not a concern, and it is clear that one of the main aims of this imagery is to inspire fear of the afterlife if one were to live outside of the Church and its protection.

There are other reasons for the use of hybrid imagery when depicting demons, which are less removed from the theological source material considered earlier. While twelfth-century theology did not largely support the concept of the demon as a hybrid or monstrous form, there were theological precedents for this idea within the writings of the Church Fathers. Augustine, who wrote extensively on the subject of demons and heavily influenced the twelfth-century ideas on the subject, was writing at a time of conversion. He was himself a pagan convert and much of his writing was concerned with the translation of pagan ideas into the Christian worldview. *Daimones,* neutral spirits of the Greco-Roman world which could be called upon for benign or malign purposes, had no place within Christian theology and became demons, providing the linguistic basis for the Latin *daemones.* These were aerial spirits with no form and their link to Christian demons does not contradict the idea of the latter as aerial and incorporeal. However, other elements of pagan belief were also associated with the demonic by writers such as Augustine in order to find a place for them in the

Christian world. This included many mythological creatures, whose non-existence had not been conclusively proven, including fauns, such as woodland deity Pan, sirens, and other hybrid creatures which were associated by the Church Fathers with demons. This systematic translation of problematic pagan ideas into Christian demons may also account for some of the more unusual visual characteristics we have seen in the examples above, such as horns and other animal parts. Many of the mythical creatures in the ancient world were understood as hybrid, and the desire to condemn these creatures as demonic and anti-Christian could have influenced the ongoing association between demons and hybridity.

There was therefore a twofold understanding of demons in the twelfth century with two distinct origins. On the one hand, demons were considered to be fallen angels which shared an aerial, incorporeal nature with their divine counterparts. They were able to take on the appearance of form but never had true bodies. The aerial *daimones* of the ancient world were considered to be the same beings by theologians, misunderstood by pagan intellects and wrongly considered neutral. On the other hand, demons were also strongly linked to the fantastical and monstrous forms of myth and legend rooted in the ancient world. For theologians, supernatural creatures which could not otherwise be explained were not of God and therefore had to be demonic. Similarly, the gods of pagan culture were clearly demons who had deluded humans into worshipping them and must be classified as such. This second origin of Christian demons is likely to have influenced the visual representation in medieval culture as hybrid and monstrous, especially given the increased interest in Greek works from the twelfth century onwards with their re-emergence in the West. Even within theological contexts, such as illuminations in theological manuscripts, it is very likely that the purpose of the illustrations representing demons was not to reflect theological accuracy. It would be very difficult to represent demons as incorporeal beings made of air. Similarly, showing demons as taking on specific human or animal forms would also be difficult as there would be no immediate and obvious way of determining whether they were demons in that form, or the forms themselves, outside of specific tropes such as a non-hybrid serpent in the garden of Eden.

Using monstrous, and specifically, hybrid forms demonstrates their demonic, supernatural nature to the viewer immediately.

It is clear that there is a complex and contradictory tradition around visual representation of demons which extends beyond the time period examined here and beyond the confines of formal theology. For example, a sixth-century Byzantine mosaic depicts the Devil alongside an angel and Christ in a last judgement scene. The Devil, on Christ's left, is here as an angel-like figure, almost indistinguishable from the angel sat on Christ's right-hand side and identifiable by the goats before him which have been separated from the sheep, in reference to Matthew 25:31.[38] Much later, in the fourteenth-century *Inferno* of Dante's *Divine Comedy*, the Devil is represented within hell as a monstrous, hybrid being with multiple heads, designed for causing maximum torment and punishment to those around him.[39] Both of these images represent the varying origins of the demonic discussed above, which has led to two vastly different understandings of the demonic physicality, both of which sit within Christian tradition. There is therefore significant scope to undertake further research on the dual nature of the demonic within Christian tradition, how the two tropes interact with and inform one another, and how they have both been incorporated into Christian understanding, despite their apparent conflict.

Notes

1   See Richard Landes, Andrew Gow, David Van Meter (eds.), *The Apocalyptic Year 1000: Religious Expectation and Social Change, 950-1050,* Oxford University Press, (Oxford, 2003), and Richard Kenneth Emmerson, Bernard McGinn (eds.), *The Apocalypse in the Middle Ages,* Cornell University Press, (New York, 1992).

2   Debra Higgs Strickland, *Saracens, Demons, & Jews: Making Monsters in Medieval Art,* Princeton University Press, (Woodstock, 2003), p. 61.

3   D. Elliott, *Fallen Bodies: Pollution, Sexuality, and Demonology in the Middle Ages,* (Philadelphia, 1998).

4   A. Bernau, *Bodies and the Supernatural: Humans, Demons and Angels, in A Cultural History of the Human Body in the Medieval Age* edited by Linda Kalof, (London, 2014).

5   Bernau, *Bodies and the Supernatural,* pp. 106-110.

6   C. Walker Bynum, *Metamorphosis and Identity,* (New York, 2001).

7   Walker Bynum, *Metamorphosis and Identity*, p. 31.

8   See J-P. Torrell, *Saint Thomas Aquinas, Vol. 1: The Person and His Work*, trans. by Robert Royal, 2nd edn (Washington, 2005), p. 40.

9   Little is known about the Grandisson Psalter's origins, other than that it was made in England. Its ownership by the Bishop of Exeter is documented by his coat of arms inserted at the beginning of the manuscript and its inclusion in his will. See Add MS 21926, https://www.bl.uk/manuscripts/FullDisplay.aspx?ref=add_ms_21926, (accessed 27th September 2021).

10 See M. H. Caviness, 'Anchoress, Abbess, and Queen: Donors and Patrons or Intercessors and Matrons?', in *The Cultural Patronage of Medieval Women*, ed. by June Hall McCash, (Athens, 1996), pp. 133-5, and 'Master of the Ingeborg Psalter', https://www.getty.edu/art/collection/artists/11379/master-of-the-ingeborg-psalter-french-active-about-1195-about-1210/, (accessed 27th September 2021).

11 See *Detailed Record for King's 5*, https://www.bl.uk/catalogues/illuminatedmanuscripts/record.asp?MSID=7880&CollID=19&NStart=5, (accessed 27th September 2021).

12 See *Bible (the 'Holkham Bible Picture Book')*, http://searcharchives.bl.uk/primo_library/libweb/action/dlDisplay.do?docId=IAMS040-002104030&fn=permalink&vid=IAMS_VU2, (accessed 27th September 2021).

13 *Book of Hours, Use of Sarum (The Taymouth Hours)*, http://searcharchives.bl.uk/primo_library/libweb/action/dlDisplay.do?vid=IAMS_VU2&docId=IAMS040-002354423&fn=permalink, (accessed 27th September 2021).

14 See *Six Figures: God, Good Will, the Devil, a Peasant, a Woman, and an Adulterer, In St. Anselm's 'Similitudes' And Other Works*, https://www.bl.uk/onlinegallery/onlineex/illmanus/cottmanucoll/s/011cotclec00011u00002v00.html, (accessed 27th September 2021).

15 See *Royal MS 19 C 1*, https://www.bl.uk/manuscripts/FullDisplay.aspx?ref=Royal_MS_19_C_I, (accessed 27th September 2021).

16 This study does not extend to a consideration of hybridity in other contexts beside the demonic, for example, gargoyles and grotesques in Church architecture. For more on this see M. Camille, *Image on the Edge: The Margins of Medieval Art*, (London, 1995).

17 'Dicunt quoque plurimos catholicos tractatores in hoc convenisse atque id concorditer docuisse, quod angeli incorporei sint, nec corpora habeant sibi unita, assumant autem aliquando corpora, Deo praeparante, ad

impletionem ministerii sui sibi a Deo injuncti, eademque post expletionem deponunt', Lombard, *Sententiarum,* pp. 667-8.

18 'Angeli omnes ante confirmationem vel lapsum corpora aerea habuerit de puriori ac superiore parte formata, ad faciendum habilia, non ad patiendum: et angelis bonis qui persiterunt, talia sunt observaya corpora, ut in eis possint facere, et non pati ... Angelis vero malis mutata sunt in casu corpora in deteriorem qualitatem spissioris aeris. Sicut enim a loco digniori in inferiorem locum, id est, caliginosum acrem, dejecti sunt, ita illi corpora tenuia mutata sunt et transformata in deteriora corpora et spissiora in quibus pati possunt a superiori elemento, id est, ab igne. Et hoc Augustinus sensisse videtur super. Gen. ita diceus: Daemones dicuntur aerea animalia, qui corporum aereorum natura vigent', Lombard, *Sententiarum,* p. 667.

19 'De hoc tamen plures dubitant, utrum daemones habeant corpora sibi inseparabiliter alligata, in quibus torqueantur. Sed satis planum est, quod sicut boni Angeli non habent corpora nisi voluntarie assumta, sic nec mali.' Bonaventure, *Commentaria,* p. 211.

20 Exodus 3:1–4:17; Exodus 13:21-22; Job 38:1.

21 'Si tamen ex coitu Daemonum aliqui interdum nascuntur, hoc non est per semen ab eis decisum, aut a corporibus assumptis, sed per semen alicuius hominis ad hoc acceptum, utpote quod idem Daemon qui est succubus ad virum, fiat incubus ad mulierem', Aquinas, *Summa,* p. 283.

22 Elliott, *Fallen Bodies,* pp. 52-3.

23 See Nona C. Flores, *'"Virgineum Vultum Habens": The Woman-Headed Serpent in Art and Literature From 1300 To 1700,* PhD diss., University of Illinois, 1981, p. 14.

24 'Et hoc per serpentem, quia tunc serpens erectus est ut homo, quia in maledictione prostratus est, et adhuc, ut tradunt, phareas erectus incedit. Elegit etiam quoddam genus serpentis, ut ait Beda. virgineum vultum habens, quia similia similibus applaudant. et movit ad loquendum linguam ejus, tamen nescientes sicut et per fanaticos et energumenos loquitur.' Peter Comestor, *Historia scholastica,* p. 1072.

25 H. A. Kelly, 'The Metamorphosis of the Eden Serpent during the Middle Ages and Renaissance', *Viator,* 2 (1971), 326.

26 'Sed quia illi per violentiam nocere non poterat, ad fraudem se convertit, ut dolo hominem supplantaret, quem virtute superare nequiret. Ne autem fraus illius nimis manifestaretur, in sua specie non venit, ne aperte cognosceretur, et ita repelleretur: iterum ne nimis occulta foret fraus ejus quae caveri non posset, et homo simul videretur injuriam pati, si taliter circumveniri permitteret eum Deus ut praecavere non posset, in aliena quidem forma venire permissus est diabolus, sed in tali in qua ejus malitia posset deprehendi. UT ergo in propria forma non venire, voluntate sua

propria factum est; ut autem in forma suae malitia congruenti veniret, divinitus factum est. Venit ergo ad hominem in serpente', Lombard, *Sententiarum,* p. 695.

27 A more thorough overview of this specific piece of visual imagery has been conducted by Nona C. Flores both in her above-referenced 1981 thesis: Flores, "'*Virgineum Vultum Habens*'" and in her later essay: '*"Effigies amicitae ... veritas inimicitiae": Antifeminism in the Iconography of the Woman-Headed Serpent in Medieval and Renaissance Art and Literature"',* in *Animals in the Middle Ages,* ed. by Nona C. Flores, (Abingdon, 2016), pp. 167-196.

28 *Full page miniature showing the Temptation of Adam and Eve with a serpent having a woman's face,* BL Add MS 21926 f.150v, https://www.bl.uk/manuscripts/Viewer.aspx?ref=add_ms_21926_fs001r, (accessed 27th September 2021).

29 *Eve and the serpent,* BL Kings MS 5 f.1r, https://www.bl.uk/manuscripts/Viewer.aspx?ref=kings_ms_5_fs001r, (accessed 27th September 2021). Bas-de-page scene of Adam and Eve eating the apple of the Tree of Knowledge, while a female-headed serpent coils round the tree, BL Yates Thompson MS 13 f.20v, https://www.bl.uk/manuscripts/Viewer.aspx?ref=yates_thompson_ms_1 3_fs001r, (accessed 27th September 2021).

30 *Adam and Eve eat the forbidden fruit while the serpent, with a woman's head, watches,* BL Add MS 47682 f.4r, https://www.bl.uk/manuscripts/Viewer.aspx?ref=add_ms_47682_fs001r, (accessed 27th September 2021).

31 *The Temptation of Eve,* BL MS Royal 19 C I f.66v, https://www.bl.uk/manuscripts/Viewer.aspx?ref=royal_ms_19_c_i_fs001r, (accessed 27th September 2021).

32 *Six Figures: God, Good Will, The Devil, a Peasant, a Woman, and an Adulterer,* BL Cotton MS Cleopatra C XI f.2v, https://www.bl.uk/onlinegallery/onlineex/illmanus/cottmanucoll/s/011cotcl ec00011u00002v00.html, (accessed 27th September 2021).

33 "Initial D: The Fool with Two Demons." Getty MS 66 f.56, https://www.getty.edu/art/collection/objects/127959/master-of-the-ingeborg-psalter-initial-d-the-fool-with-two-demons-french-after-1205/, (accessed 27th September 2021).

34 Walker Bynum, *Metamorphosis and Identity,* p. 31.

35 Walker Bynum, *Metamorphosis and Identity,* p. 159.

36 *Medieval wall painting, St Michael and St Mary, Melbourne, Derbyshire* https://upload.wikimedia.org/wikipedia/commons/e/e2/Medieval_wall_pa

inting%2C_St_Michael_and_St_Mary%2C_Melbourne%2C_Derbyshire.j
pg, (accessed 27ᵗʰ September 2021).

37 *Last Judgment Tympanum at Autun,*
https://www.flickr.com/photos/jimforest/3713195749, (accessed 27ᵗʰ
September 2021). For more detail on the Cathedral at Autun and the link
between the tympanum's imagery and the site's importance on the
pilgrimage routes see L. Seidel, *Legends in Limestone: Lazarus,
Gislebertus, and the Cathedral of Autun,* (Chicago, 1999), pp. 6-9.
Conques carving detail,
https://commons.wikimedia.org/wiki/File:2003_Conques_carving_detail_I
MG_6348.JPG, (accessed 27ᵗʰ September 2021). The imagery in this
tympanum is discussed at length in A. R. Stead, '"Eye Hath not Seen ...
which Things God Hath Prepared ...": Imagining Heaven and Hell in
Romanesque and Gothic Art', in *Imagining the Medieval Afterlife,* ed. by
Richard Matthew Pollard, (Cambridge, 2020), pp. 196-8.

38 *Christ separates the lambs from the goats* (prophecy of the Last Judgment,
Matthew 25: 31)
https://www.akg-images.co.uk/archive/-2UMDHUHWO7DX.html,
(accessed 27ᵗʰ September 2021).

39 *Inferno* Canto XXXIV in Dante Alighieri, *The Divine Comedy,* trans. by
C. H. Sisson, (Oxford, 1998), p. 191-2.

The First Papal Legatine Mission in Livonia: William of Modena and the City of Riga, 1225-6[1]

Mari-Liis Neubauer

University of Reading

The aim of this article is to assess the involvement of William of Modena (c. 1184-1251) as a papal legate in major matters pertaining to the city of Riga during his first legatine mission to Livonia in 1225-6.[2] In the first part of the paper, the context of legatine missions and that of the office of a legate will be briefly considered in order to better understand the prerogatives of such undertakings. It will be shown that in the case of William of Modena, he was invested with the highest authority a legate could wield, and that the circumstances in which he was commissioned on the mission to Livonia did not explicitly foresee his extensive involvement with the city of Riga. This leaves room for the interpretation that William must have personally perceived certain matters pertaining to Riga highly important, further exemplifying his influence on the early development of the city. In the second part of the article, three specific cases in which William was deeply involved will be analysed. As a result, more can be said not only about the struggles that the young city was facing, but also about its power relations with other authorities in Livonia and the importance of William as a legate in solving these conflicts amicably.

Representation through legation was a device employed by the papacy already in the Early Middle Ages.[3] The frequency of such legations started to rise with the eleventh century Gregorian reform and with the growing importance of papal decision-making, when an increasing number of litigants started to appeal straight to Rome, by-passing the courts of bishops and archbishops that would have traditionally examined the claims.[4] Partly as a counter-measure, a number of legates with extensive powers and authority were sent out from the papal curia.[5] Essentially, papal legates assumed the political and diplomatic duties necessitated by the papacy.[6] At the same time, crusading movements of the twelfth and thirteenth centuries also required legatine missions to be deployed with increasing frequency, as the popes did not accompany the crusades personally, and therefore needed a representative for the holy affair.[7] Yet, as has been pointed out by James Brundage, the Livonian mission which had begun at the end of the twelfth century, and in many respects resembled a crusade, did not get its own legate until the appointment of William of Modena on 31 December 1224.[8] There had been a number of legates sent to the Baltic rim more generally before William, but none of them were specifically named as legates to Livonia.[9] Pope Innocent III, while emphasising the work of preachers in the conversion of Livonia, had not seen it necessary to deploy a legatine mission there.[10] A refinement to this approach came with the pontificate of Honorius III (1216-1227) who seemed to have planned for a major missionary venture, not only to Livonia but elsewhere outside of Christendom as well.[11] As the framework of this idea remained ambiguous, it cannot be said with certainty to what extent the vision of the pope was utilised. Nevertheless, with his pontificate came a crucial change for Livonia in the form of legatine office.

Not all legates were perceived as equal. While Gratian's *Decretum*, the influential collection of canon law from the twelfth century, did not specify the distinction between individual types of legates, thirteenth-century popes and canon lawyers started to develop a sophisticated classification system for legatine missions. For instance, the *Liber extra*, which became the first officially promulgated canon law collection in 1234, defines the categories of papal legates through their capacity to absolve persons excommunicated for violent crimes against clerics.[12] While the specifics of such divisions of legatine missions differed from canon lawyer to canon lawyer, making the whole classification system during the first half of the thirteenth century ambiguous and confusing, the concept of a papal legate with the highest authority within the legatine office system – *legatus a latere* – had nevertheless taken root by the thirteenth century.[13]

William of Modena was assigned as a papal legate to Livonia on three occasions: in 1224, in 1234, and in 1244.[14] In the letter from 31 December 1224, Pope Honorius III states that *'commisso sibi plenae legationis officio'* [I commission him (William of Modena) with the office of full legation].[15] The same exact phrase can be found in the letters appointing him to his second legatine mission in 1234, and to his third legatine mission in 1244.[16] This seems to indicate that William was invested with the fullest powers that a legate could possibly hold. Indeed, the letters that were sent to William by Honorius III regarding his mission in Livonia did not seem to include limitations to his power but rather the opposite – they included special mandates that many legal commentators would have seen as powers reserved exclusively to the pope.[17] Thus, it seems that in the case of the legatine missions of William of Modena, he could be most closely identified with what was known as *legatus a latere*, a legate with the highest authority.

It is difficult to ascertain what exactly prompted the pope to send William to Livonia but circumstancial evidence can shed more light on this. In 1224, an envoy was sent to Rome from Livonia.[18] The chronicle of Henry of Livonia, finished in the late 1220s, states that 'miserat venerabilis Rigensis episcopus Mauritium, sacerdotum suum, in curiam Romanam, petere sedis apostolice legatum in Lyvoniam' [the venerable bishop of Riga sent his priest Maurice to the Roman court to ask the apostolic see for a legate to Livonia].[19] The highest spiritual authority in Livonia at that time was the bishop of Riga, who in 1213/14 had obtained a papal dispensation from being subjected to any archiepiscopal jurisdiction.[20] During the first legatine mission of William, the bishop of Riga was Albert of Buxhövden who held the bishopric from 1199 until his death in 1229.[21] Increasingly over time, the bishop of Riga was faced with competition for authority by the military order of the Swordbrothers (*Fratres Milicie Christi de Livonia*), founded at the turn of the thirteenth century.[22] Different royal powers were also getting involved in the power struggles in Livonia, of whom the most relevant to the legation of William were the Danes who were laying claim to northern Estonia.[23]

Although not confirmed by the papal letters that commissioned William of Modena on his missions, the report by Henry of Livonia claiming that Bishop Albert of Riga had asked for a legate has been seen as legitimate.[24] There have been various suggestions as to why the bishop requested a papal representative to be sent to Livonia, but the prevailing reason has been that he wished for the conflict between the Church of Riga and the Danes to be solved.[25] This, indeed, seems to be the case; in 1223, Honorius III had given Albert the right – a special privilege – to decide all questions and disputes 'que ad sedem essent apostolicam referende' [which ought to be referred to the apostolic see].[26] As the jurisdiction of regions in northern Estonia was contested, the bishop could not claim his universal spiritual lordship there, and required an intervention from the papacy. It was also likely that the bishop of Riga wished to be elevated to the position of a metropolitan, which would have required further investigation of the local circumstances by a papal representative.[27]

At the same time, the intents of Bishop Albert of Riga to request a papal legate do not necessarily have to correspond with the objectives that the papacy perceived for this mission. The letter of 31 December 1224 that invested William with legatine powers complicates things further, as it was ambigous and did not contain any specific instructions for his mission.[28] Claims that Honorius III intended the legate to set up some kind of papal state in Livonia, have been rebuked in recent scholarship.[29] A major part of William's mission was probably intended to be preaching and missionary activity.[30] Ernst Pitz has claimed that, in fact, preaching was the only device that William had at his disposal: '[n]ur fromme Ermahnungen standen ihm zu Gebote' [only pious exhortations were at his command].[31] This article will show that William's authority as a legate was certainly not as limited in practice.

Indeed, when Honorius III commissioned the legatine mission, he must have had in mind not only preaching but also administrative duties, such as the general organisation of the recently Christianised Livonian society and settling disputes relating to the division of contested regions.[32] As such, there were many issues in Livonia requiring the presence of a legate that were most likely brought to William's attention already before he embarked on his mission. Yet, there is no direct evidence that William was specifically tasked to intervene in the quarrels of Riga. That he chose to do so on multiple occasions, while relying on his authority as *legatus a latere*, not only indicates the discretion afforded to William as a legate to choose the issues to get involved with, but also testifies to the importance of the city of Riga in his eyes.

The majority of scholarly work pertaining to William of Modena and his work in Livonia has focused either on his preaching or on arbitration between the bishop of Riga, the Danes, and the Swordbrothers. Comparatively less attention has been afforded to the legate's involvement with the city of Riga. Furthermore, the most comprehensive works that do focus on thirteenth-century Riga date from more than half a decade ago.[33] While certainly thorough, and listing the details of many letters issued during William's stay in Livonia, these works do not tend to analyse the rationale of William behind these documents.

Founded in 1201 by Bishop Albert, Riga became the focal point from which missionaries dispersed further into the surrounding regions of Livonia.[34] Municipal legislation, including that of Riga, was a sphere in medieval society where various types of laws intersected. One way to distinguish legal spheres within a territorial unit, such as a town, was to divide it between authorities who then governed according to their own legislature. Such was the case in eleventh-century York, where the archbishop controlled one of the wards in the town.[35] In Germany, under which influence Livonia also belonged, municipal law in the Middle Ages tended to develop in broad families: the most important ones being the laws of Magdeburg, Bremen and Lübeck.[36] The Lübeck's law was based on the privileges granted to Lübeck upon its formulation in 1159, and eventually it became one of the dominant municipal laws along the south and eastern coast of the Baltic Sea, including in Livonia. How, in contrast, Riga's own municipal law developed at the beginning of the thirteenth century, deserves a closer look, not least because William of Modena played a central role in its early stages.[37]

As the young city of Riga was growing, its founder, Bishop Albert of Riga, likely felt that the best way to attract new settlers was to grant them official privileges.[38] Consequently, in 1211, the bishop granted the Gotland merchants trading in the Livonian ports – not just in Riga – various privileges.[39] The list was relatively short, consisting of eight categories of protections and privileges, such as the right to bear arms, to mint coins, and to not be subjected to the ordeal of carrying hot iron or duels.[40] Ten years later, in 1221, Bishop Albert declared that 'Rigensis civitas ad inhabitationem sui plus libertatis gratia, quam praediorum circumiacentium fertilitatem fideles alliceret' [the city of Riga attracts the faithful to (become) its inhabitants by the freedom rather than by the fertility of the surrounding estates].[41] This was a testimony to the success that the privileges must have had on the growth of Riga in its early stages.

The rights of Rigan citizens were explicitly brought to the attention of William of Modena during his stay in Riga. A dispute had arisen between the citizens and the bishop for which William's arbitration was sought for in December 1225.[42] The representative of the citizens argued that they had the right to elect their own 'iudex civitatis' [judge of the city] because, likely referring to the 1211 charter, the bishop had given Riga the code of the Gothlanders.[43] While the 1211 document had, indeed, granted the towns of the Livonian ports the opportunity to 'si poterunt componant' [solve their own controversies if they can], it had not specified the exact terms of how judges in the Livonian towns - including in Riga - should be chosen.[44] Bishop Albert, now responding to the demands of the Rigans in 1225, admitted that he had given them the law of the Gothlanders in general, '[d]ubitabatur autem inter eos, quod esset ius Gotorum' [but it is doubted among themselves, what the law of Gothlanders was'.[45] While the settlement that followed hereafter was granted with the explicit consent of the legate - 'de consensu nostro' [with our consent] - it is not presented as his judgement but rather a compromise that was reached by all parties.[46]

This fact, together with the structure of the document - both sides presenting their arguments, followed instantaneously with an agreement - allows us to assume that the document was preceded by lengthy discussions and disputations, and that William of Modena likely steered the negotiations. The compromise reached was as follows: the citizens of Riga are free to choose their own judge who will be responsible for all the temporal cases, but the elected judge has to be presented to the bishop to be invested by him.[47] This general pronouncement was followed by a listing of exemptions from this rule:

Homines autem, qui sunt de iurisdictione episcopi vel aliorum, qui ab episcopo feudum tenant, ut magister, praepositus et alii, non teneantur sub praedicto iudice respondere.[48]

[All people who are under the (direct) jurisdiction of the bishop or others who hold a fief from the bishop – that is, the master of the Swordbrothers, the provost and others – will not be held to respond to the aforementioned judge.]

Such a presentation of a rule, followed by detailed exemptions, was in contrast with the very general and short privileges granted in 1211. The document of 1225, which was the result of William of Modena's arbitration, reflects the depth and length of the talks that must have preceded the written statement. The legate could have been wary of ambiguity and uncertainty, because of his past experiences: when he became the bishop of Modena in 1222, his cathedral chapter demanded the horse that he had been riding after his consecration, as was customary in the diocese.[49] As William was not from Modena and he had no ties to it before him becoming a bishop there, he was likely not aware of the custom.[50] A legal proceeding ensued, and as a result, William was forced to give the horse to the cathedral chapter.[51] Perhaps such an experience made him vary of disparities in legal details, even when something – such as the authority of a bishop over its cathedral chapter – felt like common sense. Thus, it is also possible that it was William who highlighted the need for the Rigan document in 1225 to list exemptions in order to avoid future disputations.

Finally, and in addition to settling the dispute regarding the citizens' right to elect their own judge, the legate confirmed the bishop's exclusive right to mint coins.[52] Thereafter, it was stated that the citizens of Riga are freed from carrying hot iron, customs, *naufragius*, and duels, and that anybody who becomes a citizen of Riga is granted these rights.[53] Lastly, the document stipulates that the citizens of Riga are allowed to benefit from any rights that are enjoyed by 'the Germans staying in Gothland' [Teutonici commorantes in Gutlandia], with an exception of appointing their own priests.[54] Among the witnesses are citizens, merchants and *peregrini* which means that the settlement produced under the guidance of William of Modena was meant for a wide audience, further highlighting its significance in the history of Riga.

On the 11 April 1226, another landmark by the Rigan citizens was achieved with the help of William of Modena: a document was signed which clarified issues pertaining to the lands that were yet to be conquered in Livonia.[55] William of Modena, pointing out that the whole issue had become an obstacle to the conversion of the pagans, stipulated the following:

> Terrarum ergo, quae omnimodo auxilio Dei et praedictorum labore fuerint ad cultum fidei conversae, partem unam episcopo Rigensi et ecclesiae suae, aliam magistro et fratribus militae Christi, et tertiam partem civibus Rigensibus adsignamus, in his duntaxat, quae ad dominium pertinent temporale.[56]
> [Therefore, of the lands that, with the help of God and with the work of the aforementioned (parties), which they will convert to the cult of faith, we bestow one part to the bishop of Riga and his Church, another to the master and brothers of the knights of Christ (the Swordbrothers), and third part to the citizens of Riga, insofar in things which pertain to the secular dominion.]

The exact nature and extent of the spiritual rights of the bishops to be appointed in these new territories was then specified.[57] While reserving the future bishops all the spiritual rights in the territories that are to be conquered, this judgement nevertheless signified a serious drawback to the bishop of Riga in the secular sphere: in 1210, Innocent III had granted the Swordbrothers the right to one third of future conquests, while the other two thirds of the territory would be subject to the bishop of Riga.[58] Now, with the citizens of Riga gaining their share, the bishop of Riga had agreed to give up half his part.

Compared to the letter of December 1225, in which William allegedly did not decide himself on matters at hand but was rather an arbitrator, the legate's resolute voice – 'adsignamus' [we bestow] – is more evident in this letter of 11 April 1226.[59] The cooperation and the avoidance of future conflicts stemming from this resolution was clearly an important matter for the legate, for at the end of the letter he stated that:

Si autem contigerit, unum vel duos de praedictis portionariis
velle[nt] aliquam paganorum terram expugnare et subiicere cultui
Christiano, faciant hoc, communicato consilio praedictorum
trium.[60]
[If it occurs, however, that one or two of the aforementioned
parties (the bishop of Riga, the Swordbrothers, or the citizens of
Riga) wish to a large extent conquer the lands of the pagans and to
subject (them) to the cult of Christianity, they should, in this
matter, seek the advice of the three aforementioned parties (that
is, consult each other)].

With this instruction, William of Modena was clearly hoping to strike a
balance between the secular jurisdiction of the parties, and to elevate
them to an equal standing in this matter.[61] As time would show, however,
the tripartite division became a point of contention some years later.[62]

In connection to the division of future conquests, the document of
11 April 1226 also determined how the incoming pilgrims who were
landing in Riga from elsewhere were to be assigned.[63] The bishop of
Riga had ten days to preselect ten pilgrims from among the volunteers
for his use and for his castles. After ten days, the provost, the master of
the Swordbrothers, and the citizens of Riga were allowed to accept
voluntary pilgrims for service in their castles and works, and 'nec liceat
hoc alicui prohibere' [no one is allowed to prevent this].[64] That this
arrangement was presented in conjunction with the settlement regarding
the division of future conquests, has not yet gained scholarly attention.[65]

It makes sense that in order to have equal status in future
conquests, and so that no party would be weaker than any other, all
sides received the opportunity to recruit the best-equipped and well-
prepared forces into their ranks. As the pilgrims were explicitly
emphasised to be volunteers, the parties selecting them suffered no
monetary expenses, and were thus not reliant on their personal fiscal
reserves.[66] However, a different interpretation could be offered for such
a selection of pilgrims. It has been estimated that during any given year,
the number of pilgrims going to Livonia fluctuated between 300 and
1000.[67] Ten pilgrims pre-selected by the bishop and possibly a similar
number chosen by the rest of the parties, was not a significant number.
In this context, it is possible that the acts of choosing voluntary pilgrims

might have been performances to signify co-operation in the context of future conquests, with the bishop of Riga assuming the spiritually privileged role, as pilgrimages were first and foremost spiritual enterprises.[68]

Before departing Livonia in May 1226, William of Modena was involved in yet another significant task relating to the future of Riga. The general issue pertained to the concept of the town fringe, and documents relating to it were issued over the course of three months, from March until early May.[69] In the document of 15 March, the exact '*termini marchae civitatis*' [boundaries of the town fringe] were determined.[70] At the beginning of the document, the legate states that '*placuit praedictis omnibus nostro se committere arbitrio*' [it pleases [us] to commit ourselves to arbitration in all the aforesaid], thus identifying himself as an intermediary rather than a rigid judge.[71] Of course, William was not an uninvolved bystander either, as evidenced in the same letter:

> [N]obis et sibi ad invicem promittentes, quod quicquid super hoc ordinaverimus, perpetuo ratum habebunt.[72]
> [Promising among themselves to each other and to us that whatever we have decreed, they shall have it in perpetuity.]

It appears that while William of Modena is given the authority to finalise the agreement, the settlement was ultimately reached through a potentially lengthy debate among the parties themselves. In this respect, it is very similar to the written agreement of December 1225 pertaining to the rights of citizens, and which was preceded with a thorough deliberation by the involved sides, as shown above.[73] Yet, it seems that in determining the nature and limitations of the Rigan town fringe, the legate became even more involved in the preceding discussions:

> Nos igitur, rerum, locorum et personarum qualitate diligenter inspecta, dicimus et ordinamus ut ...[74]
> [We, therefore, having diligently inspected the quality of things, places, and persons, declare and ordain that ...]

Not only did William oversee and navigate the negotiations, but he decided to personally investigate anything and anyone pertaining to the case. It is likely, then, that he became very familiar with the structure and surroundings of the young city of Riga, and with the detailed demands for jurisdiction from all the parties involved. It is probable that such attention to detail in investigations was a characteristic William acquired not only during his time working as a papal notary and vice-chancellor, but also during his brief spell an inquisitor in Lombardy in 1224.[75] Of course, heresy is vastly different from settling boundary disputes, but skills and techniques acquired in an inquisitorial procedure could be put to use in civil cases nevertheless.[76]

Despite the meticulously laid down details, the legate was under no illusion that the document of 15 March 1226 would prevent any further disagreements from surfacing in the future. For this reason, he determined that a jury should be elected for the purposes of settling future disagreements:

> Si autem dubitation fuerit alicubi infra dictam marchiam, utrum sit locus ille cultus vel incultus; item ubi sunt arbores, utrum nova vel vetera; hoc totum trium iuratorum civium arbitrio terminetur, qui cives a domino espicopo, praeposito et magistro communiter eligantur, non tantum semel, sed quoties opus erit, si forsan morte vel absentia unus eorum impediretur vel plures.[77]
> [But if there will be doubt anywhere within the said fringe, whether these places are cultivated or uncultivated; also [places] where trees are, whether they are fields or uncultivated forests; also regarding dwellings, whether new or old; to this the total of three sworn citizens is bound by arbitration, who are jointly being elected by the lord bishop, the provost, and the master [of the Swordbrothers], not only once, but whenever there will be need, if perhaps one or many of them was impeded by death or absence.]

With this solution, William of Modena set up a judicial system to decide all disputes pertaining to the town fringe in the future. Such an arrangement gave all sides the opportunity to be involved in the decision-making: the citizens of Riga should provide the pool of judges, and the rest must elect suitable persons from among them. It was also understood that the selection should be made jointly by all the eligible parties. The system was intended to be permanent, with an opportunity to select a replacement judge in the case of death or absence of a judge. It is not clear whether an absence over a limited period, during which a temporary substitute is selected, or permanent absence, is meant here. Nevertheless, such a provision is not surprising in the context where medieval townspeople were highly mobile.[78] Additionally, with the description given to the town fringe that involved yet uncultivated lands, forests and new dwellings, the inevitable growth of Riga as a city is strongly implied. Indeed, new inhabitants are encouraged to cultivate unused land if they wish and consequently enjoy eight years of yield without taxation.[79] This is a clear indication of an attempt to increase the population of Riga, and whether willingly or unwillingly, it also encouraged the Christians of mostly German origin to cluster into their urban communities. In this sense then, the settlement of March 1226 was one of many that encouraged the development of a tiered society where the native '*Undeutsch*' [non-Germans] remained separated from the German-speaking upper class.[80]

Thereafter, in the same document of 15 March 1226, the workings of the jury-system are specified: their decisions should be made 'arbitrio' [by arbitration].[81] If the judges disagree, the unanimous decision of two shall suffice. If all three disagree, however, 'tunc sors diffiniat, cuius de tribus arbitrio stetur' [(the casting of) a lot should determine whose decision of the three should be held].[82] The casting of lots in medieval society was often met with criticism from churchmen who condemned such a form of active divination.[83] Gratian's Decretum declared that '[e]xcommunicetur clericus, monachus, laicus, diuinationes, uel auguria, uel sortes secutus' [(any) cleric, monk [or] layman who followed divinations, dreams, or lots, is excommunicate].[84] Similarly, the theologian Peter the Chanter proclaimed that 'maluit ergo ecclesia electionem praelati committi humanae rationi et discretion quam sortium incertitudini' [the Church prefers the choice of the prelates to be commited to the human reason and discretion rather than to the uncertainty of the lots].[85]

What, then, had prompted William of Modena, who had the ultimate authority of the pope himself, to find the casting of lots in Riga permissible? The natives in Livonia were known to use the casting of lots and other similar customs, and they were equally popular in the surrounding Slavic territories.[86] Traces of the use of lots, including in the Germanic regions from where the missionaries to Livonia generally came, can be found in already Christianised Europe, as well.[87] In any case, it is probable that the casting of lots was relatively common among the German settlers in Riga which is why it was chosen as a tool for the judges to secure a final verdict, if all else failed. While the casting of lots bore many similarities with the concept of the ordeal and judicial tests, which all had been outlawed at the Fourth Lateran Council of 1215, the prohibition was prescribed for clerics, not laymen.[88] As the judges in Riga were elected from among lay citizens, they were not subjected to the prohibition. However, a note that William made in another document that he issued in May 1226, helps to explain his rationale further: 'volentes tamen concordiam magis quam sententiam ... Nos autem sequitatem potius quam iustitise rigorem sequentes' [wishing rather for concordance than judgement ... we more preferably follow equity than the rigour of law].[89] It is evident that William's primary interest was achieving solutions that were acceptable for all parties involved, even if it occasionally meant straying away from strict legal prescriptions. The case of casting of lots in Riga is a prime example of this characteristic of William, as he permitted the use of the custom despite the general discomfort that canon lawyers had exhibited towards the practice.

Soon after issuing the main document pertaining to the disputes about the town fringe, the legate had to specify the working of the jury that he had helped to set up. On 22 April 1226, he thus specified that the decision of two of the judges set up to determine the town fringe is valid if the third one 'noluerit vel non poterit interesse' [is unwilling or unable to attend].[90] Additionally, on 7 May 1226, the legate decreed that sentences given by the judges ought to be observed under the penalty of excommunication.[91]

At first, it might seem odd that a harsh penalty of excommunication is imposed on anyone transgressing the ruling of judges who were specifically elected to decide in the sphere of secular jurisdiction. Yet, this decision can be interpreted as an attempt to secure further equity in decision-making. The bishop of Riga was the highest spiritual authority in Livonia, and even the military order of the Swordbrothers was subjected to him.[92] By issuing the blanket threat of excommunication, the legate made sure that no party, including the bishop of Riga, had more authority than any other in these circumstances. Perhaps the imposition of penalty was an afterthought, as it was issued more than two months after the document which had implemented the system of judges. It is equally likely, however, that William received reports of potential transgressions, and felt the need to clarify the penalties: with this, the legate removed the need to report to him any future breaches of decisions. Finally, the penalty of excommunication implies that the legate was not only interested in arbitrating disputes that had arisen at the time of his legatine mission, but he also wanted to secure the stability of the region in his absence. By imposing the threat of ecclesiastical penalty, he gave the settlement system the ultimate protection that he could offer as the representative of the papacy.

The legatine mission of 1224/5-1226 of William of Modena put his skills and knowledge to a test in a faraway corner of Christendom. As the pope did not specify the aims of William's legatine mission, it has been left for interpretation as to what the ultimate motives of the papacy were. The extant sources give no explicit indication that William was expected to settle disputes pertaining to Riga. However, as he was perceived as *legatus a latere*, in most cases he had the freedom to pick matters that he deemed worthwhile. The fact that he chose to get deeply involved in cases concerning Riga suggests that he considered it crucial for the young city to function properly and peacefully.

The appointment of William as a papal legate has been seen as a reaction to a request from the bishop of Riga, who first and foremost represented the interests of his bishopric. It certainly seems that the petition played a role in convincing the pope to finally send a representative to Livonia, which unlike many other theatres of conversion and crusade, had not yet had a legate *in situ*. As evidenced from the examples presented, the decisions that William made and the judgements that he arbitrated did not necessarily favour the bishop of Riga, who had personally sent for the legate. In fact, it seems that William did not attempt to please any specific party at all. What emerges from the documents instead, are attempts by the legate to set up a system or reach a solution which would be equitable and tolerable for all parties involved.

Notes

1   This article was completed during my doctoral studies which would not have been possible without the support of the South, West and Wales Doctoral Training Partnership. I am particularly thankful to my supervisors, Prof. Rebecca Rist and Prof. Helen J. Nicholson, who have provided me with invaluable advice and support throughout the writing process. Lastly, I would like to thank the reviewers for their thoughtful feedback and suggestions.

2   For his later legatine missions, see, for example, G. A. Donner, *Kardinal Wilhelm von Sabina, Bischof von Modena 1222-1234. Päpstlicher Legat in den nordischen Ländern* (Helsingfors, 1929), pp. 159-232 and Richard Spence, 'Pope Gregory IX and the Crusade on the Baltic', *The Catholic Historical Review*, 69 (1983), 1-19.

3   For a comprehensive overview of the beginnings and development of papal legatine missions in the Middle Ages, see K. R. Rennie, *The Foundations of Medieval Papal Legation* (Basingstoke, 2013), esp. pp. 47-87.

4   R. W. Southern, *Western Society and the Church in the Middle Ages* (Harmondsworth, 1970), p. 212. For the role of Pope Gregory VII in the transformation of the legatine office, see Kriston R. Rennie, '"*Uproot and destroy, build and plant*": Legatine Authority under Pope Gregory VII', *Journal of Medieval History*, 33 (2007), 166-80 (171-2).

5   Southern, *Western Society*, p. 212; A. A. Larson, 'Popes and Canon Law', in *A Companion to the Medieval Papacy: Growth of an Ideology and Institution*, ed. by K. Sisson and A. A. Larson (Leiden, 2016), pp. 135-57 (154). For an overview of medieval papal legatine missions, see Rennie, *Medieval Papal Legation*; H. Müller 'The Omnipresent Pope: Legates and Judges Delegate', in *A Companion to the Medieval Papacy*, pp. 199-219; R. C. Figueira, *The Canon Law of Medieval Papal Legation*, unpublished PhD Thesis (Cornell University; 1980); H. Zimmermann, *Die päpstliche Legation in der ersten Hälfte des 13. Jahrhunderts. Vom Regierungsantritt Innocenz' III. bis zum Tode Gregors IX. (1198-1241)* (Padeborn, 1913).

6   I. S. Robinson, *The Papacy, 1073-1198. Continuity and Innovation* (Cambridge, 1990), p. 170.

7   A. Jotischky, *Crusading and the Crusader States*, Second Edition (London, 2017), pp. 191-5; J. Muldoon, 'Crusading and Canon Law', in *Palgrave Advances in the Crusades*, ed. by H. J. Nicholson (Basingstoke, 2005), pp. 37-57 (43); C. Tyerman, *How to Plan a Crusade* (Milton Keynes, 2016),

pp. 66-75. Legatine missions were also employed for the purposes of crusading movements in Europe, see for example R. Rist, *The Papacy and Crusading in Europe, 1198-1245* (London, 2009), pp 45-54 and D. Dudley Stutz, 'Papal Legates against the Albigensians: The Debts of the Church of Valence (1215-1250)', *Traditio*, 68 (2013), 259-76.

8   James A. Brundage, 'The Thirteenth-Century Livonian Crusade: Henricus de Lettis and the First Legatine Mission of Bishop of Modena', *Jahrbücher für Geschichte Osteuropas*, 20 (1972), pp. 1-9. See also Marek Tamm, 'Communicating crusade. Livonian mission and the Cistercian network in the thirteenth century', *Ajalooline Ajakiri*, 3/4 (2009), pp. 341-72 (344). For the Baltic mission generally, see E. Christiansen, *The Northern Crusades* (London, 1996), pp. 93-103; W. Urban, *The Livonian Crusade* (Washington DC, 1981); I. Fonnesberg-Schmidt, *The Popes and the Baltic Crusades, 1147-1254* (Leiden, 2007); N. Blomkvist, *The Discovery of the Baltic: The Reception of a Catholic World-System in the European North (AD 1075-1225)* (Leiden, 2003); C. Tyerman, *The World of the Crusades* (London, , 2019), pp. 307-33; C. S. Jensen, 'The Early Church of Livonia, 1186-c.1255', in *Die Kirche im mittelalterlichen Livland*, ed. by R. Biskup, J. Götz and A. Radziminski (Toruń, 2019), pp. 75-103; T. K. Nielsen, 'Saints, Sinners & Civilisers – or Converts, Cowards & Conquerors. Cultural Encounters in the Medieval Baltic', in *Cultural Encounters during the Crusades*, ed. by K. V. Jensen, K. Salonen and H. Vogt (Odense, 2013), pp. 55-74. For the involvement of the military orders in the Livonian mission, see F. F. Benninghoven, *Der Orden der Schwertbrüder. Fratres Milicie Christi de Livonia* (Cologne, 1961); W. Urban, *The Teutonic Knights: A Military History* (Barnsley, 2018), pp. 79-108; Ē. Mugurēvičs, 'The Military Activity of the Order of the Sword Brethren (1202-1236)', in *The North-Eastern Frontiers of Medieval Europe*, ed. by A. V. Murray (Farnham, 2014), pp. 85-116.

9   A. Selart, 'Zur verortung Livlands in der Römischen Kirche. Legationsbezirke in Nordosteuropa im 13.-15. Jahrhundert', in *Die Kirche im mittelalterlichen Livland*, pp. 129-58 (139-40); Wojtek Jezierski, 'Forms of Social Capital in the European Middle Ages - Angels, Papal Legates, and the Scandinavian Aristocratic Elites, 12th -13th Centuries', *CERGU Working Paper Series*, 1 (2017), 1-16.

10   This distinguished the Livonian mission from the conversion of other regions, such as Bulgaria, Vlachia and Armenia, see B. Bombi, 'Innocent III and the Baltic Crusade after the Conquest of Constantinople', in *Crusading on the Edge: Ideas and Practice of Crusading in Iberia and the Baltic Region, 1100-1500*, ed. by T. K. Nielsen and I. Fonnesberg-Schmidt (Turnhout, 2016), pp. 117-33 (131). For an overview of Innocent III's

approach toward the conversion of Livonia before the Fourth Crusade, see B. Bombi, 'Innocent III and the "Praedicatio" to Heathens in Livonia (1198-1204)', in *Medieval History Writing and Crusading Ideology*, ed. by K. V. Jensen and T. M. S. Lehtonen (Helsinki, 2005), pp. 216-31.

11 I. Fonnesberg-Schmidt, 'Pope Honorius III and Mission and Crusades in the Baltic Region', in *The Clash of Cultures on the Medieval Baltic Frontier*, ed. by A. V. Murray (London, 2009), pp. 103-22 (106-11); L. Kaljundi, 'Neophytes as Actors in the Livonian Crusades', in *Making Livonia: Actors and Networks in the Medieval and Early Modern Baltic Sea Region*, ed. by A. Mänd, M. Tamm (London, 2020), pp. 93-112 (104-5).

12 'Liber extra decretalium', in *Corpus Iuris Canonici*, Vol. 2, ed. by E. Friedberg (Graz, 1959), X.1.30.9, col. 186. For a discussion regarding the classification of papal legates in the *Liber Extra*, see Robert C. Figueira, 'The Classification of Medieval Papal Legates in the "Liber Extra"', *Archivum Historiae Pontificiae*, 21 (1983), pp. 211-228.

13 Rennie, *Medieval Papal Legation*, pp. 163-164; Robinson, *The Papacy*, pp. 147-149. In practice, too, the distinction between *legatus a latere* and other types of legates with lesser authority, had manifested itself already in the twelfth century; for an example from England, see C. Morris, *The Papal Monarchy. The Western Church from 1050-1250* (Oxford, 1989), p. 218. On the careful balance between the authority and the delegation of authority in legatine missions, see K. Pennington, *Pope and Bishops: The Papal Monarchy in the Twelfth and Thirteenth Centuries* (Pennsylvania, 1984), p. 59; Franz Wasner, '"Legatus a Latere": Addenda Varia', *Traditio*, 16 (1960), pp. 405-16 (408); Figueira, *Canon Law*, p. 480.

14 The letter assigning William to his first legatine mission dates from 31 December 1224, see *Liv-, Esth- und Curländisches Urkundenbuch nebst Regesten* (=LUB), Vol. 1, ed. by F. G. von Bunge (Reval, 1853), nr. 69, cols. 73-5. The letter of his second legatine mission dates from 21 February 1234, LUB I, nr. 132, cols. 169-70; the letter of his third legatine mission dates from 15 July 1244, LUB I, nr. 179, cols. 234-6. William stayed in Livonia on three occasions: 1225–26, 1234–35, 1237–38; although invested with legatine powers to Livonia one final time in 1244, he did not go on that mission personally. To this date, the best biography of William of Modena is Donner's *Kardinal Wilhelm von Sabina*.

15 LUB I, nr. 69, cols. 73-5. All translations mine, unless otherwise stated.

16 LUB I, nr. 132, cols. 169-7; LUB I, nr. 179, cols. 234-6.

17 For example, William was invested with the power to elevate Riga to the metropolitan see if he thought it beneficial to do so; the letter of 19 November 1225, *Regesta Honorii Papae III*, Vol. 2, ed. by P. Pressutti,

(Rome, 1895), nr. 5721. For papal reserved powers and their development in the thirteenth century, see R. C. Figueira, 'Papal Reserved Powers and the Limitations on Legatine Authority', in *Popes, Teachers, and Canon Law in the Middle Ages*, ed. by J. R. Sweeney and S. Chodorow (London, 1989), pp. 191-211 (194-204).

18 Fonnesberg-Schmidt, *Popes*, pp. 134-5.

19 Henry of Livonia, *The Chronicle of Henry of Livonia* (=HCL), ed. and trans. by J. A. Brundage (New York, 2003), XXIX, 2; Henricus de Lettis, *Heinrici Chronicon Livoniae*, ed. by L. Arbusow and A. Bauer (Hannover, Impensis Bibliopolii Hahniani, 1955). The chronicle of Henry of Livonia has been seen as a narrative source that, at least in parts, was produced in response to the legatine mission of William of Modena, see J. A. Brundage, 'Introduction to the 2003 edition', in *The Chronicle of Henry of Livonia*, pp. xi-xxxiv (xxvii); A. V. Murray, 'Adding to the Multitude of Fish: Pope Innocent III, Bishop Albert of Riga and the Conversion of the Indigenous Peoples of Livonia', in *The Fourth Lateran Council and the Crusade Movement*, ed. by J. L. Bird and D. J. Smith (Turnhout, Brepols, 2018), pp. 153-70 (165); Paul Johansen, 'Die Chronik als Biographie: Heinrich von Lettlands Lebensgang und Weltanschauung', *Jahrbücher für Geschichte Osteuropas*, 1/4 (1953), 1-24 (9-18).

20 LUB I, nr. 26, col. 34; Fonnesberg-Schmidt, *Popes*, p. 85. See also HCL XV, 4, according to which the bishop of Riga had in 1210 obtained the authority to create and consecrate bishops in Livonia; Fonnesberg-Schmidt, *Popes*, p. 123.

21 For Albert and his life, see G. Gnegel-Waitschies, *Bischof Albert von Riga: ein Bremer Domherr als Kirchenfürst im Osten (1199-1229)* (Hamburg, 1958); M. Tamm, 'Mission and Mobility: The Travels and Networking of Bishop Albert of Riga (c. 1165–1229)', in *Making Livonia: Actors and Networks in the Medieval and Early Modern Baltic Sea Region*, ed. by A. Mänd, M. Tamm (London, 2020), pp. 17-47.

22 See Benninghoven for the most comprehensive work on the Swordbrothers. See also S. Ekdahl, 'Die Rolle der Ritterorden bei der Christianisierung der Liven und Letten', in *Gli inizi del christianesimo in Livonia-Lettonia. Atti del Colloquio Internazionale di Storia Ecclesiastica in Occasione dell'VIII Centenario della Chiesa in Livonia*, ed. by M. Maccarone (Vatican City, 1989), pp. 203-43. For a brief overview in English, see N. Morton, *The Medieval Military Orders, 1120-1314* (Harlow, 2013), pp. 73-74.

23 For the involvement of the Rus' in Livonian affairs, see A. Selart, *Livonia, Rus' and the Baltic Crusades in the Thirteenth Century*, trans. F. Robb (Leiden, 2007). For the involvement of the Danes in the Estonian mission,

see P. P. Rebane, 'From Fulco to Theoderic: The Changing Face of the Livonian Mission', in *The North-Eastern Frontiers,* pp. 85-116; T. Kala, 'Theory and Practice of the Baltic Crusade: The Incorporation of the Northern Baltic Lands into the Western Christian World', in *Crusade and Conversion on the Baltic Frontier,* ed. by A. V. Murray (Aldershot, 2001), pp. 3-20; N. Skyum-Nielsen, 'Estonia under Danish Rule', in *Danish Medieval History: New Currents,* ed. by Skyum-Nielsen and N. Lund (Copenhagen, 1981), pp. 112-135; Mihkel Mäesalu, 'A Crusader Conflict Mediated by a Papal Legate: The Chronicle of Henry of Livonia as a Legal Text', *The Medieval Chronicle,* 8 (2013), pp. 233-246.

24 B. U. Hucker, 'Der Plan Eines Christlichen Königreiches in Livland', in *Gli inizi del christianesimo in Livonia-Lettonia,* pp. 97-125 (115-7); Fonnesberg-Schmidt, *Popes,* p. 171-2.

25 Brundage, *Livonian Crusade,* p. 5; A. Selart, 'Confessional Conflict and Political Co-operation: Livonia and Russia in the Thirteenth Century', in *Crusade and Conversion,* pp. 151-76 (158); Tamm, *Mission,* pp. 31-32.

26 *Regesta Honorii Papae III,* nr. 4634.

27 Fonnesberg-Schmidt, *Popes,* p. 171.

28 LUB I, nr. 69, cols. 73-5; Fonnesberg-Schmidt, *Popes,* pp. 171-2.

29 For the claims that William attempted to create a papal state, see J. Kivimäe, 'Henricus the Ethnographer: Reflections on Ethnicity in the Chronicle of Livonia', in *Crusading and Chronicle Writing on the Medieval Baltic Frontier: A Companion to the Chronicle of Henry of Livonia,* ed. by M. Tamm, L. Kaljundi and C. S. Jensen (London, 2011), pp. 77-106 (97-8); cf. J. Kivimäe, '*Servi Beatae Marie Virginis:* Christians and Pagans in Henry's Chronicle of Livonia', in *Church and Belief in the Middle Ages,* ed. by K. Salonen and S. Katajala-Peltomaa (Amsterdam, 2016), pp. 201-26 (222). For a convincing argument that this was not the case, see Mihkel Mäesalu, 'Papstliche Gewalt im Kreuzzugsgebiet: Gründete Wilhelm von Modena in Estland einen "Pufferstaat"?, *Forschungen zur baltischen Geschichte,* 6 (2011), pp. 11-30.

30 Fonnesberg-Schmidt, *Popes,* pp. 171-72; Kaljundi, *Neophytes,* p. 104; Brundage, *Livonian Crusade,* pp 6-7.

31 E. Pitz, *Papstreskript und Kaiserreskript im Mittelalter* (Tübingen, 1971), p. 142.

32 C. Tyerman, 'Henry of Livonia and the Ideology of Crusading', in *Crusading and Chronicle Writing,* pp. 23-44 (41-2).

33 For example: F. G. von Bunge, *Einleitung in die liv-, esth- und kurlandische Rechtsgeschicte* (Reval, 1849); F. G. Von Bunge, *Die Stadt Riga im 13. und 14. Jahrhundert* (Leipzig, 1878); E. Winkelmann, *Livländische*

Forschungen (Riga, 1868); F. Benninghoven, *Rigas Entstehung und der frühhansische Kaufmann* (Hamburg, 1961).

34 HCL VI, 4; on the pre-history of Riga, see K. C. O'Connor, *The House of Hemp and Butter: A History of Old Riga* (London, 2019), pp. 12-38.

35 J. Barrow, 'Churches, Education and Literacy in Towns 600-1300', in *The Cambridge Urban History of Britain*, Vol. 1, ed. by D. M. Palliser (Cambridge, 2000), pp. 127-52 (133).

36 D. Nicholas, *The Growth of the Medieval City: From Late Antiquity to the Early Fourteenth Century* (London, 1997), pp. 154-5.

37 For municipal laws in the German sphere generally, see U. C. Ewert and S. Selzer, 'Social Networks', in *A Companion to the Hanseatic League*, ed. by D. J. Harreld (Leiden, 2014), pp. 162-93 (166-7); for Lübeck's law more specifically, see C. Jahnke, 'Lübeck: Early Economic Development and the Urban Hinterland', in *A Companion to Medieval Lübeck*, ed. by C. Jahnke (Leiden, 2019), pp. 226-52 (237-8); for the development of municipal law in the Livonian towns in the Middle Ages, see H. Pihlajamäki, *Conquest and the Law in Swedish Livonia (ca. 1630-1710)* (Leiden, 2017), pp. 44-46.

38 Bunge, *Stadt*, p. 9.

39 LUB I, nr. 20, cols. 25-8.

40 LUB I, nr. 20, cols. 25-8; see also: Pihlajamäki, *Conquest*, p. 44.

41 LUB I, nr. 53, cols. 57-8. For an overview of the constitutional development of Riga up until the visitation of William of Modena, see Winkelmann, pp. 25-31. For an overview of what became of Riga's urban law and how the concept of 'the law of the Gotlanders' changed over time, see Bunge, *Einleitung*, pp. 135-9.

42 LUB I, nr. 75, cols. 81-2; B. von Jähnig, 'Die Anfänge der Sakraltopographie von Riga', in *Studien über die Anfänge der Mission in Livland*, ed. by M. Hellmann, 37 (1989), pp. 123-58 (147); Blomkvist, pp. 471-4; Winkelmann, pp. 27-37, Bunge, *Stadt*, p. 12; Bunge, *Einleitung*, pp. 133-6; Donner, pp. 121-2.

43 LUB I, nr. 75, cols. 81-2.

44 LUB I, nr. 20, cols. 25-8; Blomkvist, pp. 437-8.

45 LUB I, nr. 75, cols. 81-2; Pihlajamäki, *Conquest*, p. 44.

46 LUB I, nr. 75, cols. 81-2.

47 LUB I, nr. 75, cols. 81-2.

48 LUB I, nr. 75, cols. 81-2.

49 *Catalogus Omnium Episcoporum Mutinensium*, ed. by G. Sillingardus (Modena, 1606), p. 88.

50 Donner, pp. 18-9.

51 For the trial, see Donner, p. 21

52 This has sometimes been seen as the only 'real' right that the bishop retained, see for example Winkelmann, pp. 31-7.

53 LUB I, nr. 75, cols. 81-2; *naufragius* in this context means the right of the landowner to claim shipwrecked goods, see Blomkvist, p. 472. William of Modena might have played a role in outlawing the ordeal, including carrying hot iron, in Sweden as well, see Heikki Pihlajamäki, 'Summoning to Court: *Ordines Iudiciarii* and Swedish Medieval Legislation', *Scandinavian Journal of History*, 45/4 (2020), 547-72 (555-6).

54 LUB I, nr. 75, cols. 81-1; Blomkvist, p. 472; Bunge, *Einleitung*, pp. 133-4; Winkelmann, pp. 32-3.

55 LUB I, nr. 83, cols. 99-101; C. S. Jensen, 'Urban Life and the Crusades in North Germany and the Baltic Lands in the Early Thirteenth Century', in *Crusade and Conversion*, pp. 75-94 (87); A. Šnē, 'The Hanseatic League and the Eastern Baltic: Towns, Trade and Politics in Medieval Livonia from the Thirteenth to the Mid-Sixteenth Century', in *The North-Eastern Frontiers*, pp. 353-78 (357); Benninghoven, pp. 203-4.

56 LUB I, nr. 83, cols. 99-101.

57 See Benninghoven, pp. 203-4.

58 LUB I, nr. 16, cols. 22-3 and LUB I, nr. 17, cols. 23-4. On this division, see Fonnesberg-Schmidt, *Popes,* pp. 81-1; Benninghoven, pp. 113-4. That the settlement of 11 April 1226 was not particularly beneficial for the bishop of Riga, has also been pointed out by Gnegel-Waitschies, pp. 156-7.

59 The letter of December 1225: LUB I, nr. 75, cols. 81-2; the letter of 11 April 1226: LUB I, nr. 83, cols. 99-101.

60 LUB I, nr. 83, cols. 99-101. It is not known in what capacity – whether as regular soldiers or as *crucesignati* – the Rigan citizens were envisioned to take part in future conquests, see Jensen, *Urban Life,* p. 87

61 Such a settlement has been contrasted with the situation in Estonia where the lack of co-operation between different Christian parties had clearly caused serious problems, see Benninghoven, p. 204.

62 Donner, p. 160.

63 LUB I, nr. 83, cols. 99-101. Whether they were all crusaders – *crucesignati* – is not known but this seems to be the opinion of Benninghoven, p. 204. That the pilgrims were seen more as a voluntary work-force to help their masters with all kinds of jobs, is proposed by Blomkvist, pp. 672-3. Indeed, crusaders were routinely referred to as pilgrims, see J. Riley-Smith, *What Were the Crusades?* (Basingstoke, 2009), pp. 2, 34-5 and M. Cecilia Gaposchkin, 'From Pilgrimage to Crusade: The Liturgy of Departure, 1095-1300', *Speculum*, 88 (2013), 44-91. For the use of crusading terminology by the popes, see Michael Markowski, '*Crucesignatus:* Its

Origins and Early Usage', *Journal of Medieval History*, 10 (1984), pp. 157-65. Nevertheless, even in the case of armed pilgrimage, distinguishable from crusading, the primary motif was the same: spiritual salvation, see Christopher Tyerman, 'Were There Any Crusades in the Twelfth Century?', *The English Historical Review*, 10 (1995), pp. 553-77 (555).

64 LUB I, nr. 83, cols. 99-101; Pitz, p. 146; Benninghoven, p. 204.

65 Benninghoven pointed out that pilgrims made up the largest contingent of the German armies in Livonia, and that they were a decisive power-structure in military activities, but he did not connect the allocation of incoming pilgrims directly to the tripartite decision regarding future conquests, see Benninghoven, p. 204.

66 For the finances of German troops in Livonia, see Benninghoven, pp. 400-1, who shows that pilgrims generally relied on external funding, as opposed to those who held a fief from the bishop.

67 Benninghoven, pp. 401-2.

68 For the development of the concept of pilgrimage, see D. Webb, *Pilgrims and Pilgrimage in the Medieval West* (London, I. B. Tauris Publishers, 2001), pp. 11-28.

69 LUB I, nr. 78, cols. 90-3; LUB I, nr 85, col. 103; LUB I, nr 86, col. 103. The urban fringe typically included the area immediately adjacent to the town's fortifications, extramural land belonging to the town and an area of influence extending 1-3km beyond the town walls, see D. Denecke, 'Comparative Approaches in the Historico-topographical Analysis of Towns and Cities', in *Lords and Towns in Medieval Europe*, ed. by A. Simms and H. B. Clarke (Farnham, Ashgate, 2015), pp. 33-61 (56-7).

70 LUB I, nr. 78, cols. 90-3. While containing interesting details, such as local names and significant landmarks, the exact details of the boundaries are not the focus of this article; however, for a concise description, see Donner, pp. 123-4.

71 LUB I, nr. 78, cols. 90-3.

72 LUB I, nr. 78, cols. 90-3.

73 The letter of December 1225: LUB I, nr. 75, cols. 81-2.

74 LUB I, nr. 78, cols. 90-3.

75 For William of Modena's short career as an inquisitor, see Donner, pp. 40-44.

76 For the techniques used in the inquisitorial procedure, see J. K. Deane, *A History of Medieval Heresy and Inquisition* (Plymouth, 2011), pp. 108-111. For the court procedure more generally, see C. J. Donahue, 'Procedure in the Courts of the *Ius Commune*', in *The History of Courts and Procedure in Medieval Canon Law*, ed. by W. H. and K. Pennington, (Washington DC, 2016), pp. 74-124.

77 LUB I, nr. 78, cols. 90-3; Bunge, *Stadt*, p. 362; Bunge, *Geschichte*, p. 131; Donner, p. 124.

78 For spatial mobility in medieval Livonia, see Anti Selart, 'Where Was the Home of the Livonian Merchant? Early Urban Mobility in the Baltics', *Zapiski Historyczne*, 84 (2019), 43-66.

79 LUB I, nr. 78, cols. 90-3. In comparison, cities in Europe tended to be more stringent about the requirements for newcomers, see M. Rubin, *Cities of Strangers: Making Lives in Medieval Europe* (Cambridge, 2020), pp. 37-43.

80 On the distinction between *Deutsch* and *Undeutsch*, see H. Valk, 'Christianisation in Estonia: A Process of Dual-Faith and Syncretism', in *The Cross Goes North: Processes of Conversion in Northern Europe, AD 300-1300*, ed. by M. Carver (York, 2003), pp. 571-580 (571); P. Johansen and H. von zur Mühlen, *Deutsch und Undeutsch im mittelalterlichen und frühneuzeitlichen Reval* (Cologne and Vienna, 1973).

81 LUB I, nr. 78, cols. 90-3.

82 LUB I, nr. 78, cols. 90-3.

83 M. D. Bailey, 'Superstition and Sorcery', in *The Routledge History of Medieval Magic*, ed. by S. Page and C. Rider (London, 2019), pp. 487-501 (489-92).

84 Gratian, 'Decretum Magistri Gratiani', in *Corpus Iuris Canonici*, Vol. 1, ed. by E. L. Richter and E. Friedberg (Graz, 1959), C.26 q.5 c.9, col. 1029. The *auctoritas* for this pronouncement is canon 32 from the First Council of Orléans in 511.

85 Petrus Cantor, 'Verbum abbreviatum', in *Patrologiae cursus completus. Series Latina*, ed. by J.-P. Migne, Vol. 205 (Paris, 1855), Ch. 78, col. 227. For Peter the Chanter's treatment of ecclesiastical elections and customs associated with them, see John Baldwin, 'Philippe Auguste, Pierre le Chantre et Étienne de Gallardon : la conjoncture de *regnum, studium,* et *cancellaria* au tournant des XIIe et XIIIe siècles', *Comptes rendus des séances de l'Académie des Inscriptions et Belles-Lettres, 144e année*, 1 (2000), 437-57 (451-2).

86 Henry of Livonia repeatedly depicts such customs in his chronicle, see HCL XI, 7; XII, 2; XX, 2; XXIII, 9 for the casting of lots. For pagan customs in Livonia as described by contemporary chronicles, see Shami Ghosh, 'Conquest, Conversion, and Heathen Customs in Henry of Livonia's *Chronicon Livoniae* and the *Livländishe Reimchronik*', *Crusades*, 11 (2012), pp. 87-108. For lot-casting among the Slavic peoples, see L. P. Słupecki, 'Prognostication in Pagan Beliefs among Slavs in the Middle Ages', in *Prognostication in the Medieval World*, ed. by M.

Heiduk, K. Herbers and H.-C. Lehner, Vol. 1 (Berlin, 2021), pp. 85-107 (98-9).

87 H. C. Lea, *Superstition and Force* (Philadelphia, 1878), pp. 311-5; Shlomo Eidelberg, 'Trial by Ordeal in Medieval Jewish History: Laws, Customs and Attitudes', *Proceedings of the American Academy for Jewish Research, 1979-1980*, 46/47 (1979-1980), 105-120 (107-8).

88 Canon 18, *Decrees of the General Councils*, ed. by N. Tanner, Vol. 1 (London, 1990), p. 244. See also Finbarr McAuley, 'Canon Law and the End of the Ordeal', *Oxford Journal of Legal Studies*, 26 (2006), 473-513

89 LUB I, nr. 88, cols. 104-6.

90 LUB I, nr. 85, col. 103.

91 LUB I, nr. 86, col. 103. This document was issued by William of Modena in Dünamünde, after he had departed Riga. Chronicler Henry of Livonia explains that '[s]edis apostolice legatus Lyvoniam derelinquens ad naves circa mare diu resedit, ventorum gratiam expectans' [as the legate of the apostolic see left Livonia, he remained for a long time by his ships near the sea, awaiting the gift of the winds']; HCL XXX, 1. See also Donner, pp. 130-3.

92 Generally, military orders were exempted from excommunication and interdict pronouncements by bishops, see J. Brundage, 'Crusades, Clerics and Violence', in *The Experience of Crusading*, Vol. 1, ed. by M. Bull and N. Housley, (Cambridge, 2003), pp. 147-166, (153-154). By contrast, in 1210 Pope Innocent III subjected the Swordbrothers to the bishop of Riga, see LUB I, nr. 16, cols. 22-23; Benninghoven, pp. 113-4. The relationship between the two major powers in Livonia was further refined by William of Modena in 1225, see Kristjan Toomaspoeg, 'The Military Orders and the Diocesan Bishops: A Pragmatic Relationship', *Ordines Militares Colloquia Torunensia Historica*, 23 (2018), 93-125 (111, esp. note nr. 123), esp. for comparisons with other military orders.

Jewish-Christian Relations in Medieval London: An Archaeological Evaluation

Eliya Ribak

New York University

Tracing the Jewish presence in Medieval England is a challenge. As David Hinton, in his article 'Medieval Anglo-Jewry' says, identifying the presence of a minority group in England, assessing whether its material culture can be recognized and trying to understand its effects on the general population are complex tasks.[1] The result is that thus far, the study of the Medieval Jewish community in London and in fact, all over England, has concentrated on surviving historical documents. Unfortunately, our documentary picture is far from complete. As Patricia Skinner notes in her work on Medieval Jews in Britain, the massacres suffered by the Anglo-Jewish community led to manuscripts being looted and sold to Jewish communities abroad. The community is therefore studied through the fiscal records, which 'cannot satisfactorily answer questions about everyday life for the Jewish residents and their neighbours. Our view is very limited, confined to the wealthiest and those active in dealing.'[2]

It would be inaccurate to say that we have no additional data on the lives of the Jewish community in London, however. Some archaeological data has survived and when pieced together and supported by historical records, can help us create a somewhat fuller picture on the everyday life of the Jewish community in London and their relationship with their Christian neighbours. The Jews of London arrived with William I in 1066 and were expelled in 1290 by Edward I. This provides us with a clear residential window of 220 years, which makes the accurate dating of associated material culture very important to the identification of the community. Historical records indicate that Jews and Christians lived together in a mixed neighbourhood known as 'the Jewry' in London. Please see Figure 1 for excavated Jewish sites considered.

This paper will argue that medieval Anglo-Jews formed a distinct community with some lifeways that were distinct from their Christian fellows: different burial customs and hygiene customs. Yet there are also many indications of interaction with the wider English community. Jews lived alongside Christians in the largely the same houses, using the same tools and objects, making them quite hard to distinguish one from the other. This indicates the two communities were not isolated and hostile to one another and shows some degree of peaceful coexistence, until the worsening conditions in the thirteenth century and the expulsion.

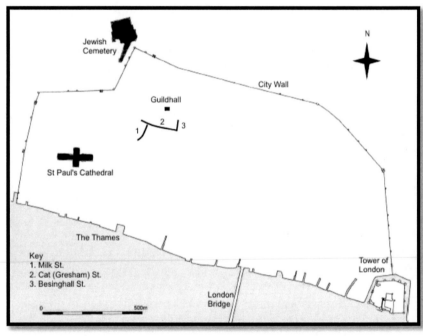

Figure 1: The city of London (c. 1270) showing the city walls and location of excavated Jewish sites; after Blair et al. 'Two medieval Jewish Ritual Baths – Mikva'ot – Found at Gresham Street and Milk Street in London', fig. 1.

Spatial Analysis

This discussion is not intended to be a site catalogue for medieval sites in London. I have chosen to concentrate on sites that contain clear Jewish presence, as indicated by material culture and documentary evidence to provide the most reliable information about the Jewish community in London in order to discuss Jewish Christian coexistence.[3]

1-6 Milk Street (MLK 76, GHT 00 - Site 1 in Figure 1)

There were two churches on Milk street: St Mary Magdalen, established by c. 1111-35 and All Hallows Honey Lane, established by 1191-1212. Property ownership records in the street indicate a mixed ownership, as can be seen in Figure 2. The churches and cemetery were under Christian ownership and are shaded in grey. Records show that Tenement 1 was also owned and used by various Christians in the 12th and 13th centuries.[4]

Tenement 2 belonged to Master Moses, Jew of London before 1076. After his death, the property was claimed by his son, Cresseus, Jew of London. After 1076, the property had passed to the crown, but Cresseus was compensated for loss of the property to Knight Stephan Chendut. The knight then sold the property to Cresseus, son of Master Elias, Jew of London after a few months.[5] Since the property was in the hands of Jews for the vast majority of the period, it is shown in the plan in white, denoting Jewish ownership.

Tenements 3 and 4 show a mixed ownership of both Jews and Christians during this period. In the plan, they are white with black dots. In 1215 Tenement 3 was in possession of John of Enefeld, Knight. By 1276 however, it belonged to Bonamicus, Jew of York.[6] Records from the early 13th century show that the property was owned by Martin the Virly, then Bernerius of Rouen, then Leo the Jew (Leo le Bland, the Jew). There was some attempt to seize the property and give it away, but Leo continued to hold it and passed it on to Joyceus, Diaya, Isaac and Samuel, sons of Abraham, Jew of London. After the death of Isaac, the king received Isaac's quarter and bought the rest of the three quarters of the property, to give it to his crossbowman Martin Seneche. Thereafter, the property belonged to Christians.[7]

Property ownership records, however, are not evidence for actual residence. Further support to the residence of Jews on Milk Street is provided by archaeological evidence. Clearly associated with Tenement 5 is a *mikveh* (ritual bath).[8] Taylor's research confirms that the property was held by Moses Crespin, of a family of leading London Jewish financiers.[9] This provides very strong evidence that Tenement 5 was not only owned by Jews but also had Jewish residents.

Two *mikva'ot* have been identified in London to date. The Milk Street *mikveh* is the more substantial of the two. It was built with high quality stone, aligned north-south and consisted of seven steps leading down to an apsidal-ended chamber. It measured 3.00 by 1.20m and its maximum internal depth was 1.45m. Later, an east-west internal blocking wall was added, but it is unclear whether this was a deliberate modification or the foundation of a later building, constructed over the *mikveh* following the expulsion of 1290.[10]

Immersion in water for purification was practiced in Judaism as early as Biblical times and the earliest constructed *mikva'ot* are known from the second half of the second-century BC. The *mikve* continued to be an important part of Jewish life in Medieval London. Its location in a Jewish household (the Gresham street *mikve* was also found in a Jewish household) has been a cause of some speculation, since it is assumed that *miqva'ot* are usually public structures associated with synagogues. In fact, these two Medieval London examples are not uncommon. In my catalogue of archaeological sites in Byzantine Palestina, a wide variety of structures identified as *mikva'ot* were found in a variety of locations including under synagogues, under private houses or as independent structures both inside and outside settlements. It is therefore unsurprising that two *mikva'ot* were found in Jewish houses, as there is no requirement for them to be associated with synagogues, nor are there always found within a synagogue compound. This strengthens Blair's conclusion that these *mikva'ot* do not necessarily indicates the existence of private synagogues.[11]

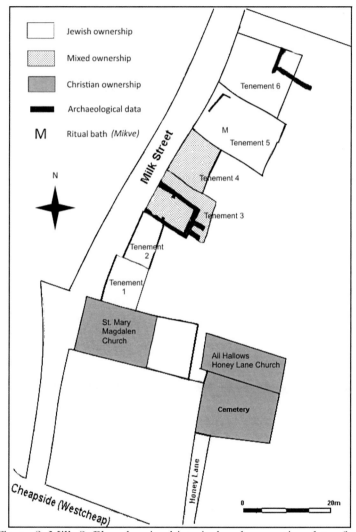

Figure 2: Milk St Plan showing historical and excavation data after figures 35, 37 and 46 in Scofield at al, 'Medieval buildings and property development in Cheapside', *Transactions of the London and Middlesex Archaeological Society*, 41, (1990) 39–238.

Dayson, in his analysis of the documentary evidence associated with the Blossom's Inn Site notes the existence of a synagogue (*scola Iudeorum*), its former existence recorded in the first half of the 14th century on Gresham Street, in the vicinity of House 6 on Milk St.[12] It must be noted, however, that this synagogue is not associated with any archaeological evidence at present. Nevertheless, evidence for a church, a synagogue and a ritual bath presence on the same street provides us with a very strong case for multiculturalism and coexistence in this part of London.

81-7 Gresham Street (GDH85, Sites 2 and 3 in Figure 1)

In close proximity to Milk St, three structures, one including a *mikveh* and a church were excavated in Gresham Street, formerly known as Cat Street. The houses were excavated in 1986. The house with associated *mikveh* is at the corner of Gresham St and a lane leading north towards Guildhall (Tenement 8 in Figure 4). The house comprised several wall foundations surrounding a feature interpreted as a Jewish ritual bath. The feature is a rectangular arrangement of two courses of stone blocks. Its original depth and the height of the associated floors is unknown. The internal dimensions are 1.64 by 1.15m, and 56cm in depth. Pottery dates the construction of the *mikveh* to the 12th century and its disuse to the 13th century.[13] As in Milk St, documentary evidence indicates Jewish ownership of the building. A charter of 1280 names the owner of the house as Aaron son of Vives. So, we have both archaeological and documentary evidence for the ownership and residency of Jews in this house.[14]

The Churchyard of St Lawrence Jewry (see figure 4), next to Tenement 8, was established in the third quarter of the 11th century and documentary evidence on its continued existence and function exist up to the 13th century.[15] Tenements 9 and 10 have no clear archaeological evidence indicating Jewish ownership. They are dated archaeologically to the same date as Tenement 8. Documentary evidence indicates that Tenements 9, 10 and 11 had Jewish owners in the second half of the 13th century.[16]

Aaron son of Vives was a prominent and important member of the Jewish community, as apart from owning the house with the *mikveh*

(Tenement 8) he is also recorded as the founder of a synagogue on the south side of Gresham Street, opposite the church of St. Lawrence, on Basinghall Street (site 3 in Figure 1). Figure 4 shows the position indicated by documentary evidence (synagogue?) as well as some archaeological evidence for the structure of the synagogue from the 12th century, despite the documentary evidence being from the thirteenth century. In 1256 Henry III gave to John son of Jeoffrey the chapel of St Mary-in-the-Jewry 'where there had once been a Jewish synagogue'.[17] Archaeological evidence in support of the identification of this structure as a synagogue comes in the shape of two twelfth-century stone buildings and an architectural fragment, which could be a voussoir from a relieving arch (see Figure 3). This provides the possibility of formal religious architecture that may well have been a synagogue.[18]

Figure 3: Possibly a voussoir from a relieving arch used by archaeologists to identify a synagogue. By permission Museum of London.

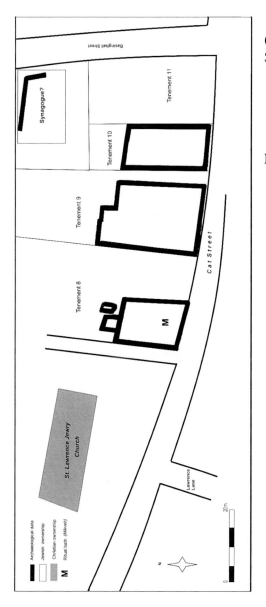

Figure 4: Gresham (Cat) and Basinghall Street Plan Showing Historical and Excavation Data after Bowsher D et al. The London Guildhall MOLAS Monograph 36, figs. 70 and 315

The documentary and archaeological data provides us with a picture of Jewish-Christian co-existence in Gresham Street. On the same block we have identified a Christian church surrounded by burials, Jewish households with one *mikveh* and a potential synagogue all in close proximity. This provides compelling evidence for religious tolerance in Medieval London, at least in the twelfth century.

Jewin Crescent/Jews' Garden (WFG58/59) – burial ground

The Jewish Cemetery of London was outside the city wall, near the Milk Street and Gresham Street sites. It was located by the north-west angle of the city wall, near Cripplegate (Figure 4). It has had various names over the years but a significant term used in 1291 and 1249-95 is '*Leyrestowe*', which means "a laying or burial place with religious significance, i.e. consecrated".[19] This indicates that at least in the early and middle twelfth century, the Jewish cemetery was considered to be sacred not just by the Jewish inhabitants but also by their Christian neighbours.

A documentary survey by Marjorie Honeybourne indicates that at least one Christian land owner was willing to rent out a part of his land to the Jewish Cemetery. At first, the cemetery was surrounded by Christian-owned houses, which were sold over time to members of the Jewish community to enlarge the cemetery. Some small evidence of legal challenges by Christians against Jews on the matter of the land also survives, yet this appears to be the exception, rather than the rule.[20]

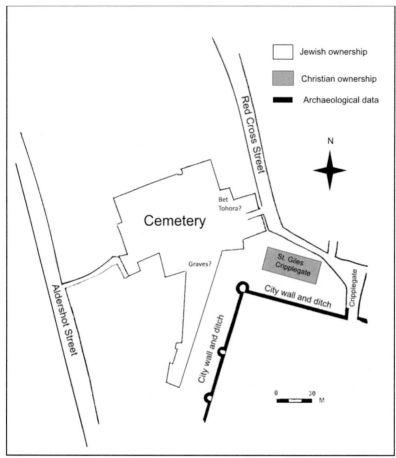

Figure 5: The Jewish Cemetery at Cripplegate and Surrounding Area
Showing Historical and Excavation Data after Honeybourne M B,
'The Pre-Expulsion Cemetery of the Jews in London', in *Transactions
of the Jewish Historical Society*, 20 (1959-61), p. 147 (plate 25).

The Jewish Cemetery will be further discussed below in an effort
to differentiate between Jewish and Christian Burial customs in
London. For the purposes of this analysis however, its location on
previous Christian land, its mostly untroubled usage, and the references
to it as a sacred place in everyday Christian parlance indicates further

evidence of mixed Jewish and Christian residence, life and indeed death in this area of London.

Since residency indicates coexistence and religious tolerance, the way Jews and Christians lived should be examined next to see if there are significant barriers between the two communities. Objects used every day reveal a great deal about the people who use them and cultural similarities and differences can be revealed by design and decorative elements.

Portable Objects

The difficulties facing us when trying to trace Jewish material culture are never greater then when attempting to find their portable objects. Hebrew texts can be found on tally sticks and seals, as well as the occasional larger object, such as the Bodleian Bowl,[21] yet few of these objects were found *in situ* and none in London. No clear Jewish symbols, such as a *menorah*, have yet been found in medieval London. This could be due to the short and transient nature of Jewish settlement and possibly removal by the owners themselves when they were exiled or the result of destruction or sale to Jewish communities outside of England.

To overcome this data shortage, Gabriel Pepper attempted to construct Jewish indicators from assemblages of everyday medieval objects such as counters, scales and lead tokens.[22] Since clear religious indicators are not archaeologically recoverable, Pepper tried to trace Jewish money lending and trade activities instead. There are considerable shortcomings in Pepper's dependence on these assemblages as indicators of Jewish presence. Hinton, the foremost authority on medieval England, said that these artefacts are far too commonly found to be a reliable indicator of Jewish presence.[23] Three of his five types of chosen artefact refer to money lending or mercantile activity, are not always closely datable to the period of Jewish occupancy and are not specifically part of Jewish culture.[24] Yet the results of Pepper's statistical analysis are interesting. All the lead tokens, 73% of the scales and 58% of the counters come from four sites, which include the sites discussed in this paper.[25] These numbers are statistically significant and while they do not help us identify Jewish presence, they provide some information about both Jews and their Christian neighbours in this part of London. Trade and banking activities are clearly attested by these objects and confirm historical claims of Jewish professions. Of course, it is entirely possible that not only merchants and bankers lived in this part of London. This data provides us with no information about other residents and their employment.

Another attempt to relate portable objects to London Jews was undertaken by Nigel Jeffries. He noted that large to very large pottery groups, containing well preserved sherds, many of them joining and with reconstructable profiles, were found around Gresham St. The shards are tightly dated to 1270/90-1300 and were found in cellars or pits which Jeffries sees as an indication of a hastily discarded and discrete assemblage. He proposes this is the result of the changes of property ownership caused by the deteriorating relations of the Jewish community with the crown, culminating in the exile in 1290.[26]

Jeffries is able to associate one pottery assemblage (thereafter PA) with a known Jewish household. Using the spatial analysis in this paper, I can link two more Jewish household to a PA. Figure 7 shows that a PA was found behind a Jewish owned house on Gresham Street, next to a house that contained a *mikveh* and a house that may have served as a synagogue. Another PA was found in a well associated with the Milk Street house containing a *mikveh* and the third in the cesspit of a house that had a mixed Jewish and Christian ownership. This analysis strengthens Jefferies' link between the pottery groups and Jewish ownership and is very valuable to our understanding of Jewish everyday life.

The likelihood that that the PAs belong to Jewish households may be strengthened by Jewish dietary law. The system of laws governing what and how Jews should eat is very complex. One of the most important laws is the one which enjoins Jews to separate milk and meat dishes.[27] Modern Jewish households usually keep two separate dining sets, one for dairy foods and the other for meat. The number of dining vessels found in a Jewish household is likely to be much larger than those found in non-Jewish households. If this practice was also followed in medieval England it would help to explain the unusually large size of Jefferies' pottery groups.

Jefferies notes that wine jugs provide a "major signature and are present in large quantities" in the PAs. Please see an example of the type of jugs identified in Figure 6. He rightly observes that these jugs are indicative of large-scale entertaining.[28] Families who live in expensive stone houses, have strong royal connections and in at least one case can afford to build a *mikveh* for their own personal use are probably important members of the community. Entertaining friends, family and business associates, especially around the numerous Jewish holidays is highly likely. Even if not linked to a Jewish household, large numbers of pottery used for entertaining is likely in this wealthy area. Yet the location and numbers of pottery are strongly supportive of Jewish association.

Pepper and Jeffries' work helps to fill out the lack of clearly identifiable Jewish objects. The very deficiency is significant. It can be explained by the short term of Jewish residency, the exile and the state of the archaeology in London. An additional possibility is that Jewish everyday life was very similar to their Christian neighbours. Despite the links made between the pottery, lead tokens, scales and counters, none of these objects had Jewish identification. While it is possible that those were sold or destroyed after the exile, it is also possible that London Jews did not try very hard to differentiate their portable objects from those of others. This indicates the community was less differentiated and isolated than is usually postulated. On the one hand these objects do confirm the life of Jews as outlined by historical documents, that of wealthy bankers and merchants. On the other hand, there is nothing in the objects they used every day that distinguishes them from their Christian neighbours (with the possible exception of pottery quantities). Having examined as much as we can from the evidence of how Jews and Christians in the area lived, an examination of burial costumes may shed more light on the differences and similarities of the two communities.

Figure 6: Example of the type of jugs found in the pottery assemblages
identified by Jeffries; KING fabric code; Height 330 mm.
By permission Museum of London. Catalogue number A200 (no
context number available).

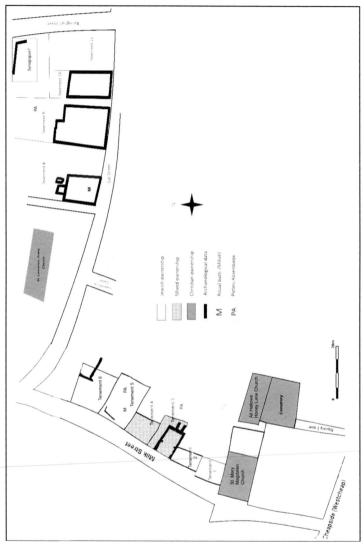

Figure 7: Locations of pottery assemblages in the study area

Burials

We are very fortunate in having any archaeological data about Jewish burials in London. This has only been possible due to the excavation of the Jewish Cemetery at Cripplegate by William Grimes in 1961. The site was identified by Marjorie Honeybourne using an extensive documentary survey.[29] The cemetery site was outside the city wall, (see figure 5) The earliest reference to the site in historical records appears to be in 1218, according to Honeybourne. Records appear to indicate continuous use of the cemetery by the Jewish community until 1291, a year after the Expulsion, when Edward I granted the site to William de Montfort.[30] No chronological dating evidence is available from the excavation. Grimes proceeded to excavate available parts of the site, since bomb rubble covered the area. The general impression received from the limited publication of the excavation, is of disappointment.

In Grimes' words:

...It was found everywhere that the cellar floors rested immediately upon undisturbed natural brickearth or gravel. The upper parts of which had already been removed. In the northern part of the site, around Jewin Street, the effect of this was to destroy all traces of graves or of any structure earlier than the eighteenth century. In the narrower strip on the south side, between Well Street and St. Giles churchyard, the results were more rewarding. Here was found a series of seven graves in all. They were closely set, in an irregular line, oriented east-west and rather larger than most graves[31]...

Grimes goes on to say that he was very surprised to find no human remains in the graves at all, and that they were emptied at some point and refilled with what he called: 'garden soil'. An additional, less well-defined group of graves were found nearby, and appeared to share the same east west orientation, and the lack of any clear human remains. Grimes attributes this removal to Jews at the time of the expulsion, or Christians. Yet Jews were unlikely to disturb any Jewish human remains, considering it a desecration.[32] So, the more likely culprits are Christians. Interestingly, Grimes comments on the fact that in one of the graves the skeleton of a small dog was found, but he does not assign it a date and while it could be an attempt to desecrate the site by non-Jews, it could also be naturally occurring, considering the cemetery site was later used as a garden.

As noted above, the Cripplegate cemetery excavation was poorly published. Honeybourne's article on the documentary sources and the history of the site is extensive, but the archaeology is only very briefly mentioned by both Honeybourne and Grimes, in his page and a half's account of the excavation in his book on Roman and Medieval London. Attempts to recover plans and field notes in the Archaeological Archive and the archive of the Jewish Historical Society of England (the sponsor of the excavation) garnered limited success. No real site plans and field notes survived, though copious correspondence regarding the excavation did. I have been able, however, to piece together the following sources: Honeybourne's article, a pre-excavation site plan and a small sketch of the burials found in the Archaeological Archive at MOLA, as well as Grime's limited description. The combination of these sources allowed me to construct the overall plan shown in Figure 5. The exact location of the graves is an estimation. One of the archive photographs has been reproduced as figure 8. No gravestones were found, although Jewish gravestones have been found in secondary use in London.

Figure 8: Cripplegate Cemetery Burials, © Museum of London

Christian medieval burials in London are more numerous and less problematic than Jewish ones. For the purposes of this study, I have chosen to concentrate on the burials found in St. Lawrence Jewry, since it represents the closest burials found to the Cripplegate cemetery and it is located within the mixed Jewish Christian residential area I explored in the spatial analysis above. The St. Lawrence Jewry burials begin in the eleventh century. Yet since the Cripplegate cemetery is dated by historical records to the 13th century, I will focus the study on the St Lawrence Jewry burials dated to the 13th century.

In the thirteenth century, the churchyard of St. Lawrence Jewry saw an intensive burial phase. Many of the 13th century graves disturbed the earlier twelfth century ones. 18 people were interred in this phase of the churchyard burials (see Figure 9). The burials were all single and oriented west-east, with the head to the west. They had a wide variety of traits, and included biers, coffins and planks. Tree ring dates suggest they took place between 1200 and 1250. No gravestones are noted in the publication.[33]

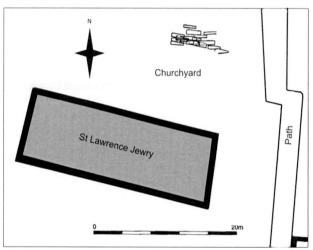

Figure 9: St. Lawrence Jewry Burials, based on fig. 103, pp. 106-7 in the London Guildhall

The data available does not allow us to compare the size of the burials. Grimes notes that the Cripplegate burials were 'rather larger than most graves' but since no actual measurements are associated with this assessment and the plans and photographs lack a scale, it is impossible to compare the size of the burials in the Cripplegate Cemetery with the St. Lawrence Churchyard burials. Even if we may rely on Grime's assessment of the size, since the burials were emptied and then refilled, it is hard to trust that the dimensions of the burials excavated by Grimes are the same as the dimensions of the original burials. Similarly, we cannot compare the number of skeletons, their sexes and ages and any burial traits, as these were not found in the Cripplegate cemetery.

It is, however, possible to discuss several interesting features of both burial sites. Discussion of burial location, orientation, shape and intercutting can be used to understand the degree of shared custom and influence or separateness of the two communities. The location of the two burial sites, although close in proximity, is also very distinct from one another. Cripplegate cemetery lies just beyond the city wall and ditch, and could be easily accessed through Cripplegate. The cemetery formed a distinct burial site and was surrounded by secular houses and gardens, (see Figure 5) but did not appear to include any religious houses, although historical descriptions include a cemetery building (described as a dovecote by later authors) and water streams used for the purification of the dead in Jewish burial rituals (later described as a pond).[34] Jewish cemeteries are usually located away from population centres. In fact, the three other Jewish medieval cemeteries, in Oxford, Winchester and Northampton, were all located outside the city walls.[35] The reason appears to be rooted in Jewish purity laws since a cemetery is considered to be impure and not fit for people to live nearby. *Cohanim* (the decedents of Israelite priests), for example, may not enter a cemetery. This may be rooted in the practical considerations that prompted Jewish sources to recommend surrounding the cemetery or the burials themselves with protections against anything that may harm the dead.[36] Since those will include animals, it may be easier to understand why custom dictated that it is safer for the living to stay away from the dead and keep cemeteries away from population centres.

By contrast, the St. Lawrence Jewry churchyard burials are located inside the city walls, and lie in close proximity to St Lawrence church (see Figure 9). A Jewish synagogue may have stood at the other end of the block, in Basinghall Street (see Figure 4). Not all Christian burials took place in Churchyards in Medieval England, burials also took place in hospital grounds as well as cemeteries. However, all these locations were within population centres and not outside the settlement walls, as in the Jewish case. Christian burials took place near churches, as in the St. Lawrence Jewry case, because the church consecrated the burial.[37] The location of Jewish and Christian burials in London and indeed elsewhere does show a considerable divergence in practice between the two communities. However, burial is an undeniably religious rite, so it is unclear to what extent the burial location would have indicated or created an estrangement between the two communities.

Interestingly the orientation of the burials was the same in both the Cripplegate Cemetery and in the St. Lawrence churchyard. The burials in the two sites were oriented in the same direction, west-east. With no actual remains found in the Cripplegate cemetery, we have no idea where the head lie, so the orientation could also be east-west. The St Lawrence churchyard burials were oriented west-east with the head in the western part of the grave. Burial orientation in Jewish and Christian tradition follows different traditions. Jewish graves have been argued to be traditionally aligned west-east, facing Jerusalem.[38] This tradition has not been consistently followed, even in the Holy Land, however. My research into burial orientation in Byzantine Palestina found no correlation between the alignment of the burial and any religious indicators. The east-west burial position was not found to be statistically significant.[39] Similarly, no real orientation rule exists for Christian burials either. Hadley states that near churches, as in our case, the burials followed the alignment of the church,[40] but that generally, the alignment and positioning of the bodies varied from case to case.

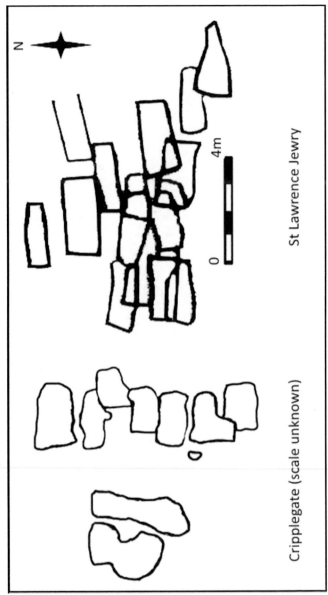

Figure 10: Shape and layout of burials

Figure 10 clearly shows that the burials are of a similar shape, although we cannot comment on the size, since that is unavailable for the Cripplegate burials. It does appear, however, that the Cripplegate burials are more uniform in both shape and size than the St. Lawrence Jewry burials. It is even clearer that the Cripplegate burials are better organised in a neat row and mostly separated from one another, especially taking into account that the burials have been removed and backfilled, which may have enlarged them. The St. Lawrence Jewry burial, by contrast are haphazard, with no clear separation between burials. As noted above, many of the thirteenth century graves disturbed the earlier twelfth century ones. By contrast the Cripplegate burials can be seen to be orderly and separate from one another with no evidence of intercutting. One may be distrustful of this distinction due to the poor quality of the Cripplegate publication. However, other Jewish burials in England have shown a notable lack of intercutting as well.[41] Yizhak Adler, in his book on Jewish burial customs, states Jewish tradition does not allow two bodies to be placed in one tomb. Nor can two burials be adjoining or one body buried on top of another. According to the *G'mara* (Rabbinic law books) this is done to separate righteous men from evil man.[42] It appears then, that in this particular case, practice follows Jewish tradition. Intercutting is, however, quite common in Christian burials.

This limited burial data appears to paint a rather distinct picture. Jews and Christians had quite different burial customs. The locations of the burials are dissimilar, showing a very different attitude to the treatment of the dead. The orientation is similar, but that could be just a matter of happenstance, since we are looking at just one example of burial for each religious group, which is not statistically significant. A future look at medieval burial orientation in England may be more profitable. The organisation of the burials also shows a distinct difference with Jewish burials well-ordered and organised and Christian burials haphazard and disorderly. Thus, limited data does show that, in death at least, the two communities appeared quite distinct from one another, echoing different religious customs, that had a great deal of influence over the treatment of their dead. Since the communities were quite different in death, it behoves us to find out more about their lives.

Health is a very important part of life and can help us see if the two groups also lived in distinctly different ways.

Health and Diet

Archaeological data from our study area provides the possibility of discussing the hygiene and diets of the Jewish community in London.

Hygiene and Parasites

Anecdotal accounts claim that due to Jewish purity laws, Jewish people kept better hygiene then their Christian neighbours and had better health as a result. Due to the skills of the excavators of Cheapside, it has become possible to test this theory. The excavators state that 'the recovery of parasitic eggs from archaeological deposits is a useful technique for determining patterns of sewage disposal in the past.'[43] and so it is, since parasitic worms, particularly *Ascaris lumbricoides* (maw worm) and *Trichuris trichura* (whip worm) have been shown to be wide spread in medieval populations.[44] But Clare de Rouffigac's analysis of parasitic eggs in Cheapside is even more valuable to us since '[t]hese worms... result from poor standards of hygiene and unsanitary living conditions.'[45] If one accepts that Jewish purity laws, which include regular use of the *mikveh* facilities, as well as regular hand washing,[46] will result in higher standards of hygiene and more sanitary living conditions, then we should expect to see fewer parasitic eggs in samples taken from Jewish households.

The Cheapside excavations took place in four different sites, which make out four of our spatial analysis sites. Of the four sites, we have confirmation by documentary analysis that Well Court and Watling Court were owned by Christians. No correlation between excavated structures and historical documents exists for Ironmonger Lane and Milk St shows evidence for a mixed Christian and Jewish ownership. Of particular importance is Tenement 5 in Milk St which contained a *mikveh*, confirming that Jewish people did, in fact live there. The results of the parasitic analysis are as follows:

Site	Religion of occupants	Parasites found
Milk St.	Jew/Christian	Very low, out of nine samples only one contained parasitic eggs. No eggs at all found in Tenements 4 and 5. Author finds this strange, blames poor conservation of samples.[47]
Well Court	Christian	Only one pit sampled, excavators claim low count due to mixed use.[48]
Ironmonger Lane	No correlation between structures and historical records	Very mixed results from high concentration to low. Author claims poor preservation and mixed use.[49]
Watling Court	Christian	A mixture of low and high concentration of parasitic eggs found. Low parasitic concentration claimed to be because of poor preservation or mixed use of pits.[50]

It appears, then, that these limited data can neither confirm nor deny the connection between the numbers of parasites and the religion of the inhabitants. Our most useful samples from Milk St are badly preserved, which casts doubt on the reliability of the information provided. As de Rouffigac rightly cautions in her report, we must consider the preservation of the samples and its effect on the quality of the data. Of course, this data sample is quite small, and more evidence is needed for better analysis. Yet it may be possible to cautiously add another explanation for the low parasitic count on Milk street. We may be also be seeing the effect of Jewish purity laws on the health of its Jewish residents. Unfortunately, no parasitic analysis has been conducted for the Guildhall and Blossoms Inn excavations. Future research may provide further information on this question.

Animal Bone Studies

In secular domestic contexts, animal bone studies (when available) may provide a good indicator of religious presence due to Jewish dietary laws. Among other laws, Jews abstain from eating pig meat as well as sea food except for fish. Animal bone and shell are archaeologically recoverable and Jewish presence can be discerned where there are large quantities of these finds. Hesse and Wapnish have shown that settlements with known Jewish populations did not engage in pig farming in the Ancient Near East.[51] My study of animal bone evidence and religious identity in Byzantine Palestina confirms their conclusion.[52] Closer to home, Gerard Ijzereef's study of 100 cess pits from seventeenth and eighteenth century sites in Amsterdam showed that *kashrut* laws were observed, not merely by the species of the animal bones found but also in the lack of non-kosher parts of animals (hind limb bones of cattle and sheep) in the Jewish areas.[53]

Unfortunately, the faunal data from our London sites is more severely limited than the parasitic data above. The Gresham Street property with the *Mikveh* is too small to be significant and the animal bones from the 1976 Milk Street fieldwork have never been analysed. Due to the proximity of Jewish and Christian domestic arrangements, there is also a good chance of mixed Christian and Jewish usage of the same features for waste disposal, which negates the usefulness and reliability of this form of evidence for identifying Jewish residents. Hopefully, future work on this aspect of Jewish diet will provide more extensive and useful data, that may allow us to distinguish between Jews and their Christian neighbours in London.

Conclusion

Archaeological evidence, despite its paucity in London, provide us with additional information on Jewish Christian relations. This allows us to supplant the available fiscal records and create a fuller picture of the Jewish community in London and their relationship with their Christian neighbours. As can be expected of this complex topic and period, it appears that the picture is not straightforward. The Jewish community clearly retained its uniqueness. They kept at least some purity laws and perhaps more which were not archaeologically recoverable and their burial customs were very different. These lifeways would have made the community separate from their Christian neighbours and raised barriers to Jews Christian relationships and acceptance. Yet there are also indications that the Jewish community was, to some extent, a part of London life. They lived in a mixed neighbourhood, with church and possibly synagogue within one block of each other. Jewish symbols cannot be found in any portable object with a known provenance and context, so they were may have been using the same tools and artefacts as other Londoners. This new analysis allows us to see the nuances and complexities inherent in life in the multicultural neighbourhood in our study area.

A great deal more can be done to add to this picture and clarify it. Further analysis of parasitic data from other sites and the study of faunal data from our sites. A study of illuminated manuscripts produced in London can help us see how Christians and Jews saw themselves; what they looked like and how they dressed. A study of these images would be useful to place infamous medieval caricatures in context. A linguistic study of surviving documents would also allow us to look at the languages and names used by the two communities, both very important cultural indicators.

Notes

---

1   David A. Hinton, 'Medieval Anglo-Jewry: the Archaeological Evidence', in *Jews in Medieval Britain: Historical, Literary and Archaeological Perspectives, ed. by Patricia Skinner* (Woodbridge, 2003), pp. 97-111 (97).

2   Patricia Skinner, 'Introduction: Jews in Medieval Britain and Europe', in *Jews in Medieval Britain, ed. by Skinner,* pp. 1-12 (5-7).

3   For information on the present state of published excavations in Medieval London, see J. Schofield, P. Allen and C. Taylor, 'Medieval Buildings and Property Development in the area of Cheapside', *Transactions of the London and Middlesex Archaeological Society,* 41 (1990), 39–238, and D. Bowsher, I. Howell, T. Dyson, N. Holder, *The London Guildhall: An Archaeological History of a Neighbourhood from Early Medieval to*

Modern Times, MoLAS (Museum of London Archaeology Service) Monograph 36 (London, 2007), parts 1 and 2.

4 Schofield et al, pp. 135-6.
5 Schofield et al, p. 137.
6 Schofield et al, p. 140.
7 Schofield et al, p. 142.
8 MoLAS, 'Blossoms Inn, 30 Gresham Street EC2, A Post Excavation Assessment' (unpublished, 2004), p. 33.
9 Joe Hillaby, 'London: The 13th Century Jewry Revisited', *Jewish Historical Society of England,* 32 (1990-92), 89-158 (128-30).
10 I. Blair, J. Hillary, I. Howell, R. Sermon and B. Watson, 'Two Medieval Jewish Ritual Baths – Mikvaót – Found at Grehsam Street and Milk Street in London' in *Transactions of the London and Middlesex Archaeological Society,* 52 (2001), 127-137 (132).
11 Eliya Ribak, *Religious Communities in Byzantine Palestina: The Relationship between Judaism, Christianity and Islam, AD 400 – 700,* BAR International Series 1646 (Oxford, 2007), 115-235 and Blair et al., p.134.
12 MoLAS, 'Blossom's Inn, 20–30 Gresham Street, 20–23 Lawrence Lane, 3–6 Trump Street, 1–10 Milk Street & Mumford Court, London Ec1: Documentary Survey, by T. Dyson' (unpublished, 2001), 1.
13 Blair et al., pp. 130-1.
14 Bowsher et al., pp. 117-119.
15 Bowsher et al., pp. 21-3.
16 Bowsher et al., pp. 120, 338.
17 *Synagoga Judeorum,* Cal Close R 1254-6, 369-70 cited in Bowsher et al., p. 337.
18 Bowsher et al., p. 337.
19 P.N. Soc, 1924, pp. 45, 57 cited in M. B. Honeybourne, 'The Pre-Expulsion Cemetery of the Jews in London', in *Transactions of the Jewish Historical Society,* 20 (1959-61): 145-159 (146).
20 Honeybourne, pp. 146-149
21 Joe and Caroline Hillaby, *The Palgrave Dictionary of Medieval Anglo-Jewish History* (Basingstoke, 2013), pp. 366-7, 332-3, 57-9.
22 G. Pepper, 'An archaeology of the Jewry in medieval London', *London Archaeologist,* 7 (1992), 3-6.
23 Hinton, p. 100.
24 Blair, 2001, 129.
25 Pepper, p. 6.
26 N. Jefferies, 'Late 13th-Century household 'clearance groups' on Gresham Street and the London Jewry', *London Archaeologist,* 13 (2012), 127-31 (pp. 128-29).

27 משפטים פרשה כ' במכילתא דרבי ישמעאל

28 Jefferies, pp. 128-29.

29 Honeybourne, p. 146-149.

30 Honeybourne, p. 146.

31 W. F. Grimes, *The Excavation of Roman and Mediaeval London*, (London, 1968), p. 181.

32 אדלר י, תשמ"ז, לעת מצוא – דיני הקבורה והקוברים, ירושלים, עמוד ס"ו

33 Bowsher et al., p. 105.

34 Honeybourne, p. 151.

35 D.M. Hadley, *Death in Medieval England – An Archaeology*, (Stroud, 2001), p. 51.

36 אדלר, עמוד נ"א- נ"ב

37 Hadley, p. 17-55.

38 J.M. Lilley, G. Stroud, D.R. Brothwell and M.H. Williamson, *The Jewish Burial Ground in Jewbury*, York (York, 1994), p. 299.

39 Ribak, p. 42.

40 Hadley, p. 25.

41 See for example, Lilley et al, p. 332.

42 אדלר, עמוד נ"ב-נ"ד

43 Schofield et al., 229.

44 Jones 1982 and de Rouffignac 1987 in Schofield et al., p. 229.

45 Schofield et al., p. 229.

46 See משנה, סדר טהרות

47 Schofield et al., p. 230.

48 Ibid.

49 Ibid.

50 Schofield et al., p. 229-230

51 B. Hesse and P. Wapnish 'Can pig remains be used for ethnic diagnosis in the ancient Near East?' *Journal for the Study of the Old Testament Supplement Series* (1997), 238-270.

52 Ribak, p. 48-50.

53 F. G. Ijzereef, Social Differentiation from Animal Bone Studies, in *Diet and Crafts in Towns*, ed. by D. Serjeantson and T. Waldron, (Oxford, 1989), pp. 41–53.

Devotional practice and emotional response to the Veronica in Middle English

Maria Luisa Maggioni

Università Cattolica del Sacro Cuore, Milano

Signatum est super nos lumen vultus tui Domine. Dedisti laetitiam in corde meo. (Psalm 4:7)

Introduction[1]

This present study was suggested by a project called *Veronica Route*[2], whose aim is to compile an online catalogue of the artistic and literary works concerning the Roman "Veronica", i.e. the medieval relic preserved in St. Peter's Basilica in Rome. This project, which consists primarily of iconographic research, tries to rediscover the lost traits of the medieval relic by comparing its copies and its main variants; *Veronica Route* includes more than five thousand works and is continuously being updated. Medieval *vernicles* (e.g. pilgrim badges) and other artifacts portraying Veronica and her veil are frequent items in the catalogue, witnessing the propagation of this devotion, which started to spread after the efforts of Pope Innocent III (who reigned between 1198 and 1216) to promote devotion to the Roman Veronica, giving rise to a liturgical veneration of the Holy Face of Christ which was soon to filter into the devotional practices of the laity. In fourteenth- and fifteenth-century England there was a significant production of vernacular texts, inspired by the Veronica legend and devotion to the Holy Face, which form the corpus on which this work is based.

The aim of this research is to investigate how the emotional and devotional drive of the Veronica theme was expressed in Middle English texts. After summarizing the development of the Veronica

Reading Medieval Studies, 47 (2021): 131-51

legend in medieval England and after presenting a brief reconstruction of the etymology of the word *vernicle*, vernicles as objects of devotion are discussed, on the basis of Middle English texts. The theme of the Holy Face in Middle English prose and poetry and the presence of Veronica in popular piety is then taken into consideration. A brief commentary on the vocabulary used to express devotion and emotion concludes the paper.

The Veronica legend in medieval England

In Anglo-Saxon England the narration of the Veronica legend circulated as it is told in the Latin *Vindicta Salvatoris*, a later addition to the body of texts known as the *Pilate Cycle*.[3] The apocryphal work commonly known today as the *Gospel of Nicodemus* (*Evangelium Nicodemi*)[4] 'has been part of the living Christian culture for over a millennium and a half. Originally composed in Greek and well attested by the last quarter of the fourth century, it migrated quickly into other Christian vernaculars.'[5] As a matter of fact, 'the first vernacular translation of *Evangelium Nicodemi* in medieval Europe, the one into Old English, was carried out in the early to mid-eleventh century.'[6] The *Pilate Cycle* introduces Veronica as the woman afflicted with an issue of blood and healed by Christ (related in Matthew 9, 20-22 and Luke 8, 43-48). This text gained early popularity and was soon vernacularized. Veronica's association with the Instruments of the Passion was already present in Anglo-Saxon England, but it was only in the twelfth century that this theme became dominant in popular piety, perhaps due to the popularity of the *Gospel of Nicodemus*.

As Swan maintains, in the late Anglo-Saxon period

> [...] saints' cults generated some of the most public, social and
> organised activities of the Christian Church in Anglo-Saxon
> England [...]. Closely tied to the cult of saints is that of relics:
> material objects believed to be either a part of the body of a saint,
> or a part of an associated object.[7]

Because of its popularity in England and early vernacularization there, mid-nineteenth-century scholars even suggested an insular origin for the legend. As demonstrated by twentieth-century scholarship[8], an eleventh-century version of the eighth-century Latin text of *Vindicta Salvatoris*, probably contains the first mention of Veronica in English:

> And sum wyf wæs þoliȝende blodes fleusan huru xii winter, seo wæs Veronix ȝenemned[9]
> [And there was a woman who had suffered from overflux of blood for 12 winters (years); she was called Veronica]

In the *Gospel of Nicodemus*, Veronica is introduced in a similar way and is said to have gone to speak in favour of Jesus during his trial, although her witness was dismissed as being provided by a woman.[10] After the fall of Jerusalem, the leprous emperor Tiberius (in other texts Vespasian) dispatches one Volosianus to fetch a disciple of Christ. When Volosianus then arrives in Palestine, he obtains the image of Christ from Veronica. The emperor sees the image, worships, is healed, believes and is baptized. In the narrative, Volosianus orders Veronica to hand him the image of Christ that she has with her:

> Ic hate þe Veronix þæt ðu aȝif me þa haliȝnysse þa þu myd þe hæfst[11]
> [I enjoin you, Veronica, that you give me the holiness (holy image) that you have with you]

The Veronica legend gained popularity in Middle English, and was recorded for example in the late-fourteenth-century alliterative *Siege of Jerusalem*, which relates the healing power of this 'lykenesse of Crist', 'the kerchef that kevered [cured/redeemed] the sike' and the beginnings of its cult in Rome.[12] Another very popular text featuring the same episode is the *Legenda Aurea*, allegedly compiled by Jacobus de Voragine, Archbishop of Genoa, around 1275. In England it was the indirect source of many hagiographical works and was anglicized in the first decades of the fifteenth century in a text known as *Gilte Legende*[13]. The English version by William Caxton, first published in 1483, gained such great popularity that it was reprinted up to 1527, reaching its ninth edition. Thanks to this version, the full account of the narrative of the

Veronica legend was further popularized. It offers the following account of the image of the Holy Face:

> [...] volusien fonde an old woman named veronica / whiche had be famylyer and deuoute with Ihesu Cryst he demaūded of her / where he myght fynde hym that he sought / She thenne escryed and sayd Alas [...] my lord and my maistre whan he wente prechyng / I absente me ofte from hym I dyde do paynte his ymage / For to haue alway wyth me his presence / by cause that the figure of his ymage shold gyue me somme solace / And thus as I bare a lynnen keuerchief in my bosome oure lord mette me / and demau[n]ded whyther I wente / and whan I had told hym whyther I wente and the cause / he demaunded my keuerchief / And anone he enprynted his face and fygured it therin.[14]

In the centuries that followed the year 1000, Mary had become increasingly the centre for veneration and expressions of emotion, offering a possibility of identification, above all for her affliction during Christ's Passion: 'Marian lyrics and prayers, as well as visual representations, like the wooden statues so common in French parish churches, became available to lay people in local idioms and in familiar settings in the course of the late-twelfth and thirteenth centuries'.[15] The growing devotion to Mary and her sufferings as a mother easily expanded to all aspects connected to the Passion; as Rubin states '[n]ew ways of experiencing Mary and the Passion were evolving in the vernacular usages'.[16] From the Early Middle Ages, the cult of the Instruments of the Passion was at the basis of devotional focus, with a more personal and intense relationship between the individual Christian and God, which was to find its best-known expression in devotional practices from about the twelfth century. Women's devotion was particularly widespread and intense, and it was extended from Mary to other female figures in the Gospels, including Veronica in her 'motherly' role, with 'an intense devotion arcing from the Blessed Virgin to St. Veronica, both revered for how they carry Christ in "true" effigy: Mary bears the Child in her womb; Veronica bears the holy face on her cloth.'[17] Through them women had '[...] the chance to create, through a deep concentration on the Passion, a devotional object – Christ – in their own image, as someone bleeding, powerless and subject to others.'[18] This vision of Christ's helplessness and of Veronica's piteous, instinctive, feminine gesture is well illustrated in this passage taken from the fifteenth-century anonymous English prose translation of Roger d'Argenteuil's *Bible en François* (mid-thirteenth century):

> Then þere went toforn oure Lord an holi woman callid Veronica, þat bare a couerchif [kerchief] to selle at the cheping [market]. And when she saugh oure Lord so foule brought and vilanously, she made gret sorou and wepid and toke him the couerchif and seid, "Iesu, . . . I am right sory of this martirdom þat thou suffrist without reson. But hold this couerchif and wipe awey the swet and the blood from thi blissid visage." And so he did. And therewithall sodeinly was the visage of oure Lord purtraied in the couerchif as like it had ben his said visage fleishly. And than oure Lord toke to Veronica hi. couerchif ageyn and bad hir that she shuld kepe it wele, for it shal hele many sekenessis.[19]

Perhaps the best know English example of this passionate participation is the fifteenth-century 'autobiography' of the Lynn burgess Margery Kempe, who would 'lay in contemplacyon, sor [painfully] wepyng in hir [her] spirit [...] cryin, roryn [crying out loudly], and wepyn'.[20]

In these narratives, Veronica is consistently presented as a woman who had been devoted to Christ and who had wiped his face on the *Via Dolorosa*. She is very conscious that her veil bearing Christ's image would be a testimony of how the guiltless Son of God had been condemned to peerless suffering. This seems to be confirmed by Jesus himself:

> "Veronyca, þi whipyng doth me ese.
> My face is clene þat was blak to se.
> I xal [shall] þem kepe from all mysese [suffering]
> þat lokyn on þi kerchy and remembyr me."[21]

Vernicles as objects of devotion

In the Middle Ages Veronica's veil (*vernicle*) was venerated as the visible, miraculous memorial of the Passion of Christ and hence of his saving work.[22] As Veronica herself says in the *Golden Legend*: 'the figure of his ymage shold gyue me somme solace'.[23] And it is not only spiritual healing to be granted by its contemplation, but it could also heal the bodies, provided it was contemplated with devotion." The origin of the noun *vernicle* is illustrated in the *Siege of Jerusalem*:

> The Vernycle after Veronik Waspasian hit called.
> Garde [watch] hit gayly agysen [richly decorated] in gold and in
>   selvere.
> Yit is the visage in the vail [veil],as Veronik hym broght;
> The Romaynes hit holdeth at Rome, and for a relyk hit holden.[24]

The mid-fourteenth-century noun *vernicle* - 'picture of the face of Christ' – derives from *veronicle*, Old French variant of *veronique*, indicating St. Veronica's cloth. With the propagation of devotion to the Stations of the Cross, the French proper name *Veronique* – a variant of the Greek name *Berenike* – was interpreted by folk-etymology as derived from Latin *vera* (true) + Greek *eikon* (image). The evolution of the word and its meanings is clearly illustrated in the *Middle English Dictionary* (*MED*)[25], in which the relevant entry lists five meanings of *vernicle*:

(a) The cloth or kerchief, preserved as a relic at Rome, said to have belonged to a woman usu. identified as Veronica, upon which an image of the face of Christ had been impressed, veronica; also, the image on the veronica;

(b) the altar at Rome dedicated to devotion of the veronica;

(c) the stylized image of the veronica; a representation of the veronica on a chalice, seal, pilgrim's token, etc.;

(d) ?a blemish or birthmark resembling a veil [prob. mistransl. of L *verruca* 'blemish'];

(e) as surname.

Definitions (a), (b), and (c) are, of course, the ones pertinent to this study. Representations of the veronica met the needs of popular piety for visible objects to venerate.[26] In the Middle Ages pilgrim badges were probably the most sought-after souvenirs of pilgrimages, to be brought back home as signs of a successful ending to an often dangerous journey and as tangible tokens of devout religious practices. From the exotic shell of Compostela to the more familiar sword of Canterbury, it was possible to buy such badges at most Christian shrines. They were often treasured items, mentioned in wills or listed among precious or cherished properties. Vernicles were a very popular subject in medieval England, appearing on badges or rings. In the *Paston Letters* 'a gret sygnnet [seal] of goolde with the vernycle'[27] is mentioned while lead badges that had been used for memento or meditative purposes were often buried with the devotee.[28] They were also common subjects on paxes, allowing the faithful and the clergy to kiss Christ during the service. Indulgences were granted for prayers in devotion to vernicles, such as *Salve Sancta Facies,* whose English translation by John Audelay will be dealt with below.[29] They were also used for solemn vows, as in the *Alliterative Morte Darthur*[30]

> He [the Baron of little Britain] said, "I make myn avowe verreilly
>   to Cryste
> And to þe haly vernacle þat voide [abandon] schall I neuere,
> For radnesse [fear] of na Romayne [no emperor] þat regnes in
>   erthe,
> Bot ay be redye in araye [in proper order] and at areste [ready for
>   battle] founden.
> (lines 308-11)

> Thereto make I myn avowe devottly to Cryste
> And to the holy vernacle, vertuous and noble,
> (lines 347-8)

Vernicles, which must have been a common sight in fourteenth-century England, were even mentioned in portraits of fake devotion. The most popular example of a hypocritical use of this religious symbol is the one contained in the description of the Pardoner in Chaucer's *General*

Prologue.[31] The description of this character, usually associated with the sin of *Avaritia*, commonly attributed to corrupt members of the clergy[32], is an indirect criticism of the simoniac practice of the commercialization of indulgences. The Pardoner would probably be well provided with (fake) documents granting an indulgence (i.e. indulgence rolls), often featuring a drawing of Veronica's cloth, above all after Pope John XXII (1316-1334) had granted an indulgence of ten thousand days for a prayer to the Veronica. In the well-known *Ellesmere Chaucer* illumination, a vernicle is clearly reproduced on the Pardoner's hat, reflecting Chaucer's verbal description[33]:

> Dischevelee [with the hair hanging loose], save his cappe, he rood
>   al bare.
> Swiche glarynge eyen [eyes] hadde he as an hare.
> A vernycle hadde he sowed upon his cappe.
> His wallet, biforn hym in his lappe,
> Bretful [brimful] of pardoun [indulgence rolls], comen from
>   rome al hoot.
> (lines 683-7)

Perhaps less well-known is the description of another deadly sin, *Accidia*, in *Piers Plowman*.[34]

> Apparailled as a paynym [pagan] in pilgrymes wise.
> He bar a burdoun [pilgrim's staff] ybounde with a brood liste
>   [stripe]
> In a withwynde [woodbine] wise ywounden aboute.
> A bolle [bowl] and a bagge he bar by his syde.
> An hundred of ampulles[35] on his hat seten,
> Signes of Synay and shelles of Galice,
> And many a crouch[36] on his cloke, and keyes of Rome,
> And the vernicle bifore, for men sholde knowe
> And se bi hise signes whom he sought hadde.
> (Passus V, 517-525)

The fake pilgrim here described wears symbols on his garments – 'And the vernicle before' – indicating he has visited the most renowned shrines many times (Mount Sinai, with its Monastery, Rome, and Compostela) walking 'ful wide in weet and in drye' (V, 530) and claiming to have venerated 'goode Seintes for my soule helthe' (V, 531). It must be remembered that both Chaucer and 'Langland' lived in a period of crisis for the Church and that both may have been influenced – to different degrees – by John Wyclif, whose critique of a 'blatantly corrupt church' was probably shared by many educated contemporaries.[37]

The Holy Face in Middle English prose and poetry

The contemplation of the Holy Face – especially in its representation in vernicles, which made it familiar and almost tangible – suggested expressions of mystical fervour in fourteenth- and fifteenth-century religious writing. The relationship between Veronica's veil and devotion to the Holy Face is of course obvious: in manuscripts a drawing of Christ's Face on Veronica's cloth often appeared with the text of prayers, offering 'a visual meditative site to accompany the verbal exercise'.[38] The Veronica image is designed to elicit affective response and participation in Christ's pain and to bring consolation, comfort, but also contrition and repentance. It is an invitation to gaze on Christ: Richard Rolle prays to Christ while contemplating how he suffered shame and anguish and implores Christ to grant him to see his 'blisful face in heuene'.[39]

Relevant passages in the works of Rolle and Julian of Norwich are well-known. In Rolle's emotional prayer to Christ, the author takes his inspiration from a representation of the face of Jesus (possibly a *veronica*, since images of the Holy Face frequently appeared not only on pilgrim medals but also in other artifacts, such as manuscripts) for moral considerations to be applied to the life of a Christian. Rolle's prayer insists on the sweetness of Jesus and on his sufferings as they appear from the image:

> SWete Ihesu, I ȝelde [give] þee þankingis for al þat schame & anguisch þat þou suffridist whanne þei spitten in þi face, / in þat swete myrrour & bodili blis of heuene, upon which aungels & seintis haue deinte [delight] to loke. / Now, swete Ihesu, ȝeue me

grace to haue most deinte inwardli to loke & þenke upon þat
blissid face; / and, swete Ihesu, restore þe liknes of þi face in my
soule þat foule synnes han faded [caused to fade]; / &, leue [dear]
lord, lete me neuere haue likinge in þe face of synne in
temptacioun, & graunte me grace neuere to assente to lust of
synne; & ȝeue me grace to worschipe þee in ech creature; & lete
me neuere haue pride of chere [aspect] of my face, ne lust to
synne for semblaunt [deceptive appearance] of ony oþirs face;
and, swete Ihesu, graunte me to se þi blisful face in heuene,
amen. Pater noster. Et ne nos.[40]

Julian of Norwich, introducing her second *shewing*, says

[...] I saw with bodily sight, in the face of the crucifix that henge
before me in the which I behelde continualy, a parte of His
passion – despite spitting and sollowing [soiling], and buffetting
and many langoryng [distressing] peynes, mo than I can tel, and
often changing of colour.[11]

She explicitly refers to 'a figure and likenes of our foule dede hame
[flesh?], that our faire, bright blissid Lord bare for our sins' (375-5),
which made her think of the:

[...] holy vernacle of Rome which He hath portrayed [impressed]
with His owne blissid face whan He was in His herd passion
wilfully going to His deth and often chongyng of colour. Of the
brownehede and blakehede, reulihede [sadness] and lenehede
[leanness] of this image, many mervel how it might be, stondyng
He portraied it with His blissid face, which is the faire hede of
Heavyn, flowre of erth, and the fruite of the mayden wombe.
Than how might this image be so discolouring and so fer fro
faire?
(375-81)

Julian here introduces the theme of the changing colour of Christ's face,
implying that this is related to his likeness to man's countenance, which
is sometimes 'darkened' by sin:

I saw His swete face as it was drye and blodeles with pale deyeng
[dyeing], and sithen [afterward] more pale, dede, langoring
[languishing], and than turnid more dede into blew [bluish], and
sithen more browne blew, as the flesh turnyd more depe dede.
For His passion shewid to me most propirly in His blissid face,
and namly in His lippis. There I saw these four colowres, tho that
were aforn freshe, redy [red], and likyng to my sigte [sight]. This
was a swemful [piteous] chonge to sene, this depe deyeng [intense
colouring], and also the nose clange [?] and dryed [shriveled], to
my sigte, and the swete body was brown and blak, al turnyd oute
of faire lifely colowr of Hymselfe on to drye deyeng.
(589-97)

The Holy Face as source of inspiration and consolation is also invoked
by the early fifteenth-century priest and poet, John the Blind Audelay,
in his version[12] of the hymn by Pope Innocent III from the year 1216,
Salve sancta facies nostri redemptoris (see above):

> *Salve*, I say, Holé Face of our Saveour,
>   In the wyche schynth [shines] to us an hevenly fygure,
> An graceus on to se!
> *Salve*, thou settis thi prynt on lynin cloth of witlé [whitish] coloure,
>   And betoke hit Veroneca fore love and gret honoure
>   Upon here sudoré [sudarium][13]
> (1-6)

In Audelay's collected poems another work expresses a salutation to the
Holy Face[14], again explicitly mentioning Veronica's *sudarium* carrying
the image of Christ's face as traced on Veronica's veil and depicted in
the original manuscript's sole large drawing (Oxford, Bodleian Library,
MS Douce 302 (Audelay manuscript), fol. 27va):

> O Jhesu, fore thi blesful *Face*,
> Thou betoke [gave] Veroneca bi grace
>   Upon here sudaré;
> That Face be me consolacion,

And to the Fynd confusion,
  That day when I schal dye.
(67-72)

The legend of Veronica, which stresses the healing power of the cloth
and its image, contributed to its popularity in English medieval
devotions; even viewing the image of the Vernicle was sometimes
considered to grant pardon of sins:

Sepulcrum Christi
And for the vernicle haue he may
Fourty dayẏes eueryche day[45]

The *Symbols of the Passion* (Royal MS. 17 A 27) is a short poem in
honour of the vernicle, presented as a remedy for the sins committed
with the mouth (namely slandering, taking false oaths, backbiting, and
boasting of one's sins):

O vernacule, i honoure him and the,
Þat þe made þorow his preuité [divine secret];
Þo cloth he set to his face,
Þe prent laft þere þorow his grace,
His moth, his nose, his ine [eyes] to,
His berd, his here [hair] dide al so.
Schilde me for al þat in my liue
I haue singud [sinned] with wittus [senses] fiue,
Namlich with mout of sclaunduring [calumny],
Fals othus and backbiting,
And made boste with toung al so
Of sinnus þat i haue do;
Lord of heuen, for-ȝeue it me
Þorow syht [sight] of þe figur þat i here se.[46]

In the manuscript, which contains twenty-four colourful miniatures with
leaf decoration of the symbols of the Passion, the opening lines of this
excerpt are preceded by the miniature of two angels holding the cloth
of Veronica (f. 72v).[47] Similar drawings were also commonly found on

indulgence rolls, with lyrics to go with each illustration.[48] Viewing these images of the vernicle was understood to grant pardon for sins.

Veronica and popular piety in Late Middle English: Mystery plays, pilgrims' guides, the *Golden Legend*

According to Sansterre, '[d]ans les derniers siècles du Moyen Âge, l'image du Christ appelée Veronica connut une extraordinaire vénération en Occident.'[49] Late mediaeval 'traditional religion' in England found one of its most characteristic expressions in religious drama, which was deeply embedded in and congruent with the intense spirituality of the age. As Davidson, puts it: 'the plays were designed to promote emotional involvement with the events being staged. Most intensely, the suffering and Crucifixion of Jesus were even to be *felt* as *necessary* for Salvation.'[50] No wonder the Veronica episode is to be found in both the *York plays* and in the N-Town Cycle.[51] The veil with which Veronica cleansed Christ's face is referred to as 'this signe', whose contemplation will 'kepe from all mysese [suffering]':

> VERONICA A, 3e synful pepyl, why fare þus?
> For swet and blood he may not se.
> Allas, holy prophete, Cryst Jhesus,
> Careful [sorrowful] is myn hert for the.
> And sche whypyth his face with here kerchy [kerchief].
> JESUS Veronyca, þi whipyng doth me ese.
> My face is clene þat was blak to se.
> I xal [shall] þem kepe from all mysese
> þat lokyn on þi kerchy and remembyr me.
> (Play 32, lines 40-8)

In the following excerpt from the *York Plays*, the act normally assigned to Veronica is transferred to the third Mary, one of the women at the tomb of Jesus on Easter Sunday. Jesus' face makes an imprint on the cloth, which becomes a sign [signe] – and a valued relic – of the Passion.

Maria 3
Allas, this is a cursed cas.
He that alle hele [salvation] in his hande has
Shall here be sakles [guiltless] slayne.
A, lorde, beleue [stop] lete clense thy face-
Behalde howe he hath schewed his grace,
Howe he is moste of mayne [power]!
This signe schalle bere witnesse
Vnto all pepull playne,
Howe Goddes sone here gilteles
Is putte to pereles payne.
(Play 34, lines 180-9)

Surprisingly enough, in *The Book of Margery Kempe*, the 'dense account of Margery's experiences in Rome does not mention the many relics, artefacts and indulgences that the Eternal City had to offer to the pious, such as the famous Veil of Veronica, referenced by Julian of Norwich from her cell in England.'[52] As a matter of fact, the vernicle was one of the best-known and most revered relics and its ostension was attended by pilgrims because of the indulgences granted to the onlookers. Pilgrim guides to Rome never fail to mention this. Capgrave's *Solace of Pilgrimes* (c. 1450) reads:

> Whann so euyr þe uernacle is schewid iii Ml ȝere [years] is graunted to þe romanes. And to hem alle þat dwelle ouyr þe mowntis [mountains] ix Ml ȝere. And to þoo þat dwelle be þishalue [this part of] þe mowntis xii Ml ȝere.[53]

The rhymed version of another popular fifteenth-century guide – *The Stacions of Rome* – is even more detailed:

> Whon þe vernicle schewed is.
> Gret pardoun . forsoþe þer is . I.-wis
> Preo þousend ȝer . as I. ow [you] telle
> To Men þat in . þe Cite dwelle.
> And men þat dwelle be sideward [nearby].
> Nyne þousend ȝer . schall ben heore part.

And þou þat passest ouer þe séé.
Twelue þousend ȝer . is grauʒnted to þe.
And þerto . þow schalt winne more.
Þe þridde part for-ȝiuenes . of al þi sore.
In lentone [Lent] is . an holy grace.
Vche [each] pardon is doubled . in þat place [54]

The healing, salvific power of Veronica's veil is also referred to in *Polychronicon*. In this history of the world originally written in Latin by Ranulf Higden (d. 1364) and translated into plain, narrative English prose a few years later by John Trevisa (d. 1402), the episode of Volusianus and Veronica is narrated as follows:

> The forsaide Volusianus took aqueyntaunce and knowleche of a noblewomman þat heet [was called] Veronica, so þat he brouȝte hir to Rome to the emperour wiþ here lynnen cloþ, in þe whiche cloþ sche hadde þe prynte of þe liknesse of oure lordes face. Þe emperour byheld þis cloþ, and was hool anon. [55]

In Caxton's *Golden Legend* Veronica's answer to Volusian underlines the exclusively spiritual value of the relic, which can not be bought by gold or silver, but can only heal those who contemplate it devoutly and with 'grete affeccion':

> And yf thy lord had beholden the fygure of Jhesu Chryst deuoutly / he shold be anon guarisshed and heled / And Volusien axid is ther nether gold ne siluer that this fygure may be bought with / She answerd nay / but stroonge of corage /deuoute and of grete affeccion / I shal go with the / and shal bere it to themperour for to see it /and after I shal retorn hether agayn [56]

Conclusion

In a period that stretches for about two hundred years the language used by the various Middle English authors doesn't dramatically change. In the quotations discussed, the image of Jesus and his body is always associated with sweetness ('swete Ihesu', 'His swete face', 'the swete body'), beauty and light ('our faire, bright blissid Lord') as opposed to unjust extreme suffering ('this martirdom þat thou suffrist without reason'), that causes his countenance to change colours because of 'spitting and sollowing [soiling], and buffetting and many langoryng [distressing] peynes', representing humanity's sins. Perhaps, the most significant association with the contemplation of Christ's suffering and the image of his face are the ones 'depicted' by the great Middle English mystic writers Richard Rolle and Julian of Norwich, in spite of their not explicitly mentioning the Veronica image. Rolle contemplates the 'schame & anguisch þat þou [Jesus] suffridist whanne þei spitten in þi face' and prays to Jesus 'to se þi [Christ's] blisful face in heuene'. Even more touching is Julian's contemplation of 'the face of the crucifix that henge before me in the which I behelde continualy, a parte of His passion'.

According to Windeatt '[o]ne might say there are at least *three* Veronicas. First, there is Veronica's existence in narratives, her legend. Second, there is the material relic, in Rome. And thirdly, there is the tradition of replicating the relic.'[57] Bearing this division in mind, the Middle English passages discussed in this paper can help readers understand how emotional devout reactions could be elicited by the narration of the Veronica episode and by the contemplation of 'veronicas' ('the holy vernicle, virtuous and noble').

In what is probably the first mention of Veronica herself in English, she is associated with suffering (in her case an illness associated with the female body). She is later described as 'sum wyf wæs þoliȝende [suffering from] blodes fleusan'. Later texts speak of her as 'an old woman named veronica', a 'noblewomman þat heet [was called] Veronica', 'an holi woman callid Veronica', who 'had be famylyer and deuoute with Ihesu Cryst'. When Veronica met Jesus 'so foule brought and vilanously, she made gret sorou and wepid and toke him the couerchif" and told him: 'Iesu, . . . I am right sory of this martirdom þat thou suffrist without reson. But hold this couerchif' because she wanted to wipe away 'the swet and the blood from [his] blissid visage.' Interestingly, the word *swet* (sweat) in all the texts considered is a homograph of *swet* (sweet). The lack of graphical distinction between the two words (typical of Middle English spelling) creates significant lexical contrasts.

The instinctive, 'motherly' reaction of Veronica ('Careful [sorrowful] is myn hert for the') eases Christ's suffering ('Veronyca, þi whipyng doth me ese./My face is clene þat was blak to se'). He is so grateful for this simple act of piety that he imprints his face on Veronica's cloth ('Þe prent laft þere þorow his grace') not only as a memorial of his suffering to be contemplated, but also as a healing relic. This is often mentioned in Middle English texts: Jesus says: 'I xal [shall] þem kepe from all mysese /þat lokyn on þi kerchy and remembyr me.' Provided the faithful 'beholden the fygure of Jhesu Chryst deuoutly', they are 'anon guarisshed and heled.' As a matter of fact, the fusion of text and image had a strong evocative, communicative power; devotion to the image, which had been initially cultivated in monastic circles, percolated into prayers and devotions of the laity and into literary texts, thus creating a continuum from liturgy to popular expressions.

Vernicles, tin badges, golden rings were not only objects of devotion, but also treasured souvenirs of the pilgrimage to Rome: according to the *Siege of Jerusalem*, Vespasian '[g]arde hit gayly agysen in gold and in selvere. / Yit is the visage in the vail, Veronyk hym broght; / The Romaynes hit holdeth at Rome, and for a relyk hit holden' (262-4). The Veronica – the 'Holy Vernacle at Rome, which He hath portrayed with His own blessed face' – was displayed in St. Peter's and granted great indulgences, for 'Whon þe vernicle schewed is./ Gret pardoun . forsoþe þer is', but it should be contemplated with genuine devotion. The pilgrim badges were, therefore, often proudly exhibited as proofs of the accomplished pilgrimage, as Langland and Chaucer say: 'the vernicle bifore, for men sholde knowe / And se bi hise signes whom he sought hadde'; 'A vernycle hadde he sowed upon his cappe.'

The Veronica was therefore an invitation to gaze on Christ, creating a desire to be like him and a longing for virtue; it was venerated as the visible, miraculous memorial of the Passion of Christ and hence of his saving work and contemplated as the sign that 'schalle bere witnesse / Vnto all pepull playne'.[38]

Notes

1   An initial version of this paper was presented by Amanda Murphy and the
     Maria Luisa Maggioni at *Emotion and Devotion in Medieval Europe The*

GCMS Summer Symposium, Reading, 21 June 2018. M.L. Maggioni wishes to thank A. Murphy for her invaluable support.

2   *Veronica Route*, https://veronicaroute.com/

3   Discussed by Barry Windeatt,"'Vera Icon'? The Variable Veronica of Medieval England" in *The European Fortune of the Roman Veronica in the Middle Ages*, ed. by A. Murphy, H. Kessler et al. (Turnhout, 2017), pp. 59-71. The material is translated in *B. Harris Cowper*, (ed.), *The Apocryphal Gospels and other Documents Relating to the History of Christ* (London, *1867*).

4   "The *Gospel* as it came to the hands of the Old English translator was already a combination of two separate pieces: the first the "Acts of Pilate" or "Gospel of Nicodemus"; the second, the "Descent into Hell." The fusion of these two pieces into one *Gospel of Nicodemus* took place not later than 425. T. P. Allen (ed.), *A Critical Edition of the Old English 'Gospel' of Nicodemus*. Unpublished PhD dissertation (Rice University, 1968), p. 1. Available online https://scholarship.rice.edu/bitstream/handle/1911/14416/6815601.PDF?sequence=1&isAllowed=y

5   A-C. Baudoin, Z. Izydorczyk, 'The Acts of Pilate and the Evangelium Nicodemi in the Age of Manuscripts', in *The Oldest Manuscript of the Acts of Pilate: A Collaborative Commentary on the Vienna Palimpsest*, ed. by Baudoin and Izydorczyk (2019), hal-02378821, pp. 13-21, (p. 14).

6   Z. Izydorczyk, 2019, 'Revised in Translation: Vernacular Legacies of the Evangelium Nicodemi', in *The Oldest Manuscript of the Acts of Pilate,* pp. 43-50 (p. 45).

7   M. Swan, 'Remembering Veronica in Anglo Saxon England', in *Writing Gender and Genre in Medieval Literature: Approaches to Old and Middle English Texts*, ed. by Elaine Treharne and Greg Walker (Cambridge, 2002), pp. 19-39. (p. 19).

8   For an overview, see Zbigniew S. Izydorczyk, (ed.), *The Medieval Gospel of Nicodemus: Texts, Intertexts, and Contexts in Western Europe* (Tempe AZ, 1997).

9   '*Legende von der Heiligen* Veronica', in *Angelsächsische Homilien und Heiligenleben*, ed. by B. Assmann (Darmstadt, 1889), pp. 181-192 (p. 182). All translations are my own.

10   'Item et mulier quaedam Veronica nomen a longe clamavit praesidi: Fluens sanguine eram ab annis duodecim et tetigi fimbriam vestmenti eius, et statim fluxus sanguini mei stetit. Dicunt Iudaei; Legem habemus mulierem ad testimonium non venire', Allen 1968, p. 102.

11   *Legende von der Heiligen* Veronica', p. 189

12 *The Siege of Jerusalem*, ed. by Michael Livingstone (Kalamazoo MI, 2004), lines 249, 211.
13 *Gilte Legende*, ed. by Richard Hamer and Vida Russell, EETS OS315, 327, 328, 339 (Oxford, 2000, 2006, 2007, 2012). 4 vols.
14 Jacobus de Voragine, *Legenda aurea sanctorum, sive, Lombardica historia*, trans. by William Caxton (London, 1483), f. XVIIv.
15 Miri Rubin, *Mother of God: A History of the Virgin Mary* (New Haven, 2009), p. 85.
16 Rubin, p. 102.
17 S. Fein, 'Mary to Veronica: John Audelay's Sequence of Salutations to God-Bearing Women', *Speculum* 86 (2011), pp. 964-1009 (p. 965).
18 Swan, p. 20.
19 P. Moe, (ed.), *The Middle English Prose Translation of Roger d'Argenteuil's Bible en François* (Heidelberg, 1977), p. 72.
20 Barry Windeatt, (ed.), *The Book of Margery Kempe* (Cambridge, 2004), p. 191.
21 'Play 32, Procession to Calvary; Crucifixion' in *The N-Town Plays,* ed. by Douglas Sugano (Kalamazoo, 2007), lines 45-8.
22 See U.M. Lang, 'Origins of the Liturgical Veneration of the Roman Veronica', in *The European Fortune of the Roman Veronica*, pp.144-157.
23 *Legenda aurea sanctorum*, f. XVIIv.
24 *Siege of Jerusalem*, lines 261-64.
25 The *MED* reconstructs the etymology of *vernicle* as 'OF vernicle, veronicle, vars. of veronique; cp. AL vernicula, vernaculum, vars. of Veronica'.
https://quod.lib.umich.edu/m/middle-english-dictionary/dictionary?utf8=%E2%9C%93&search_field=hnf&q=vernicle
26 For a recent study on the Veronica Image of Christ in thirteenth-century England, see N. Morgan, 'Veronica' images and the office of the Holy Face in thirteenth-century England', in *The European Fortune of the Roman Veronica* pp. 84-99.
27 Quotation from the *MED*.
28 See D. Brunda, *Enseignes de Pelerinage et Enseignes Profanes* (Paris, 1996) and D. Webb, *Pilgrims and Pilgrimage in the Medieval West* (London, 1999).
29 *The incipit of Salve Sancta Facies* explains that the prayer carries an indulgence authorized by Boniface IV: '*Quicumque hanc salutacionem in honore Salvatoris per xx dies continuo devote dixerit, Bonefacius papa quartus concessit omnibus vere confessis et contritus plenam remissionem omnium peccatorum et hoc scriptum est apud Romam in ecclesia Sancti Petri coram altare salvatoris.'*

http://manuscripts.org.uk/chd.dk/tutor/veronica.html
30 V. Krishan, (ed.), *The Alliterative Morte Arthure: A Critical Edition* (New York, 1976).
31 *The Riverside Chaucer*, ed. by L. Benson and F. N. Robinson (Oxford, 1987).
32 The well-known *Incipit* of the Pardoner's *Prologue* quotes the Latin saying *Radix malorum est cupiditas*, ironically to be applied to the Pardoner himself.
33 San Marino, Huntington Library MS EL 26 C 9 (f. 138r). A reproduction is available at https://hdl.huntington.org/digital/collection/p15150coll7/id/264
34 W. Langland, *The Vision of Piers Plowman*, ed. by J.M. Dent and E.P. Dutton (London and New York, 1978).
35 Small flasks of consecrated water or oil commonly carried by pilgrims returning from a shrine.
36 Possibly miniatures of a pilgrim's staff or crosses, probably indicating the number of pilgrimages undertaken.
37 W. Kamowski, 'Chaucer and Wyclif: God's Miracles against the Clergy's Magic', *Chaucer Review* 37 (2002), 5.
38 John the Blind Audelay, *Poems and Carols* (Oxford, Bodleian Library MS Douce 302), ed. by Susanna Fein (Kalamazoo, 2009), https://d.lib.rochester.edu/teams/text/fein-audelay-poems-and-carols-salutations
39 C. Horstmann, (ed.), *Yorkshire writers: Richard Rolle of Hampole, an English father of the church and his followers* (London, 1895-1896), p. 95.
40 Ibid.
41 *The Shewings of Julian of Norwich*, ed. by Georgia Ronan Crampton (Kalamazoo, 1994), lines 346-9 https://d.lib.rochester.edu/teams/text/the-shewings-of-julian-of-norwich-part-1
42 John the Blind Audelay, *Poems and Carols*, W27.
43 A piece of linen used in Biblical times to wrap the head of a corpse before burial. Here: the cloth of St. Veronica, on which an image of Christ's face was believed to be imprinted.
44 John the Blind Audelay, *Poems and Carols*, W4.
45 *Legends of the Holy Rood; Symbols of the Passion and Cross Poems*, ed. by Richard Morris. (London, 1871), p. 192
46 *Legends of the Holy Rood*, pp. 171-172.
47 The image is reproduced in *Legends of the Holy Rood*, p. 170.
48 The relationship between images and indulgences is treated for example in F. Lewis, 'Rewarding Devotion: Indulgences and the Promotion of Images', *Studies in Church History*, 56 (2016), 179-194. For a general view on

English indulgences, see N. Vincent, 'Some Pardoners' Tales: the earliest English indulgences', *Transactions of the RHS*, 12 (2002), 23-58.

49 J-M, Sansterre, 2013, 'Variation d'une légende et genèse d'un culte entre la Jérusalem des origines, Rome et l'Occident : quelques jalons de l'histoire de Véronique et de la Veronica jusqu'à la fin du XIIIe siècle', in *Passages. Déplacements des hommes, circulation des textes et identités dans l'Occident médiéval*, ed. by J. Ducos and P. Henriet (2013), pp. 217-231 (p. 217). [In the last centuries of the Middle Ages, the image of Christ called Veronica enjoyed extraordinary veneration in the West].

50 C. Davidson, (ed.), *The York Corpus Christi Plays* (Kalamazoo, 2011) https://d.lib.rochester.edu/teams/publication/davidson-the-york-corpus-christi-plays

51 The earliest evidence for the existence of the cycle at York dates from the late 14th century; the only extant manuscript (British Library Add MS 35290) was made between 1463 and 1477. The *N-town Plays* appear to have belonged to a group of travelling players; the manuscript (British Library Cotton MS Vespasian D VIII) was put together by a scribe in the late 15th century.

52 E. Klafter, 'The feminine mystic: Margery Kempe's Pilgrimage to Rome as an *imitatio Birgittae*', in *Gender in Medieval Places, Spaces and Thresholds*, ed. by V. Blud, D. Heath and E. Klafter (London, 2019), p. 124.

53 John Capgrave, *Ye Solace of Pilgrimes*, ed. by C. A. Mills (London, 1911), p. 63.

54 F. J. Furnivall, *The Stacions of Rome*, EETS, o.s. 25 (1867), p. 3.

55 Ranulf Higden, *Polychronicon Ranulphi Higden maonachi Cestrensis; together with the English translations of John Trevisa and of an unknown writer of the fifteenth century*, ed. by Churchill Babington and Joseph Rawson Lumby (London, 1865-86), vol. 4, p. 323.

56 Jacobus de Voragine, *Legenda aurea sanctorum, sive, Lombardica historia*, trans. by William Caxton (London, 1483), f. XVIIv.

57 Windeatt, 'Vera Icon?', p. 59.

58 See Lang, 'Origins of the Liturgical Veneration'.

The Relationship of Brontology and the 'Regimen of Health' in the Later Middle Ages

Janet Walls

University of Reading

Introduction

The subject of this article is the contextual relationships of late-medieval brontologies (or thunder prognostics) to regimen of health texts, which is a notable occurrence in later manuscript examples. The brontology is a text of ancient origin which makes predictions from the timing of thunder events, surviving in several types of manuscript into the Late Middle Ages.[1] The 'Regimen of health' texts are treatises known by several names, including *Regimen Salernitatem, Conservanda sanitatis,* Governal of health and the Dietary, referred to hereafter as 'the regimen'. The material is derived from Galenic teaching on the governing of health by the four elements from which the universe is made (earth, air, fire and water).[2] It advises for and against certain activities and practices of diet, exercise, even commerce and education according to the months of the year (on the supposition that they were differently affected by planetary influences). It was supplemented and developed through the Middle Ages, culminating in a large number of late-medieval English versions.[3] Brontologies in English date from as early as the tenth century, but were little regarded until the late nineteenth century when they became subject to scrutiny by scholars of philology, Old English, and folklore, over a period of around fifty years.[4] These writers approached the function of the brontology as naturally of interest to those involved in day-to-day responses to the weather, principally farmers or estate managers. Max Förster, writing on Middle English 'thunder books' in the early twentieth century, treated the brontology separately from the compilations of texts on broader topics of astromedicine or practical science with which they are associated, terming them *kleinliteratur* (or 'lesser writings').[5] However, with regard to the late-medieval manuscript contexts of brontologies and regimen in the same textual groupings, there is no association to agriculture.[6] Latterly, Heinrich Henel, then Curt Bühler, realigned brontology to such groupings of astrological texts, particularly those in the field of medicine, and more recently, Roy Liuzza has written on the difficulty of categorising brontologies and identifying their sources.[7] He suggests the great variety of the late-medieval brontology texts, and the manuscripts in which they are found, is evidence of individualised uses of the texts, rather than a large range of differently defined genres, in the same manner that Clare Lees defines homilies as unique speech events.[8] It is in this textual environment that brontology was often grouped with regimen.[9]

The history of the regimen, prior to this point in time, also one of adaptation and revision, was investigated by Luis García-Ballester in the 1990s, in a study of the influences of Islamicate physicians on the formation and interests of later-medieval regimen texts.[10] Carole Rawcliffe has also written on the wide-ranging applications of the regimen texts, from the political sphere (in the context of wider works of governance), to the maintenance of the balance of mind and body and even public health, through advice on hygiene.[11] Marilyn Nicoud defines the thirteenth to fifteenth centuries as the apogee of the text's popularity throughout mainland Europe, the different contexts there resulting in many attributions becoming attached to them. Christopher Bonfield's PhD thesis deals with this phenomenon in England, in particular, its popularity at times of outbreaks of plague, or other dread diseases.[12]

In a definitive work on all types of Anglo-Saxon prognostic up to the twelfth century, Sándor Chardonnens shows that early brontologies and a single contemporary regimen text were grouped with other prognostics in manuscript compilations, but not with each other.[13] He discusses the origins of these groupings in relation to Faith Wallis' theory of 'associative attraction', in which the use of the lunar months as time markers for prognostication, or advice, explains the inclusion of the texts into groupings of computus material. This indicates that the appropriate rules and practices for the maintenance of one's health which the texts offer were to be applied on this monthly basis with the same expectations as a prognostic. Although they may have these origins in the regulation of time by computus, in the later-medieval texts the choice of months as time markers is more clearly integrated into astromedicine by skilfully delineating the fluctuating, physical influences of the moon upon health during its cycle. The 'Sphere of life and death' (also known as the 'Sphere of Apuleius') is another text closely associated with astromedical practice and the subject of Joanne Edge's doctoral thesis and recent article.[14] The increasingly secular and applied, professional role of 'the sphere' which she discovered resonates with the manuscripts containing both brontology and regimen, and indeed, a number of manuscripts with 'sphere' texts also have both these texts within the same grouping (MSS A, B, E, H, I, K, L, P – see manuscript key at conclusion of this paper).[15]

Characteristics of the texts

Regimen texts prescribe seasonally appropriate food, drink, modes of living and medical treatment using a framework of monthly administration. This aimed to not only alleviate physical conditions, but actively improve the quality and length of an individual's life by preventing people from dying of something preventable, or strengthening their overall physical condition thereby improving their ability to fight disease or overcome injuries. The texts in question are now described in outline, firstly, with an examination of their dates and secondly, their use of language. The samples are difficult to date precisely, due to the composite nature of the manuscripts in which they are found, in some cases material spanning hundreds of years is contained within one volume.[16] Where there is no firm dating evidence recorded by cataloguers over time, palaeography and references to the time of composition of associated calendar texts were referred to. The texts are all from the fourteenth and fifteenth centuries, a time of notable increase in the number of surviving brontology texts from England, from only handfuls previously. Before the end of the thirteenth century none of these texts were associated with regimen. The regimens survived in larger numbers, though there are still less than twenty dating from the thirteenth century; like the brontologies, there was a steady increase in copying from the end of the fourteenth century. The dates are distributed as follows: of sixteen sample manuscripts, two have predominantly fourteenth-century brontology and regimen texts and one other has texts datable to the cusp of the fifteenth century. All of the remaining texts are fifteenth century, therefore the phenomenon of placing brontology and the regimen in the same textual groupings is very much of that century.

Middle English is by far the most common language for the texts, but Latin versions can be found in both the fourteenth and fifteenth centuries, as follows; fourteenth century brontology (2), regimen (1), all in the same manuscript; fifteenth century brontology (3), regimen (3), spread over four manuscripts. The fifteenth-century examples show that the Latinity of one of the texts does not mean the manuscript employs Latin universally, highlighting the probability of different sources within manuscripts, down to the level of individual texts in groupings. Overall, the selection of texts does not seem to rely on a preference for one language over another, but is most likely attributable to the availability of a chosen text in that form. For example, there are two regimens in a fourteenth-century manuscript (MS A), one is a form called the 'dietary', the other a 'governal of health', the first is in Latin, the other in English, but they are quite different – the English does not translate the Latin.[17] Both MSS C and O have Latin brontologies, as does MS G, along with two English ones and each is different from the others.

This scope of readership in vernacular writing has been discussed by Päiva Pahta and Irma Taavitsainen, and Clare Jones, in relation to discourse communities.[18] Pahta and Taavitsainen make the important point that, apart from the choice of language, the level of technical detail and didactic explanation are also significant in determining who was using texts and how and it is true that the sample textual groupings do display this sort of detail. Jones describes practices involving the collection of material (and ideas) by gift or exchange and a resultant interest in *experimenta*, in the sense of practical approaches to medicine, in response to epidemics, which fits very well with the use of regimen for prophylaxis. Similarly, Nancy Siraisi's assessment of the relative sophistication of English texts in medical books in the fifteenth century also aids understanding of this material, in diminishing the perception of vernacularisation as a simplification of learned material for the less educated.[19] We can see a glimpse of this sort of milieu in MS H, a sample providing rare evidence of the people involved in the book's production. It was written in a single hand, in Latin. The colophon identifies the scribe as Simon Wysbech, student of canon law at Cambridge, and states that he wrote the book for Robert Boxford, a local landowner.

To give an idea of the composition of a manuscript with brontology and regimen in their diverse textual contexts, vignettes of two of the samples follow: MSS C and G.

MS C is a good quality, composite volume from the late fourteenth century, too large to be easily portable (275 mm x 215 mm), with the appearance of a reference book. A semi-quadrata book hand is used and in the textual grouping of the brontology and regimen initials are embellished with red and blue ink and major initials burnished with gold. All the texts in MS C are in Latin – there are texts of university medical training, calendar and lunar and solar eclipse tables for the meridian of Oxford University with a date of 1380. The contents table groups the texts into two parts, firstly listing a medical treatise with attributions to the works of Islamicate scholars. The second part is on humoral theory, attributed to 'Johannes Mesue', with a focus on the effects of different climates on the body. The grouping of the brontology is part of this categorised under the heading '*signa astroligica*', it commences with a bloodletting text, based on astromedicine, i.e. the safety of the practice according to lunar activity, followed by the brontology. Two more major prognostics follow; the revelations of the prophet Ezra (predictions from Christmas) and Christmas Day prognostics per se, the latter concerned with predicting the weather for the year ahead from the day of the week on which Christmas Day falls. These prognostics are the precursor to a long regimen grouping dealing with the effects of diet and temperature on demeanour, interspersed with Petrus Hispanus' (who was to become Pope John XXI) *Thesaurus Pauperum*, ff. 87v-106r).[20]

MS G is composed of two, long regimens. The book is very small (100 mm x 85 mm) and would have easily fitted into a pocket; it seems like a handy, personal manual. Its quality is good, it seems professionally produced, written in a very clear, semi-quadrata book hand. The large initials are missing (although the initial to be placed there is marked in ink), which could be interpreted as an optional extra which the person who commissioned it decided against. Despite its appearance of a personal reference book and the fact that the majority of the texts are in English, a large amount of the regimen material is on astromedical skills. The extensive grouping of the brontologies includes an abbreviated regimen attributed to 'Johnne de Burdeue' (John of Burgundy). One of the brontologies is presented in Latin and it is assumed that the text was left so because it was the language of the original exemplar (e.g. a university textbook), but that this presented no obstacle to the owner or compiler of the book. The very dark and dirty end folios indicate that it had seen some use, also showing that it did not have a binding early in its life, rather was kept directly in a pocket or bag and frequently consulted.

Another important area of research is whether there is any evidence of intended, practical associations between the texts, or was their grouping together less deliberate than that? Further to this, a change or development had taken place in the use of the texts from ecclesiastical, calendrical contexts, to a more popular, yet professional, use. The actual term 'regimen of health' only occurs as a title in one of the manuscripts samples here (MS C), it is more common amongst the wider corpus of English regimen texts without brontologies. In most sample manuscripts the term comes from earlier manuscript cataloguers' alignment of the text to the structures and strictures of ecclesiastical (and later, university-based) medical training, in which a regimen is defined as a set of rules to be followed. The 'Governal of Health', an alternative and more common title in the sample, infers that good health is within the reach of the reader if precise governance of oneself is practised, resonating with popular, late-medieval guidance on wider governance in political or commercial spheres, it resembles works such as Thomas Hoccleve's *De regimine principium,* written in the 1410s and the later work of Niccolò Machiavelli, 'The Prince'.[21] However, the regimen should not only be thought of as a self-help guide to better health, wealth and success for those without access to doctors or other advisers, but, equally, a part of the toolkit of medical practitioners, along with knowledge of astrology and humoral theory.[22] A good example of this is MS J, consisting of two, long, technical regimens with brontology incorporated (ff. 1r-39r, 41r-56v).

The Sample Texts

The total of the surviving English regimen of health and brontology texts will now be assessed, along with the proportion of manuscripts with both brontology and regimen texts to understand the extent of the texts throughout the period in question. There are two hundred and twenty-three late-medieval regimen texts from England, considerably outnumbering the fifty-seven brontologies, a big increase from the early Middle Ages.[23] Brontologies existed in rather niche and specialised astromedical contexts compared with other kinds of prognostic texts which, by the late-medieval period, number in excess of one thousand.[24] The brontologies came into contact with regimen texts as a result of groupings of applied science texts in nineteen manuscripts, giving a total of twenty individual brontologies and twenty-five regimens.

The Brontologies

Are the brontology texts in these manuscripts similar to each other, or is a degree of individualisation evident? If so, to what extent? This query does not seek analogues or exemplars of the texts, but to identify areas of interest and practice to explain textual relationships to regimens. Bearing in mind that each brontology covers several matters of concern for the future, the texts can be categorised using the following broadly defined attributes;

    a)   showing classical, or Mediterranean influences
    b)   referring to medical or health matters
    c)   having meteorological details
    d)   referencing travel and merchant activities
    e)   focused on agriculture

The sample manuscripts are listed below, according to these categories:

	showing classical or Mediterranean influences	referring to medical or health matters	having meteorological details	referencing travel and merchant activities	focused on agriculture
A	✓				
B		✓			
C			✓		
D					✓
E 1		✓			
E 2			✓		
F					✓
G					✓
H		✓			
I					✓
J				✓	
K					✓
L				✓	
M					✓
N	✓				
O					✓

Although medicine is not an overall preoccupation within these brontologies, they all incorporate some health issues (both mental and physical and especially in seasonal contexts), which makes them relevant to the concerns of the regimen. For example, the August entry in **MS D** (rendered in modern English); '(thunder in) August betokens great heart's envy and sickness and much pilgrimage' (f. 60r) and the September entry in **MS E (2)**; 'Thunder in September signifies many men shall be sick, great winds, plenty of corn and much striving among the people and much envy' (f. 70r). The most individual of the brontology texts in the sample are found in MSS E and I, and appositely, they are also regimen texts, the brontologies are incorporated into the regimen of health treatises themselves, thereby creating a multipurpose reference tool. This is demonstrated in the entries for January (Aquarius in the case of MS E) which consist of the following combinations of items:

MS E (1 of 2 brontologies)
- list of perilous days when the sun is in Aquarius (approximately, from the third week of January to the third week of February)
- brontology
- the humours of Aquarius
- the element of Aquarius (air)
- favourable activities for the period: build castles or houses, marry, let blood, begin long-term projects
- unfavourable activities: do not do medicine to the legs, from the knee to the ankle, do not go on a short journey or commence anything short-term, do not cut the thighs, or their sinews down to the last part of the ankle

MS I
- drink white wines
- forbear bloodletting
- list of perilous days in the month
- brontology
- mist prognostic (very rare)
- lunary, or moon prognostic

The respective scribes express quite different concerns, with few points of reference between the texts. Even the advice for bloodletting is contradictory, at least for some part of January (as they are not dealing with precisely the same month period). In MS E, bloodletting is advised throughout the zodiac period of dominance of Aquarius, but advised against throughout January in MS I. Other contrasting points are the very specific medical advice in MS E, explaining how to avoid unsafe cutting into the body, with the injunction to avoid bloodletting altogether in MS I and the lack of reference to dietary matters in MS E. Although offering different approaches as regimens of health, the texts concur in the inclusion of brontology and its placement after the texts on perilous days. They speak of quite different practices, the second does not need to be applied by a medical professional, but the first certainly does, very probably a surgeon.

The other examples of brontologies in textual groupings with regimen share some basic prognostications with each other, forewarning of great winds, the state of the grain crop and the likelihood of battle if thunder is heard in the early part of the year. However, notably different elements arise in each grouping as the entries progress through the year, evincing the individual interests of their compilers. Starting with the two above manuscripts, MS E has a unique pilgrimage text and the mist prognostic in MS I is virtually unknown anywhere else.[25] MS A has an uncommon reference to large numbers of creeping creatures in Aries and given that the few current species of native British reptiles inhabit only the warmer parts of the country in small numbers, this prognostic speaks of the text's origins in the warmer, drier countries of the classical, or Mediterranean, world. The MS B entry for June contains the political hot potato of the likelihood of the equalisation of the balance of wealth between rich and poor. The MS J entry for August rather starkly evokes the realities of medical practice, 'sickness of many folk, there shall the common profit be done'. MS K is another brontology integrated with regimen, featuring, amongst other things, travel advice, for example, when the sun in Gemini, the traveller should undertake a journey as they will find a friend. In MS L, rhyming verse resonant of 'occupations of the months' texts (in which advice is given for seasonally appropriate activities) is incorporated, stating that if thunder is heard in February, the rich will lie low and (it will be) a good year to sow.

The Regimen

A high degree of individualisation is found in the brontologies grouped with regimens, including in the elements of combined brontology and regimen texts such as MSS E and I, above, so is it the case that the regimen texts are equally personalised? The first piece of evidence for this is in the naming of the texts. There is only one example originally called 'the regimen of health' and not so-termed by the cataloguers, in the Latin version, '*De regimine sanitatis et de dieta*' in MS C (ff. 107r-123r). Three others are called 'governals', MSS A, G (1) and J, highlighting a concern with long-term care and maintenance of the body. The one example of a *conservanda sanitatis*, MS A (regimen 1) is similar in tone to this and there is one dietary, MS G (2), (which does not only refer to food and drink, but the regulation of health more generally). Otherwise, the scribe, or compiler of the work simply incorporated the text into longer health treatises of their own composition for their own use, as discussed above, without the need for a title. There is no set placement of the brontologies in regimen groupings, they appear both before and after the regimen texts. When this is the former, it could be argued that they were intended for reference before seeking advice in the regimen, if after, as a check and balance on the regimen and so reinforcing the favourability, or otherwise, of medical procedures such as bloodletting. In both cases, a dynamic interaction of the brontology with the regimen is indicated.

Regimen attributions provide further evidence of the individualisation of the texts. Thirteen of the twenty-five regimen texts have an attribution of some kind. Such attributions can be understood as devices to enhance the authority of the text and, at the same time, advertise the education and training of the scribe. The most frequently occurring are the three regimens attributed to Galen, a Greek physician active in the second and third centuries CE.[26] This attribution indicates a formal, medical training, as Galen's anatomical and medical works were part of the university medical curriculum.[27] The next most common attribution is to John Lydgate (mentioned twice). This is to be expected, as Lydgate, a prolific fifteenth-century writer, was the author of a popular Latin regimen of health (from which he made his own English translation), known in English as the 'Dietary'.[28] Lydgate's regimen concludes with a sceptical commentary about the commercialisation of medicine, at the expense of an apothecary and two medical masters.[29] One of the two regimens in MS H also has this title, without attributing it to Lydgate. A further attribution is to John of Burgundy, known by various Anglo-Norman sounding versions of his name, such as 'John de Bordeue'. He was another fourteenth-century writer on health matters, famous for a plague treatise and works on epidemiology.[30] Other attributions also refer to medical practice and training, for example, MSS B and C are formed as a letter containing medical advice allegedly brought from Hippocrates' tomb by 'Caesar'.[31] Like Galen's, the much earlier works of Hippocrates were a prominent feature of the medical curriculum. Similarly purporting to be a record of the medical advice of an ancient 'doctor' to a famous, historical figure, a letter is also attributed to Aristotle, writing to Alexander, on this occasion via the translation of 'John of Spain' which traces it back to Islamicate Spain.[32] An attribution to Arnaldus de Villa Nova in MS C also provides a putative connection to medical education as he taught for many years during the thirteenth and early fourteenth centuries at the University of Montpellier medical school, where he also translated medical works from Arabic. MS F has a much less common attribution to Thomas Forestier.[33] His fame came from his expertise with the sweating sickness, a disease first encountered in England as a virulent epidemic in the late fifteenth century. This piece of evidence, of course, places the composition of this regimen firmly at the end of the period. Fundamentally, then, these various attributions are advertising the medical credentials of the regimen and its compilers. Do the companion brontologies also display similar medical provenances?

Brontology attributions

Commencing with the title 'verse from Salerno' (the famous, medieval medical centre in Italy), the MS A brontology clearly belongs in a medical grouping, it has an identified patron (or renowned person) to endorse it, '*ad Countissam de Hermand*', with a further attribution to one 'Thomas'.[34] In addition to the attribution to John of Burgundy, as noted above, the MS G brontologies are part of a regimen grouping supplied with several attributions; 'after the description of many other diverse doctors, that is to say, Bernard, Austin, Plato, Ptolemy, Sydrac, Aristotle, Avicenna, Galen and Hippocrates'. MS I is also integrated into a regimen and has an explicit stating that the prognostics were found in 'books written and found by wise clerks to teach unlearned men and to make them wise'.[35] The explicit in MS J is very similar to MS G, in emphasising medical authorities, but without the reference to Hippocrates; 'following antique doctors. A worthy doctor made this little treatise after the description of diverse doctors, Saints Bernard,

Augustine, Plato and Ptolemy, Aristotle and Galen, Sydrac and Avicenna and many other doctors according with the same'.[36] The majority of the brontologies, however, are unattributed, which may, again, simply be because they were the personal compositions of various practitioners recording and expounding aspects of medical care and long-term wellbeing appropriate to their own practice or interests.

Since most brontologies do not have clear attributions to authoritative sources, should the reason for the text's inclusion in professionally focused regimen textual groupings be sought in its nature as a special, meteorological influence on the humours in their governing of health and wellbeing? If so, were other types of weather prognostic also referred to in this way? The balancing of the four humours was regarded as an important astromedical skill in the Late Middle Ages, essential for both long and short-term health. For some practitioners, an understanding of all aspects of weather influences (based on the four seasons, corresponding to the four humours) would have been an important part of this. In the sample manuscripts, this interest is demonstrated in MS K, which has a specialised text on dispositions and qualities of the weather within the regimen and brontology grouping and MSS B, C, F, G, O, which have further weather prognostics, with the brontology, based on either winds or sunshine.[37] What can be discerned about these groupings from the way the weather texts are used? Perhaps they represent a belt and braces approach, where multiple weather texts were available for comparison. As is usually the case in this sample of manuscripts, there is no set pattern to the weather texts' placement, although in each case the brontology takes precedence before other forms of weather. In MS B, the regimen is prior to the brontology and the brontology is followed by sunshine and wind. In MS C, the order is brontology, wind and sunshine, then regimen. In MS G brontology and a sunshine prognostic are part of a regimen grouping. A significant feature of this small subgroup with extra weather texts, however, is that they contain many apothecary and herbal texts, correlating the growth of plants, their resultant efficacy for medicinal purposes with knowledge of the weather. One reason for including a brontology in this is that the obvious ill-effects of plant damage from thunder storms would naturally have been of interest, but less well-known, is the fact that, although thunderstorms can be devastating, there is also scientific evidence that the thunder event itself benefits plants, due to a large release of nitrogen compounds into the atmosphere afterwards.[38]

Other texts

Finally, a brief survey of other material in the groupings. The most obvious texts to aid consultation of a regimen of health are other prognostics, forewarning of times of the year when health was endangered because of unfavourable planetary activity, for example. If this is the case in these groupings, which other texts were grouped together with brontology and regimen? The table, below, lists which diagnostic and prognostic texts are in the same groupings as regimen and brontology.

Manuscript	Texts grouped with, or part of, regimen, in addition to a brontology
MS A	zodiac prognostic, total of three different regimen texts (before and after brontology), 'Donet of Physic' (humoral theory for doctors), uroscopy, plague, several herbals, materia medica
MS B	zodiac prognostic, medical prognostic, Christmas prognostic, perilous days, charms
MS C	*Liber Almansoris* (medical textbook translated from Arabic by Gerard of Cremona) lunary, nativity prognostic, herbal, humoral theory, New Year prognostic, zodiac theory for medicine
MS D	herbals, Christmas prognostic, charms, uroscopy
MS E (1)	plague, zodiac theory, properties of planets, bloodletting
MS E (2)	perilous days, canicular days, onomancy, lunary, New Year prognostic, properties of planets, bloodletting
MS F	herbals, alchemy, humoral theory, practical case history guide, Christmas prognostic, solar prognostic, lunary

MS G	prognostic by dominical letter, Christmas prognostic, bloodletting
MS H	herbals, ophthalmology, New Year prognostic, perilous days, bloodletting
MS I	lunary, dominical letter, Yule, weather, perilous days, humoral theory, bloodletting, dentistry
MS J	the whole grouping is called the governal of health; Christmas prognostic, humoral theory
MS K	bloodletting, humoral theory, medical prognostic by the months, perilous days, computus, weather science
MS L	medical recipes, herbals, ophthalmology, dentistry, genital and urinary medicine, signs of life and death medical prognostic, onomancy
MS M	perilous days, bloodletting, physiognomy prognostic, onomancy, properties of planets, lunary
MS N	properties of planets, herbals, medical recipes, humoral theory, Esdras (prophet Ezra) prognostic, New Year's Day prognostic, physiognomy prognostic, perilous days, zodiac theory (how it affects the humours of the body), bloodletting
MS O	herbals, dental, genital and urinary, fevers, poisons, gynaecology and obstetrics

As expected, there are numerous prognostics and the Christmas Day and New Year's Day ones which determine the favourability for health and other matters for the year ahead are present, although their use is less frequent in astromedicine generally. The brontologies among them are usually the closest prognostics to the regimen itself, then to any herbals, perilous days and bloodletting texts. Only one manuscript context (MS O) does not display overt knowledge of the precepts of late-medieval astromedicine. The plurality of herbals is of interest in itself, displaying an academic approach in the presentation of several sources on aspects of herbs; their growth, treatment as medicines and even the best times to trade for them. Plague texts are also a feature of these groupings, bad weather was thought to have the potential to develop into bad humours in the air (known as 'miasma') which it was firmly believed caused infections. The wider groupings, therefore, are applied prognostic sections in the sense of the early groupings of prognostics identified by Chardonnens, but now interlaced with much practical, medical theory and frequent references to apothecary practice. This also includes specialist knowledge of ophthalmology, dentistry, gynaecology and obstetrics, and medicine of the genital and urinary system. It is also notable that bloodletting texts are often the last items in the groupings, so it seems in these cases that the procedure was to be carried out after all the other texts in the grouping had been consulted.

In conclusion, whether brontology and regimen had continued their journey together in English contexts from the early Middle Ages, or the association came about as a result of a continuing interest in humoral theory, in particular the balancing of the humours to maintain health, stimulated by contemporary epidemics, the grouping of months brontology with regimen, in particular, is key to its wider development from the earlier Middle Ages to a companion text for practical medicine. Another important finding is that, in these groupings, where there is one regimen, often at least one other is found and packaged with them, more than one version of relevant, useful prognostic texts, like the brontology, and in some cases, further weather texts. This multiplicity of brontology texts and other prognostics exists to a greater extent than in manuscripts without regimen and only brontology. Practitioners were giving a range of information from which to make choices about diagnosis and prognosis for individual patients, in their particular circumstances. The foundations of these groupings lie in medical education, with a historic linking of regimen and prognostics for medical purposes first found in the works of Hippocrates. So, this, along with attributions for regimen, points to late-medieval, medical practitioners as the main driving force behind such composite manuscripts and compilations; in particular, when the groupings of astromedical texts incorporate brontology. Where there are attributions in the regimen, they display the sort of knowledge seemingly designed to impress patients, or for wider public transmission. The many regimen texts in groupings with brontology without attribution also show the compilers not simply copying standard medical texts, but creating their own works. Likewise, the lack of use of the term 'regimen' in these contexts indicates incorporation into the work of those who already knew what the text was. This grouping practice culminated in the late medieval period with Swiss Army knife-style, intercalated texts, where mental boxes could be ticked during a consultation, secure in the knowledge that all areas had been covered in order to achieve the most thorough diagnosis and prognosis. The two new findings from this sample are firstly, that this type of textual grouping relates to the intricate humoral balancing required for medical specialisms and that brontology was regarded as significant in this.[39] Secondly, bloodletting texts are often closely associated, so, in terms of use, brontology is frequently positioned between the theoretical care and long-term approach of the regimen and the everyday practice of letting blood as the quickest, most practical way of balancing the humours.

MS short Reference	Manuscript
MS A	Oxford, Bodleian Library MS Digby 95
MS B	London, British Library, Sloane MS 2584
MS C	London, British Library Sloane MS 282
MS D	Cambridge, St. John's College MS K.49
MS E	London, Wellcome Library MS 8004
MS F	London, British Library, Additional MS 27582
MS G	London, British Library, Sloane MS 989
MS H	San Marino, Huntington Library MS HM 1336
MS I	San Marino, Huntington Library MS HM 64
MS J	Oxford, Bodleian Library MS Radcliffe Trust e30
MS K	Oxford, Bodleian Library MS Bodley 591
MS L	New Haven, Yale University, Beinecke Rare Book and Manuscript Library, Takamiya MS 61
MS M	London, British Library, Sloane MS 213
MS N	London, British Library, Sloane MS 1609
MS O	London, British Library, Egerton MS 2852
MS P	Cambridge, Gonville and Caius College MS 457/395

Notes

1   *Vade mecum* (or physicians' portable reference books), university textbooks, household books, folded almanacs.

2   'the regimen from Salerno', 'the conservation of health'. Medieval doctors
were concerned with the four elements' control of the four bodily humours:
black bile, yellow bile, blood and water.
3   Additional Moses Maimonides etc., English – for example, that of John of
Burgundy, a fourteenth-century physician from Liège, author of *De
epidemia.*
4   Commencing with B. Assman, '*Eine Regel Über den Donner*', *Anglia* 10
(1888), 185.
5   Max Förster, '*Die Kleinliteratur des Aberglaubens im Altenenglischen*',
Archiv für das Studium der Neueren Sprachen und Literaturen 110 (1903),
346-58 (p. 350), see also '*Beiträge zur Mittelenglischen Volkskunde*', 120
(1908), 45, 128.
6   Apart from a few instances of classical or mediterranean world-sounding
reference to viticulture in brontologies.
7   Roy Liuzza, 'What the Thunder Said: Anglo-Saxon Brontologies and the
Problem of Sources', *The Review of English Studies* 55 (2004), 1-23 (pp.
22-23).
8   Heinrich Henel, '*Altenglischer Mönchsaberglaube*', *Englische Studien* 69
(1934–35), pp. 329-349.
9   See C.F. Bühler 'Astrological Prognostication in MS. 775 of the Pierpont
Morgan Library', *Modern Language Notes* 56 (1941), 351-355. Bühler
notes the brontology's astrological focus, it is part of a booklet dedicated to
applied astrology, with two full-page diagrams, a zodiac man and planetary
alignment chart.
10   Luis García-Ballester in Sheila Cambell, Bert Hall and David Klausner
(eds.) *Health, Disease and Healing in Medieval Culture* (Centre for
Medieval Studies, 1992), pp. 119-131.
11   See Carole Rawcliffe, 'The Concept of Health in Late Medieval Society' in
*Le interazioni fra economia e ambiente biologico nell'Europe
preindustriale secc. XIII-XVIII* ed. by Simonetta Cavaciocchi (Florence,
2010), pp. 317-334, (pp. 317, 319, 320, 325).
12   See Marilyn Nicoud, *Les régimes de santé au moyen âge: naissance et
diffusion d'une ecriture medicale en Italie*, I-II, *Ecole Francaise de Rome*,
(Rome, 2007); Christopher A. Bonfield, *The* Regimen Sanitatis *and its
Dissemination in England, c. 1348–1550*, University of East Anglia,
Unpublished PhD, 2006, pp. 36-44. There were three major outbreaks in
England from 1360 to 1479 (also other epidemic diseases, such as sweating
sickness, or *sudor anglicus,* arriving in 1485), *Maria A. Spyrou et al,*
'Phylogeography of the second plague pandemic revealed through analysis
of historical Yersinia pestis genomes', *Nature Communications 10 (2019-*

10-02), p. 4470. Also, note the sweating sickness (or *sudor anglicus*) of 1485 as a major contender for the later texts.

13 Lászlo Sandor Chardonnens, *Anglo-Saxon Prognostics, 900–1100: Study and Texts,* (Leiden, 2007), p. 30.

14 Joanne Edge, *Nomen Omen: the 'Sphere of Life and Death in England, c. 1200c. 1500,* Royal Holloway, University of London.

15 In sample MSS A, B, E, H, I, K, L, P – see, p. 17, for manuscript key.

16 Sloane 282, for example, material from the thirteenth to the seventeenth centuries.

17 The first commonly attributed to John Lydgate, the second to John of Burgundy.

18 Päiva Pahta and Irma Taavitsainen, 'Vernacularisation of scientific and medical writing in its sociohisttorical context' in Irma Taavitsainen and Päiva Pahta (eds.) *Medical and Scientific Writing in Late Medieval English* (Cambridge, 2004), pp. 15-17; Clare Jones, 'Discourse communities and medical texts', ibid., *passim.*

19 Nancy Siraisi, *Medieval and Renaissance Medicine: An Introduction to Knowledge and Practice* (Chicago, 1990), pp. 52-53.

20 Arnaldus de Villa Nova, *De regimine sanitatis et de dieta,* ff. 107r-123r; Aristotle's letter to Alexander the Great, *Epistola de sanitate tuenda ad Alexandrum,* translated by John of Spain, f. 123r.

21 Morgan 775 does contain a regimen of health text, but not in association with its brontology.

22 The range of people engaged in this is quite wide and the terminology for, and definition of, medical and paramedical practitioners at this time is varied and obscure, fully university-trained doctors were physicians, surgeons received their education from a craft guild, some were interested in both aspects (see the renowned, late-fourteenth-century surgeon John of Arderne, see Oxford Dictionary of National Biography entry https://www.oxforddnb.com/view/10.1093/ref:odnb/9780198614128.001. 0001/odnb-9780198614128-e-636?rskey=N4ja2n&result=2) and there were others who practised a combination of these skills (along with astrology) and who may have received some university tuition, but not a full degree, simply calling themselves 'doctor', or 'leech'. Also, some apothecaries did not limit themselves to the preparation of medicines, but took a more hands-on approach.

23 From the eTKeVK2 database of medical and scientific works.

24 This is the count of those listed in the eTKeVK2 database for the period, in English and Latin.

25 An early, twentieth-century reference gives a provenance for this text in Islamicate learning, but it was clearly not well-known or used in England;

Edward Robertson, 'Arab Weather Prognostics', *The Journal of the Royal Asiatic Society of Great Britain and Ireland*, 2 (1930), 377-389 (p. 384).

26 MSS I, K, L

27 Michael McVaugh, 'Galen in the Medieval Universities, 1200-1400' in Petros Bouras-Vallianatos and Barbara Zipser (eds.), *Brill's Companion to the Reception of Galen* (Leiden, 2019), 381-392 (pp. 382-383).

28 See Jake Walsh Morrissey, 'To Al Indifferent': The Virtues of Lydgate's 'Dietary', *Medium Ævum*, 84 (2015), 258-278 (p. 258).

29 Ibid.

30 Lister M. Matheson, '*Médecin sans Frontières?* The European Dissemination of John of Burgundy's Plague Treatise', *ANQ*, 18 (2005), 19-30 (p. 19). Another instance of concern for public hygiene.

31 See Pearl Kibre, 'Hippocratic Writings in the Middle Ages' *Bulletin of the History of Medicine*, 18 (1945), 371-412 (p. 392).

32 This is probably John of Seville (*Joahnnes Hispalensis*) sometimes mistranslated as 'John of Spain' (from a reading as '*Johannes Hispanus*', or '*Hispaniensis*'), a twelfth century scholar who translated works from arabic into Latin and produced a version of the *secreta scretorum*, which deals with regimen matters, see Lynn Thorndike, 'John of Seville', *Speculum*, 34 (1959), 20-38.

33 See Christie's auction catalogue for the first edition of his work in French, this has details of regimen recommendations in the book: https://www.christies.com/lot/lot-le-forestier-thomas-d-before-1513-contre-5573361/?

34 'From the Countess of Hermand', possibly a reference to the popular work of Thomas le Forestier on epidemic illness, see above.

35 Here in modernised English.

36 f. 39v

37 Twenty-four manuscripts.

38 D.G. DeCoursey et al, 'Thunderstorm in Agriculture and in Forest Management' in *Thunderstorms: The Thunderstorm in Human Affairs*, ed. by Edwin Kessler (Norman OK, 1981), pp. 85-112.

39 See MSS A, H, I, L, O.

Pleasure in Knighthood: The Private Construction of a Social Identity in *Partonopeu de Blois* and its Middle English Adaptation

Lucie Kaempfer

University of Düsseldorf

The construction of chivalric identity in medieval romance often exposes a conflict between private and public realization, or, in other words, pleasure and duty.[1] The hero must find fulfilment in the private sphere of love as well as assume his social and militant role. The chivalric hero thus becomes 'a divided self', as Simon Gaunt puts it, 'split between an impulse towards social integration and a counter-impulse towards socially alienating, but privately fulfilling desires.'[2] While this tension is certainly at play in the popular twelfth-century Old French romance *Partonopeu de Blois*, this coming-of-age story suggests that the experience of private pleasure enables the public performance of knighthood.[3] Before becoming a high-performing knight of the French army, the young Partonopeu is brought to a beautiful and exotic town where he discovers love and wallows for a year in the pleasures of sex, hunting and eating. His chivalric education thus appears to coincide with his sexual education, which is more broadly an education in pleasure. The present article argues that this romance places a particular emphasis on the private, the feminine and the emotional in the hero's construction of his knightly identity, suggesting a potential continuity between individual pleasure and the social performance of chivalric identity. A comparison with its fifteenth-century Middle English adaptation, which displays some unease with these elements, showcases the significance – and particularity – of the role of pleasure and the private sphere in the romance's depiction of masculine identity.[4] Having been written more than two centuries later, the Middle English version can be seen to follow some of the recognised trends of romance adaptation. Helen Cooper has thus shown that Middle English romances tend to be more pious than their continental sources, to display greater plausibility and to emphasise action.[5] The Middle English *Partonope of Blois* indeed follows some of these tendencies, while remaining mostly faithful to its source's plot and characterisation. By focusing on the private and emotional sphere, the present comparative study suggests that the romance, in both of its versions, offers an original model for the construction of chivalric identity, based on pleasure.

My analysis focuses on two sections of the plot that are crucial to developing Partonopeu's knightly identity in the Old French and Middle English versions of the romance, both of which happen outside the public realm of masculine knighthood. The first one is found at the start of the story and encompasses the introduction of the hero and his getting lost in a forest while hunting, up to his miraculous arrival in Chef d'Oire, where he meets the invisible Melior and remains for a year. This part of the tale constitutes the preparatory phase of Partonopeu's career as a knight. The second section of the tale that I will consider has many parallels with the first one. It starts after he has broken his promise to Melior to never try to see her and, having been rejected by her, flees alone into the forest to let himself die in despair. At this point, our hero is back in the forest where his knightly quest started and is once again rescued, put in a boat, and brought to a haven of safety and comfort by a lady – this time Melior's sister Urraque. This rescue is followed by the knighting ceremony, which makes official Partonopeu's identity as a knight. Both moments are thus crucial to the construction of his social identity as a man and a knight and yet they both happen in complete isolation from what Simon Gaunt calls 'the masculine social', in the feminine sphere of 'the supernatural and private'.[6]

Gaunt has famously argued that, while identity construction is monologic in the *chansons de geste,* male characters defining themselves 'in relation to other men', it is dialogic in the romances: 'a relationship with a woman thereby becomes a prerequisite of masculine [identity]'.[7] Love and the feminine bring the hero on a path of self-discovery that is private rather than group-motivated.[8] Yet that individuation can potentially alienate him: medieval romance often rests on a conflict between a process of individuation, actualized in a relationship with a woman, and one of integration in masculine society.[9] This contrast is exacerbated in the Partonopeu romance which famously blends features taken from the *chanson de geste* genre with courtly romance and the fairy lover motif.[10] It thus features long passages where the protagonist evolves in the masculine society of the battlefield and establishes homosocial bonds, alongside passages where he is completely removed from such society, in the sole company of women. These spaces appear incompatible throughout the romance until the final tournament that sees knights competing for Melior's hand in marriage. Interestingly, however, the identity of the male hero is mostly shaped within those feminine spaces. As has often been noted, Partonopeu is highly dependent on women in his self-actualization. Hosington thus argues that in both the Old French and the Middle English versions, 'the three main female characters – Melior, Uraque, Partonopeu's mother – influence him by each providing him with an identity': Melior that of secret lover, his mother the social identity of son, nephew of the King of France and 'defender of home and country', while Uraque helps him to find his own identity between 'love and social duty'.[11] I argue that, rather than each forcing a specific identity on him, Melior and Uraque provide the hero with spaces outside of masculine, chivalric society where his individual pleasure comes first. It is within these spaces that he can individually and emotionally adopt the social identity of knighthood. The fulfilment of his personal desires through material, sensual and emotional pleasure indeed play an unusually big role in this romance and seem to foster rather than hinder the formation of his social identity as a knight, a nobleman and ultimately a husband and emperor.

To become a knight, Partonopeu must first become a man: the story starts when Partonopeu is very young – only thirteen years old in the original French version. As Penny Eley notes, most of the translations make him less precocious, which suggests that Partonopeu's young age is 'a departure from [...] an accepted literary paradigm'.[12] Despite his young age, Partonopeu exhibits an impressive array of qualities: he is brave and valiant, humble and sweet (A 545-7), but above all he is extremely handsome.[13] Having spent three lines describing his moral qualities, the narrator quickly moves on to a long and detailed physical description. Here we find a second surprising element: Partonopeu is portrayed in a sexualized and feminized way, including sensual features, such as a kissable mouth. Eley and Simons have shown how this passage displays elements typical of portraits of women and argue that it contributes to turning Partonopeu into a sex object.[14] Throughout the first part of the French romance, Partonopeu thus possesses a dual status as a young boy (*damoisel* A 564, *enfant* A 629), and an object of sexual desire. Knighthood, and manhood, are not yet part of his identity.

The English adaptor, by contrast, substantially revises this first introduction. Significantly, he raises the age of the hero from thirteen to eighteen. Gretchen Mieszkowski proposes that this radical change might in fact be a scribal error.[15] The translator, she argues, does still refer to the protagonist as a child, and retains the plot elements that require Partonope to be very young: namely, that he has not yet been knighted and must thus wait several years before he is fit to marry Melior and become emperor. Yet, Mieszkowski does not entirely rule out the possibility of a deliberate change of age, noting that, as we shall see, the translator does seem 'uneasy about the initial bedroom scene', a discomfort that might justify the change.[16] For my part, I would argue that it emerges more clearly that the change is deliberate if we look to its direct context, as well as the other changes the translator makes. Most significantly, he first introduces Partonope as a man rather than a child ('thys manne' 506 and 522), although his youth is nonetheless acknowledged: he is a 'yonge man' (508) and 'off hys age he had no pere' (519).[17] Secondly, the translator entirely omits the long physical description present in the French version. This striking omission may indicate a reluctance to overtly sexualize the young protagonist: by making him an eighteen-year-old man and concentrating on his moral qualities, the translator resolves any uneasiness that may arise with regards to the sexualization of a child. Partonope, unlike his French counterpart, is, at the start, a manly hero: he is not a child and in no way feminized or sexualized.[18]

Masculinity in fact appears as a more important concept in the Middle English translation: the terms *manhode* and *manly* are firmly embedded in the construction of knighthood, while they lack any equivalent in the French original.[19] The word *manhode* appears twenty-one times in *Partonope*, rhyming six times with *knyghthode* and appearing a couple of times in close proximity to the term *chivalry*. All in all, the English adaptation makes much more explicit the question of gender identity and its significance in the construction of knightly identity. The term *manhode*, in Middle English, encompasses the implicit qualities and behaviour displayed by an exemplary man, defined by the *Middle English Dictionary* (*MED*) as 'manliness' as well as 'chivalric nature', 'courageous behaviour' or 'courteous behaviour'. Manhood and knighthood thus appear as interconnected forms of identity, which entail a form of social behaviour. This change in the conceptual terminology of chivalric identity makes the category of manhood much more explicit within the chivalric ethos and therefore impacts the representation of Partonope's coming-of-age and the formation of his adult, masculine identity.

The English version emphasizes the transition of the young protagonist from child to man in the first part of the romance, revealing a hesitation between wanting to depict a manly hero and following the original coming-of-age plot. After the introduction, the narrative begins with Partonope and his uncle Clovis, King of France, going boar hunting in the Ardennes, during which Partonope gets lost and ends up spending the whole night alone in the forest. Here, Partonope is referred to as a child for the first time: 'Thys was welle don, as of a chylde,/[...] He ys ryghte lyke to ben a man' (556-9). As he performs the 'manly' act of killing a boar, the hero is revealed to not actually be a man, but rather a 'chylde', which can refer to a 'young child' or a 'young man, youth' according to the *MED*, who is almost *like* a man. The following lines depict the hero's lonely, terrifying night in the forest and his discovery of a magical ship, which brings him to the marvellous, but entirely empty, city of Chef d'Oire. Here, Partonope is no longer described as a man but as a lost *chylde*. This episode is central to the presentation of Partonope's inner, emotional identity as that of a boy who is becoming a man, since he is absolutely alone, and does nothing more than react emotionally to what is happening to him. Neal describes the English Partonope's 'acquiescence to his journey' as 'a giving over of the self to something that is inevitable, unknown, but possibly pleasurable.'[20] I argue, however, that the English adaptor reduces his complete passivity as well as the emphasis on pleasure.

The English translation first follows the French text relatively closely, as both versions offer a poignant and realistic picture of a lost, scared child. The Middle English version, however, demonstrates a preference for speech and action over description, a tendency that is typical of such romance adaptation.[21] But while Helen Cooper has argued that English romances tend 'to indicate emotion more by action and statement than by soliloquy', this English adaptor introduces numerous first-person prayers and emotional soliloquies in lieu of the French version's visual descriptions of the crying Partonopeu. The English Partonope is thus able to voice some resistance to what happens to him, by expressing his fears and praying to God for help. Rather than complete passivity, he displays a form of reflexive coping mechanism as well as decision-making. While the French Partonopeu 'Pleure des iols, ne set que faire,/Car n'ert apris de nul mal traire.' (A 659-60 *He cries his eyes out, now knowing what to do, because he is not used to suffering*), the English one expresses his dismay: 'what may I do? [...] Helpe me lorde Gode' (658-661) and then takes a decision: 'the yonge man wyste not what to do,/But at the laste he drew hym to/An olde tre, an holowe thynge,/Ther-in to have his loggyng.' (664-67). Interestingly, the added direct speech also allows the translator to make explicit the emotional transition from youth to man that occurs in the first part of the romance. Once in the empty palace, upon entering the chamber, Partonope exclaims: 'I wolle as ny as euer I can/Take herte to me, and be a man' (1120-21). Yet even as he professes to be a man, he is referred to as 'the chylde' by the narrator only eight lines later and is, in fact, almost exclusively referred to as such throughout this passage. The identity categories of man and child, or at least youth, are thus explicitly emphasized and problematized in the English version of the romance, which highlights the unusual presence of such a young and passive hero in the romance genre. Partonope may be presented as an eighteen-year-old man at the start of the story, fit to be its manly hero, but he must still undergo a coming-of-age, which is a key element of the French version's plot. The English Partonope, at the start of the story, is alternately a *man* and a *chylde*, oscillating between youth and manhood, as he learns to overcome his fear.

While fear is an important part of the young man's self-discovery during his first adventure in the forest and his arrival in Chef d'Oire, it is soon replaced, or at least accompanied by pleasure.[22] In the French version, fear is consistently mixed with awe and pleasure. As he discovers the city, his *dolor* and *peor* are mixed with his great *joie* at the place's beauty and wonder (A 874-77). The city, whose splendour is described at length, forms part of the sensual seduction of Partonopeu, substituting itself to Melior's physical beauty which remains invisible.[23] As he goes to sleep in the magnificent bed – also described at length – he is afraid of devils (A 1050), but also experiences intense pleasure (*loisir* A 1056). Partonopeu's transition from child to man involves overcoming his fear, but also the discovery of luxury and its pleasures. The Middle English version does not mention any joy, only the measured comment that Partonope's 'herte sum-what be-gan to lyghte' (941) at the beautiful view of the town. The translator refuses to dwell on the visual description of the chamber and the bed (1153-55), only mentioning the richness of the clothes laid out for him. Significantly, there is no mention of pleasure or leisure at this point, but only of fear ('mykell drede' 1157) and decision-making in the form of rhetorical questions ('what may I do' 1158). Fear, for the French Partonopeu, is directly mixed with pleasure in his aesthetic experience of Chef d'Oire, while for the English Partonope fear must first be overcome on its own before he can gain access to (sexual) pleasure.

The sexual encounter between Partonopeu and Melior is quite extraordinary in its graphic detail and violence. In both versions, the act is presented as a rape: Partonopeu overcomes his fear as he is driven by desire and forces himself on the mystery lady who has climbed into the bed. In the French romance, this is the first scene where Partonopeu speaks – finally becoming an actor after having been a silent spectator for so long. Though the scene clearly is a rape, Partonopeu learns afterward that Melior was, in fact, the instigator of his coming to Chef d'Oire, with the plan of marrying him. By contrast, while the English adaptor conveys the violence of the French version, he also reveals Melior's thoughts beforehand and posits her more strongly as a desiring subject.[24] This important passage thus problematizes the notions of female desire and male passivity: the woman performs passivity while she actually is the desiring agent, so that the young man can perform masculine agency. While she does desire him, the decision of whether or not she will have sex with him that night, well before they can get married, is not hers. She can only worry and lament about the loss of honour that it would entail for her.[25] The young man, on the other hand, needs only worry about his pleasure.

Vines has analysed this scene as it appears in the Middle English text, arguing that it needs to look and feel like a rape to the young man, because 'male sexual aggression' is a 'fundamental aspect of establishing chivalric identity.'[26] While I agree that sexual desire brings the hero to action and thus helps him establish his manhood, I believe that the most important element of the sex scene, with regards to the hero's identity, is not the violence but the novel experiences of desire and pleasure – described as 'deduit' (A 1302) in the French text, and as 'game' (1573) in the English one. The sex scene marks the starting point to the year he will spend in the empty city of Chef d'Oire, a year during which he adopts the social identity of chivalry by being trained in pleasure rather than aggression. This is done in complete social isolation: because he is still too young to be an acceptable husband for Melior, their relationship must remain secret. His only social contact is Melior, who he can hear and touch, but not see. Chef d'Oire here corresponds to a representation of the Orient as an idyllic space dedicated to love and eroticism, as Catherine Gaullier-Bougassas argues: the Orient in *Partonopeu* is a place where the hero withdraws into himself, rather than opens up to others.[27] Until it becomes the 'real' place of which Partonopeu becomes emperor, the Orient is a fairy kingdom of beauty, sensuality and femininity. His becoming an adult and a nobleman, and his preparation towards knighthood, happen within this sensual sphere of pleasure, in isolation from the social world, and through the fulfilment of his personal desires.

After the sex scene, Melior explains to her young lover how she planned all of this and how she wants him to become, in two years and a half, her husband and the Emperor of Byzance. She reveals her plan to him so that he will become a 'cevaliers eslis' (A 1495 *elite knight*), 'a knyghte/A more a-beller' (1838-9). Interestingly, in practice, the programme consists almost exclusively of leisure. The first day, Partonopeu puts on the magnificent clothing laid out for him (FR A 1587-1594; ME 1953-1968) and is served a magnificent meal (the English translator has his Partonope exclaim: 'Alle thys a-raye ys for me broghte.' 1982), before he goes out to explore the city and its surroundings, which are described at length. When he comes back to Melior in the evening, she explains that she chose this perfect setting and had the most magnificent city built, all for him and for his 'deduit et giu' (A 1734 *pleasure and play*), his 'playe' (2136): the city's entire purpose is his own pleasure.[28] All of this must have the desired effect of instilling in the young man a powerful sense of his own importance. Indeed, the construction of this sense of entitlement can be read as one of the main goals of his stay in Chef d'Oire. In this magical kingdom, the young man 'is encouraged to imagine himself as an adult and, more importantly, as the ruler he will one day be.'[29] But instead of being confronted with his potential future subjects and the city's administration, the life he leads there is one of pure, material pleasure. He enjoys Melior's (invisible) company every night and, during the day, is provided with access to hunting dogs, birds and horses, luxurious forests and rivers. Melior describes to him the noble dogs and birds he can use for his hunting amusement: she uses the adjective *gentil/gentyll* to refer to the animals (FR A 1792, 1797; ME 2211), thus emphasising the nobility of the activity and everything associated with it. The Middle English translator makes this link more explicit: when all the hounds run to Partonope because they have found a boar, the narrator writes: 'The crye to here yt were a feste/For an emperor an for a lorde' (2250-51). During his stay in Chef d'Oire, Partonopeu thus learns how to perform the social identity of the noble knight by participating in its pleasures.[30] As he cannot see anyone nor be seen, these pleasures are entirely material, sensual and aesthetic rather than social, yet they correspond to the social identity of the nobleman.

In both versions, Partonopeu's nobility is a key building block in the formation of his chivalric identity. Melior chose him for his nobility and his beauty, with the assumption that knightly 'prowess [is] expected as the corollary of his beauty'.[31] Partonopeu's noble lineage, as Vines notes, is presented as the very reason why he must pursue chivalry.[32] Melior, who takes on the role of mentor, reminds him of this noble lineage, which she invokes as a guarantee of his future knightly identity:

Car ja li sans ne mentira,
Mais Nature tos tans fera.
Ne souferra la gentillece

> Que ja faciés fors noblece. (A 1505-1508)
> *Because Blood will never lie, Nature will prevail and Gentility will*
> *never allow that you do anything without nobility.*

By this logic, as a descendant of Hector, who only loved chivalry (A 1501-03), Partonopeu too will prove a great and noble knight, since blood, nature and nobility never lie. In this passage, *sang, nature* and *gentillece*, which can mean nobility in both the social and moral sense, are personified as objective and innate qualities, which ensure that Partonopeu shall always behave nobly. The personification is removed in the English version, where Melior instead asks him to act in accordance with his noble blood, which means dedicating himself to knighthood: 'Loke ye sewe forþe þat no-belle blode,/And sette yowre herte euer in cheualry.' (1852-3). While the English translator diminishes somehow the passivity implied in the personification of blood nobility, both versions have Melior deliver an emotional rather than practical education. What matters here is that Partonopeu *love* chivalry, set his heart in it: he must adopt chivalric identity not through prowess and masculine validation yet, but through individual, emotional commitment. This request for commitment comes with a recipe on how to behave to be a good knight. This does not include fighting skills, but rather social skills for the performance of the social and moral identity of a knight.[33] She instructs him to be humble and pleasant with everyone, rich or poor, to give freely and be generous with knights – for which she will give him the material means – to honour God and the Holy Church and, finally, to be valiant in battle (FR A 1913-1930; ME 2405-2422).

The fact that the young man receives chivalric education and sponsorship by his lady is not uncommon in romance. A similar scenario is at play in the popular story of Lanval/Launfal. The hero, who is already an established knight, loses the favour of the king and queen and therefore both his material and social status at court. It is his fairy lover who provides him with the (mainly material) means to gain his identity back. During his secret love affair – he is forbidden to reveal the existence of his lady who remains invisible to anybody but him – he moves back and forth between the fairy's magical, and private, world and the 'masculine social' world of the court. In that way, he can enjoy the fairy's company at night and perform his newly re-acquired social status in chivalric society during the day. In this fairy story, the knight regains his access to courtly society through his secret association with the fairy lover. The process does not entail a period of isolation until the very end of the story when he retires to a life of pleasure with his fairy mistress, forever removing himself from court.[34]

Partonopeu's education in the social behaviour of chivalry, on the other hand, is coterminous with his education in the private realm of love. Melior's teachings on chivalric behaviour form part of Partonopeu's life of sensual pleasures in Chef d'Oire: after a full day of hunting, he comes home and have his 'delit' (A 1857), 'joye and delyte' (2300) of Melior, followed by further 'joie' and play in the form of pleasant and educational speeches: 'Et de deduit et de grant sens/Et des fais de l'ancien tens' (A 1861-62 *And pleasant and meaningful stories of ancient history*), 'And she hym tellyth nobel storyes,/Off love of knyghthode olde victoryes./Hym to dyporte faste besyeth sche' (2307-09). The pleasure of chivalric education thus overlaps with sexual pleasure. Her teachings are part of the 'parler et juer et sentir' (A 1447), 'playe, speche, and felynge' (1806) that he can have of her. The young man's initiation to chivalric identity thus happens in complete isolation from chivalric, homosocial society: it relies uniquely on private, sensual and material pleasure.

After a year of 'joie bien pleniere' (A 1884), 'joye fulle playnere' (2353), thinking of nothing else than his personal pleasure, his lady and his hunting dogs, and thus forgetting 'de son païs/De ses parents, de ses ami' (A 1889-90 *of his land, his parents, his friends*), 'alle hys kynne' (2358), the young man remembers himself and where he comes from ('De soi qui est et dont est nés' A 1886). While his stay in Chef d'Oire was a key milestone in his identity formation, allowing him to become an adult and a nobleman, it isolated him from his community, making him lose sight of his group identity as Frenchman and count of Blois. With Melior, he discovers himself as an individual, a (noble)man and future husband and emperor through private gratification, but he must still realize his knightly identity within the 'masculine social' and through a demonstration of practical martial skills. As Aisling Byrne has shown, 'absolute gratification' in fairy lovers romances would only stunt narrative progression and therefore individual growth: the 'stasis of fulfilled desire' can only last so long.[35] Partonopeu thus eventually asks Melior for the permission to go back to France and help the French army in its war against Sornegur. This long war episode offers an exclusively masculine space typical of the *chansons de geste*, where the young man can be seen and recognized as part of a 'brotherhood', a 'community of fighting men'.[36] Here, after a year immersed in sensual pleasures and social entitlement, Partonopeu appears to have somehow gained the skills necessary to discharge the duties of knighthood: he battles against Sornegur's army and quickly becomes an outstanding soldier and leader in the French army – although he has not yet been awarded the title of knight.

When he arrives in Blois, he is first welcomed by one of Melior's knights who brings him horses carrying gold and silver. The knight explains that he should now behave like a knight, and do everything that knights do, except actually becoming one: 'Ses vos envoie Melior,/Et prie vos d'armes porter,/De tornoier et de joster,/Fors que ne soiés cevaliers.' (A 2010-13 *Melior sends you these and requests that you bear arms, tourney and joust, but without becoming knighted*; ME 2544-2549). This is a key aspect of the plot: Melior wants to be the one to 'çaindre l'espee' (A 2015), to gird his sword (ME 2551-2), on the day of their wedding. Partonopeu's official identity as a knight is thus dependent on his lady and on his own status as a lover. The intersection of chivalric identity with that of lover is a prerequisite of medieval romance: knightly prowess must be inspired and witnessed by a lady. In the Partonopeu story, this link is made explicit and official as the protagonist can only be knighted by his lady.

In France, he acts like a knight and becomes recognized as a worthy warrior and generous leader. However, Partonopeu then goes through a dramatic loss of identity and must reacquire both his identities of lover and nobleman before he can formally acquire the status of knighthood through a dubbing ceremony. Having betrayed his lover's command to never trying to see her, Partonopeu is first chased out of Chef d'Oire, before leaving his own family, knights and home in Blois to disappear into the forest – the same forest where he got lost at the start of his identity quest. During his suicidal wandering in the Ardennes, he becomes unrecognizable: he is dirty and extremely thin, his hair is long and messy and when Urraque, Melior's sister, finds him she first identifies him as a 'caitis' (A *5952 slave or exiled; by extension a miserable*), 'caytif' (7296). Here, Partonopeu suffers a self-imposed loss of identity, consciously describing himself as a miserable and an outcast ('un bricon', 'un musart' A *5995*; 'a knave/a brothel, an oute-caste fro all thing' 7356-7). The terms used here imply a change in his social identity: from aristocratic knight and lover, he is become a social outcast and a poor miserable. This form of violent retreat out of society into wilderness and the incumbent loss of social identity is a common result of love betrayal in medieval romance. Such 'flight to wilderness', as Robert Hanning puts it, is a 'metaphor for the flight from the self' that the hero has started to hate.[37] Hanning assimilates this episode to the famous madness episode found in Chrétien de Troyes' *Yvain*. There is an important difference between the two exiles, however: while Partonopeu 'assumes the appearance of the madman' he does not seem to lose his mind.[38] Yvain explicitly loses his reason and his senses on top of his social identity: when he is finally found, naked in the forest, by a lady, he has no memories of his mad episode.[39] In the Partonopeu romance, on the other hand, the protagonist loses his social identity of nobleman, knight and lover but not his senses: this identity loss is self-enacted. Because he adopted chivalric identity by emotionally committing to it rather than through 'objective' masculine validation, he can also consciously, subjectively, uncommit.

This different type of identity loss also means a different form of recovery. When the lady finds Yvain in the forest, he is unconscious: she covers him with an unguent that makes 'la rage et la melencolie' (3007 *the rage and melancholy*) disappear from his brain and lays clothes next to him before leaving, only coming back when he is dressed and back to his senses. The knight thus first comes back to himself and gets dressed in proper clothing before he has any social interaction. After that, the young woman brings him back to her lady's castle, where they wash and feed him, and procure him armour and a horse. The emphasis is on getting the knight his physical strength back: 'Qui tant a esté sojornez/Qu'an sa force fu retornez' (3155-6 *Who stayed there until he was back to his old strength*). Women thus restore his mental health and his physical strength and appearance, yet as soon as this is done, he will reclaim his knightly identity through the display of prowess within a masculine social space. After a very short convalescence, knightly action literally comes knocking at the door: thieves attack the castle. Yvain goes out after them and violently kills one of them, after which he is soon recognized by the knights of the castle as a great knight. It is this validation of male peers that actualizes the recovery of his social, knightly identity, not womanly care and his passive stay in the feminine private realm.

Partonopeu, on the other hand, is conscious and conversant when Urraque finds him in the forest. He knows who he is – or was – but refuses to be that person anymore, answering 'traitor' when Urraque asks him for his name (FR A 6001-2; ME 7367). The gracious lady still reveals who she is, however, which brings about her own recognition of Partonopeu. Fearing for his life, she decides to lie to him and tell him that Melior has forgiven him and loves him, thus effectively restoring his identity as lover and as a man.[40] The second step is to reconstruct his identity as a knight – or more precisely as a young warrior ready to be knighted – which primarily involves a physical transformation and a lot of leisure. In contrast with Yvain, who remains in the presence of women just long enough to get back on his feet and into the masculine world of knightly aggression, Partonopeu recovers his social identity through an extended and pleasurable stay in the sole company of women: Urraque and Persewis, a cousin of the two sisters who falls madly in love with Partonopeu. Urraque brings the young man to Salence, a small, paradisal island full of vegetation and crowned with a magnificent palace. Critics have often contrasted Salence to Chef d'Oire as a more simple and natural setting, a fertile *locus amoenus*, where the empty Chef d'Oire represents sterility and artifice.[41] The two places nonetheless seem to perform the same function: establish (or restore) Partonopeu's social identity through private, material, and sensual pleasures. Urraque makes sure that nobody else on the island can see or talk to him except her and Persewis (FR A 6214; ME 7606-7) and that all his desires are satisfied: 'Molt i sejorne a grant delit/Et tot a son plaisir i vit.' (A 6199-6200 *He remains there pleasurably, living only for his pleasure*), 'She made hym have all maner delite' (7590). Much of this pleasure comes from the fake love letters that Urraque forges for him. The rest has to do with restoring his appearance through care and luxury: the ladies patiently untangle his hair, or, in the English version, wash it so that it goes back to its natural colour, and dress him with the most beautiful clothes.

Finally, Urraque provides him with extraordinary armour, which is described in great material detail as being the best and the finest that he has ever seen. When he tries it on, thus effectively putting on the costume of the knight in the scene that precedes his dubbing, he is still in the sole company of the two doting women. Once he is armed and mounted, Partonopeu goes out to test his armour and his horse and, more prominently, to offer a spectacle of knightly glamour to the two maidens. Indeed, the narration focuses on Urraque's and Persewis' admiring gaze: the French narrator explains how Persewis falls deeper in love as the suit of armour makes him look even more beautiful (A 6893-95) and the English adaptor repeats how much they enjoy seeing him ride and how he is the most beautiful armed man they have ever seen (8440-45). Overall, the construction of his physical identity as a knight taking place in this scene is focalized through their loving, feminine eyes; here, his armour, horse and shield – all the attributes needed for the military function of knighthood – only serve to enhance his attractiveness as a lover.

When he finally officially becomes a knight and is girded by Melior herself, it is indeed his identity as lover that prevails. Excited and terrified at seeing his beloved again, the young man behaves more like a conventional lovesick lover than a lusty and valiant knight, turning red and lowering his head for shame, and fleeing to his room to vent his anguish as soon as it is done. The Middle English version expands the portrait of the typical lovesick lover, emphasizing his complex emotional state through his changing hue (8973). During the final tournament, Partonopeu offers a perfect display of knightly prowess ignited by love. Yet he ultimately wins Melior's hand not because he is the best knight, but because he is the prettiest. The tournament indeed ends with a beauty contest, in which the final competitors are stripped of their suits of armour. Partonopeu thus approaches the panel of judges unarmed, wearing only a tunic and girdle: his beauty and his shamefulness are emphasized over his manliness or prowess. Once again, the English translator dwells on Partonope's emotional state and how it is visually expressed on his face (12063-68). Bruckner argues that 'the transformation of the tournament into a kind of beauty contest has the effect of intertwining beauty and prowess, birth and individual performance, as complementary, rather than contradictory, values, equally necessary in a comprehensive social system.'[42] The tournament indeed brings together the different facets that form knightly identity and that are successively emphasized throughout the romance. It also reconciles the feminine, private sphere with the masculine, social one. Ultimately, however, the fact that Partonopeu is successful because of his beauty highlights the unusual role that (aesthetic) pleasure, female desire, and male passivity and emotionality play in the construction of chivalric identity in this romance.

To conclude, the romance offers an original representation of the chivalric identity quest through its problematizing of knighthood as dependent on female influence and desire and its foregrounding of the private, feminine sphere as a locus of social, masculine formation. Whereas some critics have described Chef d'Oire as 'hedged round with prohibitions' and antagonistic to the social world of honour, turning the young man into a 'kept man' and Melior's 'powerless dependent', I argue that it is the place of both the fulfilment of his personal desires and the construction of his social identity.[43] Before he becomes a knight in practice – by fighting in a war and eventually being formally dubbed – Partonopeu constructs his knightly identity not by acquiring the skills necessary for performing knighthood as a military function, but by adopting the social identity of a nobleman, involving spending considerable leisure time dedicated to hunting, lovemaking and cultivating a sense of self-importance. Pleasure becomes a crucial notion, bringing together the identity strands of lover and of nobleman (both necessary in chivalry), reunited in a sense of gratification and entitlement. Similarly, in Salence, the preparation for the social rite of passage that is knighting consists in building Partonopeu's confidence up again as an attractive young man and a successful lover. The Middle English adaptation follows the Old French plot closely and also posits personal, private gratification as the key building block to the young man's construction of his social status as nobleman, lover and, ultimately, knight. I therefore do not wish to overstate the differences between the two versions. However, a comparative approach helps highlight the significant and unusual elements of the original romance. The translator's unease with the emphasis on pleasure and aestheticism or with the hero's young age and attractiveness is one such indicator. The Middle English version indeed constructs Partonope's knightly identity with more emphasis on manly behaviour and less on his status as an object of contemplation and desire; in doing so it makes more explicit the hero's emotional transformation from *chylde* to man, and on to lover-knight.

Notes

1 This research was generously supported by the Swiss National Science Foundation (SNSF).

2 Simon Gaunt, *Gender and Genre in Medieval French Literature* (Cambridge, 1995), p. 109.

3 The twelfth-century Old French, anonymous romance *Partonopeu de Blois* was a remarkably popular text, which was continuously adapted throughout the Middle Ages, resulting in translations into at least six Western European languages. The romance is usually dated from around 1150-1180. It was long thought that the author of *Partonopeu* wrote after and under the influence of Chrétien de Troyes, but more recent studies have argued for the possibility of the romance to be a precursor of Chrétien. See Penny Eley and Penny Simons, '*Partonopeus de Blois* and Chrétien de Troyes: A Re-Assessment', *Romania*, 117 (1999), 316-341.

4 Two Middle English versions exist, one which exists only in fragmentary form (only 308 verses are extant) and which departs from the Old French narrative structure, and a longer version, which follows the French plot faithfully and which is the one this article studies.

5 Helen Cooper, *The English Romance in Time: Transforming Motifs from Geoffrey of Monmouth to the Death of Shakespeare*, (Oxford, 2004), see pp. 30 and 130.

6 Gaunt, p. 108.

7 Gaunt, p. 96.

8 See Robert W. Hanning, *The Individual in Twelfth-Century Romance* (New Haven, 1977), p. 215.

9 See Gaunt, p. 109.

10 On the romance's 'fusion' of genres see Penny Eley, *Partonopeus de Blois. Romance in the Making* (Cambridge, 2011), pp. 6-7.

11 Brenda Hosington, 'Voices of Protest and Submission: Portraits of Women in *Partonopeu de Blois* and its Middle English Translation', *Reading Medieval Studies*, 17 (1991), 51-75 (pp. 65 and 70).

12 Eley, p. 20.

13 I use Olivier Collet and Pierre-Marie Joris (ed. and trans.), *Le roman de Partonopeu de Blois* (Paris, 2005). Modern English translations are mine.

14 Penny Eley and Penny Simons, 'Male Beauty and Sexual Orientation in *Partonopeus de Blois*', *Romance Studies*, 17 (1999), 41-56 (pp. 45-49).

15 Gretchen Mieszkowski, 'Urake and the Gender Roles of *Partonope of Blois*', *Mediaevalia*, 25 (2004), 181-195 (pp. 182-83).

16 Mieszkowski, p. 183.

17 For the Middle English version, I use Trampe A. Bödtker (ed.), *The Middle-English versions of Partonope of Blois* (Oxford, 1912). Electronic Edition (Cambridge, 1992).

18 On (reversed) gender roles in the romance's depiction of the love story, see Matilda Bruckner, *Shaping Romance: Interpretation, Truth, and Closure in Twelfth-Century French Fictions* (Philadelphia, 1993), pp. 109-156; and Mieszkowski.

19 The words *masculinité* or *virilité* do not appear in twelfth-century French literature. The examples found in the *Dictionnaire du Moyen Français* all date from the fourteenth and fifteenth centuries.

20 Derek Neal, *The Masculine Self in Late Medieval England* (Chicago, 2009), p. 195.

21 Cooper, p. 30. On the preference for direct speech and dialogue over descriptions see for example A. C. Spearing's detailed analysis of English translations of Marie de France's *lais*. Spearing, 'Marie de France and her Middle English Adaptors', *Studies in the Age of Chaucer*, 12 (1990), 117-156. Sif Rikhardsdottir notices it with regards to the Partonopeu romance but does not comment on it further, arguing that both the Old French and the Middle English versions paint a realistic image of a scared, lost child. Rikhardsdottir, *Medieval Translations and Cultural Discourse: The Movement of Texts in England, France and Scandinavia* (Cambridge, 2012), 123 and 136.

22 Albrecht Classen, in a study of the German version of the romance, argues that fear is a key element in the protagonist's quest for self and identity. Classen, 'The Struggle Against Fear as a Struggle for the Self in Konrad von Würzburg's *Partonopier und Meliur*', *Mediaevalia*, 25 (2004), 225-252.

23 See Esperanza Bermejo, 'Chef d'Oire dans *Partonopeus de Blois*: La ville comme espace de totalisation', *Mediaeval Studies,* 63 (2001), 223-244 (p. 229).

24 Helen Cooper has argued that the representation of 'active female desire' is more characteristic of English than French romances, Cooper, p. 220. On the emphasis on Melior's active desire in the Middle English *Partonope* see Rikhardsdottir, pp. 141-142.

25 On the treatment of female reputation and honour in both versions of the romance see Ronald M. Spensley, 'The Courtly Lady in *Partonope of Blois*', *Neuphilologische Mitteilungen*, 74 (1973), 288-291 and Hosington, pp. 56-57.

26 Amy Vines, 'Invisible Woman: Rape as Chivalric Necessity in Medieval Romance', in *Sexual Culture in the Literature of Medieval Britain*, ed. by A. Hopkins, A. Rouse and C. J. Rushton (Cambridge, 2014), pp. 161-80 (p. 174).

27 Catherine Gaullier-Bougassas, *La Tentation de l'Orient dans le roman médiéval. Sur l'imaginaire médiéval de l'Autre* (Paris, 2003), p. 57.

28 As Amy Vines notes, this justifies the long description of the city at the beginning of the episode: 'These resources are not present merely to be admired or wondered at, but are marshaled for Partonope's pleasure and use.' Vines, *Women's Power in Late Medieval Romance* (Cambridge, 2011), p. 93.

29 Vines, *Women's Power*, p. 93.

30 Vines goes against critics who see this sojourn in Chef d'Oire as a period of sheer inactivity and dependence with no chivalric development, by arguing that it is a 'crucial element of Partonope's education where his tutor and lover provides him with the personal experience and chivalric lessons he needs to succeed.' I agree with Vines and would argue further that the very inactivity that characterises his stay is part of the formation of his knightly and noble identity. Amy Vines, 'A Woman's "Crafte": Melior as Lover, Teacher, and Patron in the Middle English Partonope of Blois', *Modern Philology*, 105 (2007), 245-270 (p. 258).

31 Bruckner, p. 120.

32 Vines, 'Woman's "Crafte"', p. 255.

33 Ryan Naughton, in his thesis 'The construction of Knightly Identity in late Middle English Romances' ProQuest Dissertation Publishing (Ann Arbor, 2010), demonstrates 'the primacy of lineage and natural nobility in the matrix of knightly identity construction', but also argues 'that the performance of a particular social role is key in constructing and maintaining an individual knight's knightly identity' (p. 12). He thus defines 'natural nobility' as stemming both from 'lineage and proper behavior' (p. 17).

34 On the power and influence of the fairy lover in Marie de France's *Lanval* and Thomas Chestre's Middle English *Sir Launfal*, see Vines, *Women's Power*, pp. 115-140.

35 Aisling Byrne, 'Fairy Lovers: Sexuality, Order and Narrative in Medieval Romance', in *Sexual Culture in the Literature of Medieval Britain*, ed. by

A. Hopkins, A. Rouse and C. J. Rushton (Cambridge, 2014), pp. 99-110 (pp. 105 and 109).

36 Gaunt, pp. 23 and 26.

37 Hanning, p. 216.

38 Hanning, p. 82.

39 Chrétien de Troyes, *Yvain ou le Chevalier au Lion*, 3022-25, from Daniel Poirion (dir.), *Chrétien de Troyes. Oeuvres Complètes* (Paris, 1994). All subsequent quotes are from this edition, English translations are mine.

40 Gretchen Mieszkowski argues that 'by telling Partonope that Melior loves him as he needs to be loved, as "hir lorde," her husband, no longer as her kept man, Urake liberates his manliness.' Mieszkowski, p. 186.

41 See Hanning, p. 87 and Hosington, p. 62.

42 Bruckner, p. 131.

43 Hanning, p. 215; Mieszkowski, p. 184.

Reading Medieval Reviews

B. Besamusca and F. Brandsma eds. *The Arthur of the Low Countries, The Arthurian Legend in Dutch and Flemish Literature*, Arthurian Literature in the Middle Ages, University of Wales Press, 2021

In this latest instalment of Arthurian Literature in the Middle Ages, we find a balanced volume offering a clear and complete overview of Middle Dutch and Flemish Arthuriana, the first book-length study of its type. The volume invites both experts and students to immerse themselves in familiar and unique stories with rigour and clarity. The volume addresses explicitly advances in Arthurian Literature in the Low Countries over the past forty years, and it is an essential contribution to Arthurian scholarship at large.

The Arthur of the Low Countries sets out to present an up-to-date survey of Arthurian manuscripts and texts in the medieval Low Countries to serve the needs of both Dutch Arthurian scholarship and the international community. It is the tenth instalment of the Vinaver's Trust series *Arthurian literature in the Middle Ages*. It aims to provide "a reliable and comprehensive survey of Arthurian writing in all its generic and linguistic diversity".[1] In this, the volume excels and delivers what it sets out to offer. It delves into the richness and diversity of medieval Arthuriana in the Low Countries, expanding on what had been a contribution in a single chapter dealing with this subject in *The Arthur of the Germans*. While focusing on Dutch-language, the volume covers a broader cultural perspective by considering material consumed and produced in the Low Countries written in French and Low German. Furthermore, its final chapter investigates the influence of medieval Arthuriana in a post-medieval setting. The volume is accessible to the general reader, despite being part of a series designed for Arthurian scholars.

The first chapter in the book describes the historical background and social and cultural contexts of the texts. It looks into questions of origins, the where and when of the composition of the romances. It follows a geographical approach focusing on the 'River Lands' of the Meuse and Rhine, the County of Flanders, the Counties of

Holland/Zeeland and Hainaut, and the Duchy of Brabant. Furthermore, it synthesises these regions' cultural and political situations, placing the texts within specific contexts. As such, the chapter delves into questions about audiences, concluding that the romances were probably written for wealthy and cultured laymen but not for high courtly circles. It is an interesting opening to the volume, which sets up the scene for later in-depth literary analysis of the romances.

The production of French Arthurian narratives in the Low Countries, as a by-product of the multilingual culture of Flanders, is addressed in chapter 2. The chapter argues that the highest nobility preferred French as its language of culture, which attests to the production of French Arthurian narratives commissioned in Flanders. The chapter thus focuses on a specific corpus in French, which together with the manuscripts in which it is to be found is explored carefully in this section of the book. It looks into questions of patronage, concluding that it is essential not to isolate the romances from other literary corpora for which similar logics of patronage might have been present. When looking at ownership of the books, the chapter argues that ownership of Arthurian manuscripts in French was widespread among members of the medieval aristocracy of the Low Countries, with members of the merchant class owning books as early as the beginning of the fourteenth century. According to the chapter, the production of Arthurian Manuscripts in the Southern Netherlands attests to the popularity of the *Lancelot-Grail* Cycle *c.* 1270 and 1350. The chapter concludes that Flanders became a centre for Middle Dutch Arthurian literature and that French Arthurian literature remained in circulation in the Low Countries throughout the Middle Ages.[2] A helpful list of digitised Arthurian manuscripts mentioned in the text is provided at the end of the chapter.

Manuscripts and manuscript fragments of Middle Dutch narratives are discussed in chapter 3. Here, both the most luxurious copies are considered alongside codices of lesser quality, such as the *Lancelot* Compilation, now MS The Hague, KB, 129 A 10. The chapter thus considers the overall corpus before asking when and where the manuscripts were produced. It then considers their format and appearance, highlighting interesting features of both modest copies and more lavishly illustrated codices. In the case of the famous *Lancelot*

Compilation, interesting clues are provided as to its composition, together with an analysis of key annotations made by a contemporary corrector. This analysis leads the chapter to suggest exciting conclusions about the performance of the text for a listening audience. Another section of the chapter looks into the questions of correctors for the *Ferguut* copy now in Leiden, UB, Ltk, 191, fol. 1-32. The concluding section of the chapter focuses on French Arthurian romances that survive in two types of manuscripts: single-text codices and multi-text codices before expanding on questions of transmission, the richness of the material preserved, and the loss that is thus apparent from what has indeed been preserved. The chapter also includes a section listing digitised manuscripts mentioned in the text.

Chapter 4 discusses the range of references to and stories of Arthur found in Middle Dutch historiographical sources. It begins by looking into the work of the Flemish author, Jacob van Maerlant, which include the first references to King Arthur in Middle Dutch works. Maerlant wrote works on various subjects, including a mirror of history, the *Spiegel historiael,* and his works were written to both instruct and entertain. The chapter continues its analysis of historiographical sources by discussing the work of Maerlant's continuator, Lodewijk van Velthem. Velthem completed Maerlant's *Spiegel historiael* and produced a continuation for another one of Maerlant's works, the *Boek van Merline.* Here, the chapter argues that Maerlant's initial scepticism towards the historicity of Arthurian romances is replaced by Velthem's enthusiasm and a broad mixture of references to other Arthurian narratives in his chronicles, which he does by linking Arthurian themes with King Edward I of England. Furthermore, Velthem is credited as the owner of the *Lancelot* Compilation. This chapter concludes with a brief discussion of Arthur's inclusion in poems listing the Nine Worthies and its imprint in later historiography.

Chapters 5-7 analyses Arthurian romances produced in the Low Countries based on the source material. Chapter 5 studies the translations of French verse romances. Thus, it concentrates upon Tristant, Wrake van Ragisel, Ferguut, Perchevael and Torec. These constitute the oldest translations or adaptations of the Middle Dutch Arthurian tradition. They were produced in the west, in Flanders. The chapter discusses each translation of Old French Arthurian verse texts, presented in their presumed order of composition.[3] Special attention is given to the subsequent phases in the adaptation process. For each romance, an initial introduction is included, considering the physical and contextual characteristics of the surviving fragments. A summary of the romance follows, with a subsequent discussion, including one or more sections of analysis. The conclusion to the chapter argues for standard features in these romances, such as their critical attitude toward the chivalric ideology of the Arthurian court.[4] Furthermore, the romances are presented as less complex and ambiguous but more realistic than their French sources.[5] According to the chapter, they recount good, fast-paced stories which they emphasise, resulting in more one-dimensional narratives with exemplary qualities.

Chapter 6 looks into the original compositions produced after the first translations of verse romances from Old French into Middle Dutch. It thus discusses what the chapter labels as indigenous Arthurian romances: Walewein, Moriaen, Ridder Metter Mouwen, Walewein ende Keye, Lanceloet en het hert met de witte voet. These five Middle Dutch Arthurian romances were produced in Flanders in the second half of the thirteenth century. Walewein is considered the greatest of all Flemish Arthurian literature. At the same time, the other four texts were adapted to be included in the *Lancelot* Compilation, using a standard set of characters within generic plot patterns. In the introduction, the chapter argues that these texts were written for readers and listeners who were already familiar with these texts, and which placed Walewain in centre stage. After the introduction, the chapter follows a structure similar to that found in the previous chapter. The generalities of each text are discussed, followed by a summary of the narrative and literary criticism. The conclusion poses the question of audiences by asking about the target recipients of indigenous Arthurian literature in Flemish and by discussing the literary knowledge of intended audiences. It argues that authors' choices when writing in Flemish and not in French can be seen as an act of competition and emancipation.[6]

Chapter 7 delves into renditions of the French prose romances, which included at least three independent versions of the French Prose *Lancelot*, together with the texts described as the Merlin Cycle and the Lancelot Cycle. It evinces a salient appreciation for Walewein, which is also purported in chapter 6. The chapter proposes a chronological approach to the discussion of the texts, thus starting with Maerlant's Grail and Merlin, followed by three Lancelot translations, the *Lancelot* Compilation, Velthem's *Merlin* Continuation, and finally the *Historie van Merlijn*, the only printed Arthurian text. Without standardised accompanying summaries, which only appear occasionally when needed, each section critically discusses each one of the works mentioned above, highlighting interesting motifs or relevant themes and posing comparisons to other Arthurian texts when needed. The detailed discussion of the *Lancelot* Compilation is a highlight, answering the questions of 'how?', 'who?', and 'why?' the compilation was made. It argues for the creation of a coherent cycle in which seven inserted texts find their place within the framework of a trilogy[7] and offers an in-depth analysis of the compilation process.

Following a geographical line of argument, chapter 8 discusses the considerable amount of material tending eastward and situated in the Germanic regions, especially the Rhineland, a region the chapter highlights as significant to Arthurian scholarship, being the intersection point of French, Middle Dutch and Middle High German Arthurian traditions. The chapter discusses the eastward distribution of romances produced in Flanders or Brabant and the role of the Low Countries as a transit zone in this process.[8] It showcases 'first, the direct translations of Old French texts; second, the reimportation of the Old French classics via the Middle Dutch and Middle High German adaptations; and third, the continuous tradition of scholarly Latin Arthurian texts found in monastic libraries.'[9] The chapter then proceeds to discuss Merlin, Parcheval, and Lancelot's figures and finalises with the general characteristics of the tradition. It argues for the presence of 'a wide-ranging Arthurian tradition of varied intensity and impact' in the Rhineland.[10] Latin historiography is equally present with French romances, Middle Dutch, and occasionally Middle High German adaptations. The chapter concludes that generally, the Low Countries and the Rhineland do not play a geographical or genealogical role in the German Arthurian classics. No distinct and independent regional Arthurian tradition developed in the Rhineland.

The last chapter in the book traces the development of Arthurian narratives in a post-medieval setting, discussing the re-emergence of Arthurian material in Dutch literature, particularly in the nineteenth and twentieth centuries after an apparent period of neglect. It looks into different media: novels, plays, comic strips, music, radio plays and film. The chapter proves how Arthurian stories can renew themselves, generating a significant new message for each generation.

We are dealing with a ground-breaking volume, given the scope of the material it presents and the rigour the authors bring about in their chapters. There is ample evidence of solid editorial work. The pieces are well integrated and cross-reference each other effectively. This text is not a piece-meal volume; it rather firmly stands together as a cohesive piece of work. It provides a comprehensive overview and up-to-date state of the field in Arthurian literary studies in the Low Countries. It is evidence of the richness in Arthurian scholarship both to the general reader and the Arthurian scholar.

M. Carolina Escobar-Vargas, PhD
Department of History
Universidad Nacional de Colombia, Sede Medellín

Notes

1   B. Besamusca and F. Brandsma eds. *The Arthur of the Low Countries, The Arthurian Legend in Dutch and Flemish Literature*, Arthurian Literature in the Middle Ages, University of Wales Press, 2021, p. ix.
2   Besamusca and Brandsma, p. 41
3   Besamusca and Brandsma, p. 78
4   Besamusca and Brandsma, p. 108
5   Besamusca and Brandsma, p. 109
6   Besamusca and Brandsma, p. 146
7   Besamusca and Brandsma, p. 180
8   Besamusca and Brandsma, p. 148
9   Besamusca and Brandsma, p. 195
10 Besamusca and Brandsma, p. 199

Ryan H. Wilkinson, *The Last Horizons of Roman Gaul: Communication, Coin Circulation, and the Limits of the Second Burgundian Kingdom: A prosopographical, numismatic, and ceramic synthesis (ca. 395-550 CE).* British Archaeological Reports, International Series no. 3006. Oxford: BAR Publishing, 2020.

In this revised edition of his doctoral thesis, Ryan Wilkinson offers a communication-focused approach to the end of Roman Gaul and the beginnings of its early-medieval successor polities. Wilkinson argues that the Roman empire can be seen as a network and its decline can be characterised as the moment when 'customary ties between communities broke down' (p. 1) and led to the fragmentation of the wider, inter-connected whole.

The nature of early-medieval Burgundian hegemony has not been overlooked, but it is not frequently the focus of a monograph. While Wilkinson does not seek to supplant the monograph of Justin Favrod, nearly 25 years later this book may be its closest sequel. Wilkinson offers an erudite analysis of ceramic and monetary finds across Northern Burgundy, complemented by a review of episcopal councils and movement; scholars and students of Merovingian Gaul will find much here, especially the overall contention that the most conspicuously 'Roman' region of early-medieval Burgundy was also the least connected to contemporary Roman successor states.

Of greater interest for scholars with a wider interest in the history of the region or period, however, is Wilkinson's use of communication and network theory to analyse these findings. By exploring the dynamics of power and communication, Wilkinson avoids recent emphasis on social networks as evidence for individual agency to focus on communication structures that constrained and linked individuals. Noting that so-called 'weak' ties– those between people from different social circles– are considered highly important for modern knowledge, contact and resource exchange between different social groups, he contends that a significant strength of the late-Roman empire was its decentralised, inefficient, disordered networks of communication. The increased channelling of early-medieval communication through royal embassies, abbots and bishops served to delimit communication and connectivity, as communities became less resilient to individual deaths, disputes and new borders. This trend impacted different types of exchange and community differently: although it funnelled communicative power into key elite powerbrokers who most easily integrated into new, Merovingian networks when the region was conquered, Wilkinson suggests that the manufacture and movement of goods was often more slowly affected by political transformation.

Wilkinson focuses on the area around Langres, Dijon, Autun and Chalon-sur-Saône, cities that are often ignored in analyses of early-medieval Burgundy in preference for the Rhône basin and Lake Geneva. In consequence, his study has many new offerings. Sometimes, however, it is difficult to determine how far his hypotheses can be supported without seeing a comparable study of the main Burgundian metropoles of Lyon, Vienne and Geneva. Likewise, the remit does not permit Wilkinson to consider the re-founding of the Alpine monastic nexus of Agaune under Burgundian royal control: this might have provided an interesting counter-study. More broadly, the central hypothesis of the book reifies the existence of an interconnected Roman Gaul that disintegrated in the early Middle Ages: it would be interesting to consider if the network of mobile elites and long-distance marriage alliances that Wilkinson treats as typical of Roman Gaul and the empire were, rather, a brief late-Roman anomaly not the norm from which the early Middle Ages departed.

There are occasional repetitions in phrasing and the reproduction of images does not always provide as much detail as may be desired. More painful is the lack of indices: although the book is designed to be read from cover to cover, this omission renders the print copy frustrating for checking references. These are very minor details, however, and are both outweighed by the very low retail price of this book and its inclusion in digital BAR subscription packages which leave it very accessible to many (graduate) students, scholars and libraries. Overall, it is an ambitious and exciting reframing of early-medieval Gaul and the end of the Roman empire that will hopefully spawn wider debate and case studies.

Becca Grose
University of Reading

J. Dresvina and V. Blud eds. *Cognitive Sciences and Medieval Studies: An introduction,* University of Wales Press, 2020.

Cognitive Sciences and Medieval Studies: An introduction is the most recent in the University of Wales Press' series *Religion and Culture in the Middle Ages.* The series encourages the use of a variety of tools and theoretical approaches to understanding medieval culture, this edited collection of papers turning to the neurosciences. The editors are Victoria Blud, a research associate in the English department at the University of York, and Juliana Dresvina, a member of the History Faculty at Oxford.

They begin with an introduction setting out this complex and varied material; the range of papers then starts with Part I, 'Questions of method'. In 'How Modular are Medieval Cognitive Theories?' Jose Filipe Silva finds parallels between modern and medieval models of cognition and the mind. Ralph Hood, in 'An Unrealised Conversation: Medieval Mysticism and the Common Core' looks at the psychology of religion and challenges psychology to be more open to something other than methodological naturalism, whilst in 'Questions of Value: Brain Science, Aesthetics and Art in the Neurohumanities', art historian Matthew Rampley offers a helpful note of scepticism and caution about scientific data and how it is interpreted.

In Part II 'Histories of Neuroscience, Psychology and Mental Illness' Daniel Lord Smail's paper 'Neuroscience and the Dialectics of History' suggests that a neurobiological consideration of societal stress can offer a useful explanation of violent behaviours. Wendy Turner writes on 'Medieval English Understanding of Mental Illness and Parallel Diagnosis to Contemporary Neuroscience' considering diagnoses of mental disorders arising in late medieval English legal records, in the light of modern disorder classifications. Dresvina's own article on 'Attachment Theory for Historians of Medieval Religion: An Introduction' considers medieval religiosity in the light of psychological insights from the study of secure and disrupted emotional bonding.

Part III gives 'Case Studies: Reading Texts and Minds'. Godelinde Gertrude Perk writes on 'A Knot So Suttel and So Mighty: On Knitting, Academic Writing and Julian of Norwich', examining the cognitive processes involved in Julian of Norwich's experiences as related to those of anchoritic knitting crafts, as an example of embodied cognition. Victoria Blud explains how computational brain-based models of cognition have expanded to better understand the mind in its wider physical and environmental context, in 'Making up a Mind: '4 E' Cognition and the Medieval Subject'. Cognition is here seen as embodied, embedded, enacted, and extended, an approach which more easily includes the humanities; she uses it to further explore the writings of Julian of Norwich. Antonina Harbus also uses ideas of embodied cognition in the study of the stimulation of emotion in two poems from the Exeter book, in her paper 'Cognitive Approaches to Affective Poetics in Early English Literature'. Part IV, 'Approaching Art and Artefacts' continues with 'Medieval Art History and Neuroscience: An Introduction' by Nadia Pawelchak. She combines psychological research and medieval scholarship to illuminate how a medieval viewer might have responded to an image on an ivory mirror case. In 'Spoons, Whorls, and Caroles: How Medieval Artefacts Can Help Keep Your Brain on Its Toes', Jeff Rider looks at other artefacts and records of a medieval dance, considering human interactions with objects from the perspective of embodied cognition. Finally, John Onians summarises the collection in his 'Afterword: The Medieval Brain and Modern Neuroscience'; he accepts the provisos of the more sceptical contributors but concludes 'there is no activity of the mind which cannot be illuminated by the study of the brain.'[1]

Cognitive neuroscience is the study of the biological processes underlying cognition. It is concerned with processes at the chemical, neuronal and neural network levels in tasks like memory, perception, attention, language, and processing emotion. It is a rapidly developing field, generating many insights of benefit across academic boundaries; its influence in the humanities has increased over the last twenty years, with the birth of new fields such as neuroaesthetics – the 'cognitive turn.' Smail remarks that 'history and neuroscience make strange bedfellows' but the hope, and the unifying theme of the book, is that the light that such science might shed on historical phenomena.[2] As a neuropsychologist turned medieval historian I was obviously drawn to this combination of my two passions, and hoped that it might provide insights for my own research on ideas about the brain and 'disorders of the head' in medieval medicine.

The papers cover a wide array of disciplines, with contributions from historians, art historians, literary scholars, a psychologist, and a philosopher. As editors, Blud and Dresvina lay the ground for this with an excellent, clear, introduction helping to make it more accessible. Neuroscience here is interpreted widely, including sometimes psychiatry and general human biology, but this does allow for some interesting papers. Smail suggests that state-on-subject violence in the form of public executions and other oppressions in late medieval Europe was a form of stress induction which reduced testosterone in the male population; rewards or stresses meted out by state authorities served those in power by exerting control at a neurobiological level.

Some of the strongest papers are those of the editors themselves, who show a clear understanding of current psychological research and thinking, as well as the medieval scholarship. Also impressive is the article by Pawelchak who comments on how the neurosciences can illuminate possible medieval perceptions, making this concrete in the example of an image of courtship in a hunting scene. Viewers, both then and now, would have an automatic, embodied, neurologically based mirroring response to the two lovers, to their posture and gaze direction, driven by innate processes but shaped by their own experiences. She cites psychological research on responses to eye gaze and body stance in modern research participants; at the same time, she explores medieval conventions of aristocratic courtship and the symbolic significance of the falcons depicted.

My first concern was that the utility of a neuroscience approach might be overstated, a fashionable enthusiasm provoked by a wide-eyed wonder at the advances in cognitive and brain research. Fortunately, my own hesitations are shared by several contributors, which are taken into account. Perk helpfully explains that we need to be cautious about assumptions that medieval and modern brains operate in the same, or even similar way. Although the human brain is the product of evolution, it has considerable neuroplasticity and culture and experience cause significant changes in neuronal organisation and function. Art historians have been very taken with primate mirror neurons, but these may not even be present in humans; Rampley warns of the limitations of investigative techniques like functional MRI. This all accepted, do the assembled chapters then convince us that this novel approach is a helpful enterprise? The application of neuroscience to the medieval world is sometimes pushed to the limits of its usefulness and sometimes beyond. Some papers are interesting in their own right but the addition of a neurocognitive perspective can seem tenuous and strained. In many cases however, the experiment is well worthwhile; in particular, Dresvina and Pawalchak's analyses give a fascinating and effective demonstration of a happy marriage of the two approaches. With a wide spread of contributions, this volume has something for everyone, with several gems.

Anne Jeavons
University of Reading

Notes

1   Onians, J., 'Afterword: The Medieval Brain and Modern Neuroscience' p. 234.
2   Smail, D.L., 'Neuroscience and the Dialectics of History', p. 83.